Salvation in Henri de Lubac

SALVATION IN HENRI DE LUBAC

*Divine Grace, Human Nature, and
the Mystery of the Cross*

Eugene R. Schlesinger

*University of Notre Dame Press
Notre Dame, Indiana*

Copyright © 2023 by the University of Notre Dame

Published by the University of Notre Dame Press
Notre Dame, Indiana 46556
undpress.nd.edu
All Rights Reserved

Published in the United States of America

Library of Congress Control Number: 2023937441

ISBN: 978-0-268-20553-9 (Hardback)
ISBN: 978-0-268-20555-3 (WebPDF)
ISBN: 978-0-268-20552-2 (Epub)

In loving memory of Paul G. Crowley, SJ (1951–2020)

ad majoram Dei gloriam

CONTENTS

Acknowledgments	ix
Introduction	xiii

Part One

Salvation Desired: Nature, Grace, and Competing Humanisms

1.	Saving Grace: Soteriology in the Works on Nature and Grace	3
2.	Authentic Humanism as Salvation	20

Part Two

Salvation Disclosed: Revelation and Spiritual Exegesis

3.	Knowing the Mystery: De Lubac's Paradoxical Theological Epistemology	37
4.	Spiritual Exegesis and/as Salvation	58

Part Three

Salvation Realized: Ecclesiology and Sacraments

5.	Church as the Community of Salvation	77
6.	*Corpus mysticum verumque*	94

viii   Contents

Part Four

Salvation Consummated: Eschatology and the Theology of History

7.	Salvation as the Meaning of History	111
8.	Salvation as Eschatological Sacrifice	125

Coda: *Mysterium Crucis*	140
Conclusion	150

Notes	157
Bibliography	221
Index	238

ACKNOWLEDGMENTS

You hold in your hand the culmination of nearly a decade of reflection on and apprenticeship to the thought of Henri de Lubac. Unsurprisingly, in a journey of such length, I've been helped along by a good many people, and so accrued several debts of gratitude. In the first and most prominent place, I must thank Susan K. Wood, SCL, my first teacher of de Lubac, from whom I gained the fundamental orientation toward his works that informs the present book. It was in a doctoral seminar taught by her that the seeds for this study were planted, and in the years since she's been an exemplary mentor, colleague, and friend. I'm sure she'll disagree with me here and there in the following pages, but I hope she sees the mark of her influence; I couldn't have written this without her.

Additionally, the usual rogues' gallery of names that appear in my acknowledgments belong here as well: Luke Togni, Jonathan Heaps, and Ryan Hemmer. They have all been important interlocutors as I've thought through this project at the level both of the forest and of the trees, lending me their expertise and their friendship.

I've also benefited from discussion and correspondence with Kevin Hughes, Shaun Blanchard, Ulrich Lehner, Andrew Meszaros, Jon Kirwan, and Jenny Martin. At several junctures Jordan Hillebert and Joseph Flipper encouraged me both through their own work on de Lubac and through camaraderie as fellow Lubacian scholars. I've shared a good many conversations about de Lubac and *ressourcement* with P. J. Jedlovec. Paul Schutz read and offered feedback on several chapters, in a spirit of true collegiality. Around the time I was trying to get a handle on the intellectual currents of de Lubac's day, particularly in terms of theological epistemology and the nature of "Thomism," Michel Barnes was pursuing adjacent questions and I reaped the benefit of his dogged historical investigations. Anne Carpenter has been a fellow-traveler in trying to figure out precisely what *ressourcement* means and what our relation to it here and now, amid the signs of these times, should (and can) be. I'm grateful for her friendship.

Stephen Little and John Martino were great encouragers and offered insightful guidance as I sought to discern the proper shape for this investigation and the proper home for it. I also had considerable help, on the research end of things, from several sources. The library staff at Santa Clara University (particularly Melanie Sellar and Christine Welter) made sure I had all the resources I needed, whether through acquisitions or InterLibrary Loan. The Archives jésuites de Vanves were willing to send me photocopies of documents from de Lubac's days in formation. And my daughter Evelyn frequently accompanied me to campus, where she would scan pdfs of articles for me so that I could focus on other duties. I don't expect to ever have a better research assistant than she's been.

On that note, I owe tremendous thanks to my family. They've followed me around the country for my work, supported me in it, and kept me grounded so that I've remembered that I am more than that work. My daughters, the aforementioned Evelyn and her sister, Joann, have made do with a punctilious father and the oddity of having so many of our family's social connections coming from the not-quite-real world of academe. My wife, Loren, has been my constant companion and best friend: in weal and woe on both sides of this continent. She's been there as book projects have come and gone like so many tides on a steadfast shore. Without question, she is the *sine qua non* of my work, and the highest honor of my life is to share it with her.

Finally, it is a bittersweet joy to dedicate this volume to the memory of my dear colleague and friend Paul Crowley, SJ, who died just as I was completing my initial work on this project. I first met Paul in the context of his editorship at *Theological Studies*. I'd recently submitted an essay to the journal, and he sought me out at a meeting of the American Academy of Religion, just to make contact, a practice he kept up any time I was presenting at gatherings of the AAR or the Catholic Theological Society of America. He was always an enthusiastic supporter of my work and believed in me in ways that made it easier to believe in myself. I counted him an important friend, but I never expected that we would work together on the same faculty. So it was a true joy to end up doing so, though I wound up not having as much time with Paul as I'd hoped. As Paul's health declined, his spirit never did. He remained the same steadfast friend I'd always known him to be, and I'll forever treasure the conversations we were able to share in his final months. Paul lived and died as an exemplary member of the Society of Jesus (a vocation he shared with this book's subject), entrusting himself, as well as his liberty, memory, and entire will, to his loving God. With great regularity he would observe that for the eternal God, the resurrection is always already *now*. I miss Paul dearly, but rejoice in the sure, certain hope that he is already living in that wider life toward which the entire creation strains, and at which it shall finally arrive, at which it has already arrived in Christ our Lord.

The Octave of Easter, 2022

Introduction

The writings of Henri de Lubac have left an indelible mark upon Catholic theology, preparing the ground for, giving shape to, and explaining the seminal event of twentieth-century Catholicism: the Second Vatican Council. Like the Council itself, though, de Lubac remains a contested figure, difficult to classify. Did his project of *ressourcement* break apart a moribund and decadent scholasticism, allowing for innovation and freedom? Or do his consistent and biting critiques of the implementation of Vatican II serve as a cautionary tale against half-measures from a visionary who lost his nerve and could not follow through (or as a clarion call for fidelity, depending on one's assessment of the so-called "spirit of Vatican II")? In all this, it is all too easy for de Lubac himself to become little more than a cipher: a proxy in the post-conciliar struggle for Catholic self-definition.

This is not to say that de Lubac cannot illuminate our understanding of the Council and its still-incomplete implementation, thereby informing the post-conciliar debates. Indeed, at a juncture where our context is beginning to eerily and distressingly parallel his own—down to a resurgent integralism seeking to ally the church with authoritarian political movements—de Lubac, who resolutely opposed both fascists and their integralist collaborators, seems as relevant as ever, in ways that I wish he were not. And, like ours, his was an era within which the Catholic Church struggled to articulate its relationship to social and historical change. We can indeed learn from his own navigation of such issues. But before he can inform our present context, he must be understood on his own terms, lest our engagement with him leave us staring at our own reflection, like those bygone seekers of the historical Jesus. Writing about Teilhard de Chardin, de Lubac offers a hermeneutical warning that we would do well to heed in his case as much as that of his departed friend: "It is only too easy to dismiss, in a writer's thought, anything that makes no special appeal to us, to minimize or even completely overlook its importance. This may lead us, in all good faith, to distort the whole meaning of his work, even if any analysis we include is itself accurate."[1] There has been no shortage of careful and enlightening scholarship on de Lubac, but we must be sure that we interpret him in light of his own central concerns.

The principal contention of this book is that Henri de Lubac's theological works demonstrate a soteriological preoccupation that provides a principle for integrating the concerns of his major works in the areas of the theology of the supernatural, spiritual exegesis, sacramental theology, ecclesiology, and the theology of history, as well as many of his works on particular figures and movements. While de Lubac wrote little about soteriology as a distinct locus, it provides the key content for nearly every major area of his writings. His was a thought centered around the person and act of Jesus Christ, the divine Savior who consummates history, transforming it into salvation history, who discloses and brings about the supernatural destiny of the human race, whose life is manifested in the life of the church through its sacraments and liturgy, and who, as the one who invites and brings human beings into friendship with God, is the fullness of revelation.

Irenaeus's dictum that, in bringing himself, Christ brought all newness, pervades de Lubac's works.[2] The idea of the Christian newness or novelty (terms I shall use interchangeably) is best grasped in the course of reading de Lubac's writings, since it emerges organically throughout them in the course of discussion, and not as some abstract definition. Therefore, a brief statement about it here can prime us to recognize and more readily assimilate it when we encounter it in the ensuing chapters. Most basically, the Christian novelty refers to the conviction that the coming of Jesus has indeed made a difference—in humanity's relationship to God, in the relationship between nature and grace, in the relationship between the Old and New Testaments, in history itself. His coming has brought about a change that would not have occurred apart from it. Christianity, then, is not simply more of the same, nor even an intensification of what had come before or was already the case. It is, rather, something decisively new. And yet, this discontinuity does not abrogate, but rather preserves, what had come before. It is a *renewal*, and, as such, must be renewing *something*. This Christian novelty is essentially soteriological—referring to the radical change brought about by Jesus Christ. As we shall see, it is particularly concentrated in his redemptive act, the paschal mystery. It is this renewal by Christ's redemptive death and resurrection that stands at the heart of de Lubac's theological vision. And his consistent recourse to it is, perhaps, the chief contribution he can make to our own present context.

"Organic Unity," Conciliar Anachronism, and the Nexus of Mysteries

The attempt to discern de Lubac's central concerns is no easy task. His œuvre is generally recognized to be sprawling and diverse, with Hans Urs von Balthasar likening approaching it to standing "at the entrance of a primeval forest."[3] De Lubac himself, recognizing the occasional and even haphazard character of his various works, suggested that "it would be fruitless to seek in such a diverse collection of writings the elements of any truly personal philosophical or theological—or as some have said, 'gnoseological'—synthesis, whether to criticize or to adopt it."[4] For all that, though, de Lubac's biographer and longtime friend, Georges Chantraine, suggests that de Lubac's work could be "characterized by two words: occasion and synthesis,"[5] while Balthasar suggests that, for all their diversity, these works are characterized by an "organic unity."[6] Taken together, these considerations indicate that, while we may expect to find an underlying unity within de Lubac's work, what unity we find will neither be methodologically intentional nor display the full coherence of a system, properly speaking. What we find instead is a diverse set of interrelated foci that are neither simply convertible nor only extrinsically related.

This realization of the differentiated unity of de Lubac's corpus invites us to consider the degree to which his outlook was formed not by the Second Vatican Council, with which he is so often, and rightly, associated, but by the First. This, of course, is not to suggest that we *neglect* the central importance of Vatican II to de Lubac's thought, but rather to avoid anachronism and recognize that he was primarily an inter-conciliar figure. Of the nineteen or so volumes of his major works,[7] twelve were published before or during Vatican II. While the latter Council's documents may indeed shed important light upon de Lubac's theology, especially those works written during or after it, we should avoid reading his works in light of a context that did not exist when they were being produced.[8]

xvi   Introduction

One concept from Vatican I is especially pertinent for our understanding of de Lubac's thought: the nexus of mysteries. According to the Constitution on the Catholic Faith, *Dei Filius*, because the mystery of God infinitely exceeds the capacities of our finite intellects, our knowledge of God, even when it is based on revelation, will always remain somewhat "covered by the veil of . . . faith and wrapped, as it were, in a certain obscurity."[9] Despite this recognition of our intellectual limitations, the Council also taught that a "most profitable" understanding of the mysteries remains available to reason, guided by faith along two paths: analogies drawn from things we know by natural reason and consideration of the "connexion of these mysteries with one another and with the final end of humanity."[10] The trope of the *nexus mysteriorum* parallels our observation that the Lubacian corpus is characterized by an intrinsically related diversity.

De Lubac's Own Use of the *Nexus Mysteriorum*

My appeal to the nexus of mysteries is itself fully consistent with de Lubac's thought. At several junctures, he makes explicit appeals to *Dei Filius* and to the *nexus mysteriorum*. The most significant of these is in his programmatic inaugural lecture at the Université Catholique de Lyons in 1929, which was later published as "Apologétique et théologie." This lecture indicates the direction that his subsequent thought will take, and we shall return to it in chapter 3's investigation of de Lubac's theological epistemology. At this juncture, what matters is de Lubac's direct appeal to Vatican I: "Has the First Vatican Council not summoned us to search for the links between the two of them [apologetics and theology] when it teaches that the theological method consists of studying the relationships that exist not only among the various dogmas but also between the totality of dogma and its ultimate end?"[11]

De Lubac makes explicit appeal to *Dei Filius* elsewhere in his work, drawing upon its teaching that divine truth exceeds the capacities of our finite intellects,[12] and at times directly appealing to the nexus of mysteries.[13] Especially pertinent is his statement in 1955: "This text [*Dei Filius* on the nexus of mysteries] is very dear to me. I had occasion to quote it myself, from the time of my first publication ["Apologétique et théologie"]. I have often been inspired by it since then."[14] While it never be-

Introduction   xvii

comes explicitly programmatic for him, he comes close to this in *The Splendor of the Church* when he states that the *nexus mysteriorum* "is not a luxury but a necessity" if one is to develop an understanding of the faith.[15]

Mysteries, Mystery, and Dogma

The notion of a nexus of mysteries presumes a fundamental unity to the Catholic faith, for it stresses that the mysteries are connected in an integral whole. In his mature reflections in *The Christian Faith*, de Lubac reflects upon this integral unity at length.[16] The unity of the church's belief occurs because the church receives its faith from and is "judged by one Word," who testifies to one God, the divine Trinity.[17] While the church teaches many things, holding to numerous dogmas, these all refer to and are founded in a more fundamental and singular mystery.[18] "One can," of course, "enumerate mysteries. . . . But if the 'Dogmas' find their unity . . . in their origin, the 'Mysteries' find their unity interiorly, through their substance."[19]

In this passage de Lubac signals two things. The first is important to note in passing: there is a relation of dependence between dogma and mystery. As we shall see in chapter 5, de Lubac understands dogma to be entirely derivative of the Christian mystery. Indeed, Bertrand Dumas argues that in de Lubac's usage *dogme* and *mystère* are more or less interchangeable, a contention that can be corroborated by de Lubac's appeal to the nexus of mysteries in "Apologétique et théologie," where he states that the Council had instructed theologians to consider the relationship of *dogmas* with one another and with humanity's final end.[20] The second thing is related to the first and bears more directly on our present task: the unity of the nexus of mysteries is not a mere mental construct or an imposition, but an interior feature of the mysteries themselves. They are substantially unified.

In this way, de Lubac reflects a consensus that steadily grew throughout the twentieth century and that probably owes its emergence to *Dei Filius* and its call to consider the *nexus mysteriorum*, despite potentially appearing at variance with it. The theological milieu of Vatican I tended to understand the "mysteries" in the plural, as a set of interlocked, divinely revealed realities. As theologians pursued the nexus of these mysteries, they increasingly recognized that, fundamentally, they referred to a singular mystery: the mystery of salvation in Christ.[21]

While appeal to the nexus of mysteries has perhaps fallen into desuetude in the years since the Second Vatican Council, replaced, if at all, by a more generic appeal to "mystery," the movement toward a more singular referent to the Christian mystery should not be seen as an about-face, but rather as a refinement of the viewpoint expressed in *Dei Filius*. Here a comparison with Vatican II's Constitution on Revelation, *Dei Verbum*, is instructive. While *Dei Filius* recognized that the truths of divine revelation exceed all human capacities, including propositional expression, the idiom still tends to be rather propositional, as if God has granted humanity access to a data set otherwise inaccessible, which provides additional information for our understanding of God and our relationship to him. *Dei Verbum*, on the other hand, as the fruit of the twentieth-century movement of *ressourcement*, recovers a far more vital, dynamic, and narratival account of revelation.[22] This account sets it in terms of a pedagogy of salvation beginning from humanity's creation and continuing through the Word and God's consistent call to us, through that same Word after our Fall, through the prophets of Israel, and finally through the Word made flesh.[23] The account of revelation in *Dei Verbum* is relational and soteriological because it all converges upon humanity's restoration to God through the incarnate Christ.[24] Even as we recognize the differences between the two constitutions, we must not overlook their continuity. *Dei Verbum* concerns itself precisely with the interconnection of the mysteries (e.g., the Trinity, creation, revelation, Christology, soteriology) with one another and with humanity's final end. A case could be made that it represents not a departure from but a maturation of *Dei Filius*'s account of revelation.[25] In a rather similar manner, de Lubac's works pursue the connection of their various loci to the mystery of redemption in Christ, which is, in the end, what *Dei Filius* commended: the connection of the mysteries to one another and to humanity's final end.

Immediately upon recognizing the relevance of the *nexus mysteriorum* to de Lubac's work, a qualification is needed. De Lubac was not a methodologically oriented or preoccupied thinker. His works tend to be historical in nature and are often a web of undifferentiated quotes and citations from patristic and medieval forebears. De Lubac himself accurately characterizes this tendency in the introduction to *Catholicisme*: "This book contains no more than certain materials gathered together in no very strict order and followed by certain reflections on them."[26] One will not find from him the sustained attention to method found, for instance, in his Jesuit confrère Bernard Lonergan, nor even in his erstwhile-Jesuit pupil, friend, and advocate Hans Urs von Balthasar. This being the case, we should not assume that de Lubac has self-consciously adopted the nexus of mysteries as a methodology. Though, as we have seen, he does at times explicitly appeal to the *nexus mysteriorum*, what I suggest is more along the lines of a reflexive approach, born from having had one's assumptions and horizons formed in a certain milieu within which a synthetic approach to theological loci came naturally, than a method, whether explicit or inchoate.

This more tacit influence of the nexus of mysteries can be discerned in de Lubac's first book, *Catholicisme*, which is generally considered to contain in seminal form the themes that would be unfolded over the rest of his career in his other major works.[27] This book includes forays into ecclesiology and sacramental theology, the theology of nature and grace, the spiritual interpretation of Scripture, the challenge of atheism, and the relation between Christianity and the other religions. All of these threads are gathered and woven together by de Lubac to articulate a single theological vision of the social dimensions of Catholic dogma. In this way, *Catholicisme* evinces the *nexus mysteriorum*, albeit without explicit appeal thereto.

Mysticism and Mystery

Closely aligned with the central place afforded to the Christian mystery in de Lubac's theology is his account of Christian mysticism. Writing in retrospect, de Lubac observes, "I truly believe that for a rather long time the idea for my book on Mysticism has been my inspiration in everything; I form my judgments on the basis of it, it provides me with the means to classify my ideas in proportion to it. But I will not write this book. It is in all ways beyond my physical, intellectual, spiritual strength."[28] This statement furnishes two key observations for those who would seek to account for the synthetic unity of de Lubac's theology. First, it is incumbent upon us to attend to this feature of his thought, which he identifies as its center. Second, this center remains largely unarticulated. Though, as we shall see, mysticism's influence can be discerned throughout his corpus, the fact remains that he never completed a major work on the theme; the most direct treatment we have is a single 1965 essay, "Mystique et Mystère," the title of which alone indicates the close proximity between mysticism and mystery in his thought.

Though the trope of mysticism has received relatively scant attention in Anglophone scholarship of de Lubac,[29] a significant vein of recent French-language scholarship has been developing this aspect of de Lubac's thought, attending especially to the relation between the notions of *mystique* and of *mystère* in the Lubacian œuvre. The latter term has received its definitive treatment in Étienne Guibert's *Le mystère du Christ d'après Henri de Lubac* (2006), while the former has been most fully explored by Bertrand Dumas in *Mystique et théologie d'après Henri de Lubac* (2012). Other important works have related one or the other (or both) of these terms to various areas of de Lubac's writings: the theology of the supernatural, theological anthropology, history and eschatology, and so forth.[30] Dumas, in particular, has demonstrated that, far from being an ancillary concern, *mystique* animates the whole of de Lubac's thought. Crucially, as de Lubac's thought matured, he came to understand *théologie* as itself interior to *mystique*.[31]

As we shall see, de Lubac's understanding of Christian mysticism turns primarily upon the interiorization of the Christian mystery. It names the incorporation of humanity into the life of God the Trinity through the redemptive work of the incarnate Christ. It is ecclesial in its context and sacramental in its texture. It is essentially an account of salvation. Hence, the category of mysticism allows us to clarify what is meant by *salvation*. While within the concrete world-historical order that actually exists, salvation has occurred as a remedial endeavor, a redemption following upon the sin of humanity, the concept itself, as used in this book, is broader than that. Salvation refers to humanity's coming to share in the life of God the Trinity through Christ. The full and final flourishing of humanity would have been possible only through divine grace even if our nature had remained sinless and unfallen. Even apart from any sort of healing from sin or rescue from danger, we would have still needed to be "saved."

My use of the same terminology for the realization of humanity's supernatural vocation, whether the counterfactual state of an unfallen humanity or the actual state of affairs of a post-lapsarian redemption, is intentional. It serves to foreground the absolutely supernatural character of salvation. This helps us to avoid distortions and reductions that can tend to arise when we become preoccupied with matters of remediation. As important as concepts such as guilt and forgiveness may be, they do not tell the whole story, though they are often presented and discussed as if they do. We avoid this by recognizing that even a sinless humanity depends entirely upon divine grace for its ultimate beatitude, while still concerning ourselves with the form that salvation has taken within the actual world order. The trope of mysticism, then, provides us with another conceptual framework for understanding the same reality, and so allows us to avoid simply conflating salvation with redemption.

This recognition that mysticism is essentially soteriological provides us with a means by which we can more readily account for the unity of de Lubac's œuvre and integrate the insights of others. At the same time, though, because de Lubac never completed his desired book on mysticism, we must be careful in our appeal to the concept. His works must be allowed to speak for themselves, without being distorted by a Procrustean appeal to mysticism. It is not the case that de Lubac's works were all about mysticism (or salvation) after all, rather than their ostensible topics. Dumas's contention that *théologie* is interior to *mystique*, as opposed to there being a relation of subordination, opposition, or equivalence, allows us to uphold this view. *The Splendor of the Church*, for instance, remains an ecclesiological work and not a crypto-soteriological or mystical work. And yet the inclusion of *théologie* within *mystique* can prime us to recognize the overarching concerns that drove de Lubac's project.

This study shall follow an inductive method, then, examining de Lubac's corpus on its own terms while also noting the consistent soteriological tropes upon which it, in all its variety, turns. The topic of mysticism will be broached only in those contexts in which it is explicitly invoked or directly relevant. We shall save sustained consideration of the matter for the end, in a coda, noting in retrospect how it illumines the œuvre whose lineaments we have explored on its own terms and allowing us to move into a final synthesis. By following this inductive approach, though, we shall ensure that this synthesis does not come at the expense of the specific contours and emphases of the works themselves.

For this reason, while in the end I shall present my own synthetic account of the speculative soteriology that seems to have informed de Lubac's thought, up until that point, I shall keep theological construction muted lest I occlude de Lubac's own voice. In a work of constructive theology, I would be rather more free with my own theologizing, but here the goal is to present an accurate statement of de Lubac's own thought, in view of his own central emphases and commitments.

Soteriology between Ontology and History

The soteriological focus I propose also allows for a *rapprochement* of sorts between two predominant trajectories in English-language de Lubac scholarship. One, exemplified especially by John Milbank and Radical Orthodoxy, tends to interpret de Lubac through an ontological lens, seeing in him the recovery of a lost Platonic-Christian synthesis in metaphysics and providing the means to recover an authentically Christian vision of reality, in contrast to the now-regnant secular order.[32] The other, pioneered by Susan K. Wood's study of de Lubac's theology of spiritual exegesis, interprets the French Jesuit through a more historical lens, concerned principally with the transition from the Old Testament to the New with which de Lubac's theology of spiritual exegesis was preoccupied.[33]

For a whole host of reasons that will become clearer in the course of discussion, I align myself more with the historical than the ontological trajectory. First, de Lubac is explicit in his statements distancing himself from Platonism.[34] Beyond this, de Lubac devoted thousands of pages to discussing patristic and medieval spiritual exegesis, all while insisting that we could not and should not simply attempt to re-create it. This, by the way, signals that *ressourcement* is something rather different than mere repristination or retrieval, a point to which I shall return. It also represents a real oddity unless we recognize, with Wood, that de Lubac was up to something else in those studies. An attentive reading of his œuvre shows that diachronic historical concerns pervade it and that the more static ontological reading cannot adequately account for the form or content of his thought.

Introduction   xxiii

A soteriological focus allows us to integrate the perspectives and concerns of the two disparate lines of de Lubac scholarship: the ontologically focused trajectory exemplified by Milbank and Boersma and the historical trajectory exemplified by Wood. Salvation is not an eternal principle but a historical act. It is precisely Christ's act of salvation that forms the pivot of history. The Christian newness lies in Christ's salvific achievement. And this is a salvation that affects humanity at the core of its being: calling us beyond ourselves and to God. It impinges on our nature and its end. Hence, at the nexus of history and ontology lies soteriology.

The Way Ahead

Salvation in Henri de Lubac: Divine Grace, Human Nature, and the Mystery of the Cross follows an itinerary comprised of four main movements. Part One, "Salvation Desired: Nature, Grace, and Competing Humanisms," is especially concerned with the problem of the supernatural and its relationship to two distinct and opposed humanisms: the "inhuman humanism" of atheism and the authentic humanism de Lubac sought to re-establish with his social account of salvation in *Catholicisme*.

Chapter 1 interrogates de Lubac's writings on the supernatural in order to clarify their soteriological impetus. From *Surnaturel* onward, de Lubac consistently considered human nature in terms of its finality, which is the beatific vision. This teleological account of humanity renders unnecessary and dismisses as misleading the hypothesis of a possible state of pure nature. I foreground the trinitarian dimensions of de Lubac's account of deifying grace, which incorporates humanity into the Son's filial relationship in an ecstasy of pure gift. This trope of integration into the trinitarian generosity would reappear throughout his oeuvre, and in *Surnaturel* is characterized in sacrificial terms, which shall inform our presentation throughout for two primary reasons.

First, sacrificial language appears with noticeable regularity in the Lubacian corpus, and does so perhaps more as a matter of course than anything else. Faithful to the Catholic theological tradition, de Lubac assumed a sacrificial understanding of Christ's redemptive act. However, we should not allow the popular imagination surrounding sacrifice to confuse the issue here. Within the Christian tradition, sacrifice is not simply identical to immolation or death, nor is it any sort of sacralized violence. Following Augustine and his refiner Thomas Aquinas, sacrifice is preeminently charity, love, gift-of-self. Christ has saved humanity by dying, rising, ascending to the Father, and bestowing upon it the Holy Spirit, in short, through the paschal mystery. Throughout this work, references to the cross or to sacrifice should be understood as a shorthand for this entire complex of redemptive events, not as referring to Christ's death in isolation from the rest of the mystery of redemption. Second, attention to this sacrificial language will allow us to more readily integrate the various areas of de Lubac's thought, particularly his theologies of spiritual exegesis, of history, and of the Eucharist. Further discussion of sacrifice in the course of the argument shall serve to clarify the matter further.

Chapter 2 carries forward de Lubac's theological anthropology into a consideration of his engagements with non-Christian thought, especially atheistic humanism and Buddhism. While the previous chapter clarified that de Lubac's account of the supernatural is driven by soteriology rather than ontology or the social order implied by said ontology, he clearly saw the social implications of this vision, which met the exigencies of his particular context. In contrast with the atheist humanisms proposed by Comte, Nietzsche, and Proudhon, Catholicism presented a true humanism grounded in the theological virtue of charity, which draws human beings into the life of God, because God himself is love. Once more, the charity operative in Christ's crucifixion is the means by which we are integrated into the trinitarian love.

The account of salvation in the writings on the supernatural tends to be more formal and notional. The chapters in Part Two, "Salvation Disclosed: Revelation and Spiritual Exegesis," provide material content to the account of salvation. Chapter 3 considers the soteriological focus of de Lubac's theological epistemology and its relation to his theological anthropology. For de Lubac, knowledge of God is not primarily informational but is about introducing humanity into the divine life. This is evident in his works *The Discovery of God* and *The Christian Faith*, the latter of which provides an account of revelation grounded in the Trinity's saving act in Christ. The revelation of the Trinity is soteriological both in the sense that it is revealed in God's saving acts and in the sense that it is revealed in order to bring us into the life of the Trinity.

Introduction   xxv

Chapter 4 turns from revelation as a concept to the practice of spiritual exegesis. De Lubac's theology of spiritual exegesis is soteriologically focused in two senses. First, spiritual exegesis turns upon the relation between letter and spirit, which correspond to the Old and New Testaments construed not so much as canonical texts as economies of God. To pass from the letter to the Spirit is to "pass over into Christ" such that spiritual exegesis is isomorphic to conversion to Christ. Second, the paschal mystery provides the pivotal content for Scripture. Christ's sacrifice on the cross is the act of exegesis that accomplishes the transition from Old to New Testament, from letter to spirit. Here we find perhaps the clearest expression of the "Christian newness," which stands in both radical continuity and discontinuity with what has come before. The Old Testament is both preserved in and radically transformed by Christ's saving act. The four senses of Scripture can actually be reduced to two, because tropology (the moral sense) and anagogy (the eschatological sense) are themselves interior to allegory. They unfold its meaning, but add no further content to it. This provides a crucial structure for de Lubac's theology of history.

Part Three, "Salvation Realized: Ecclesiology and Sacraments," considers the concrete realization of salvation in the Christian church. De Lubac's account of salvation is famously social, and the church is the context wherein salvation is realized. It is the community of salvation in the strongest sense of that term. As human beings are incorporated into Christ, they are likewise incorporated into the church, which is his body. Chapter 5 reprises the social vision of salvation evident in *Catholicisme* and demonstrates that this is the theological substance of de Lubac's ecclesiology. All other aspects of his ecclesiological vision serve this basic principle.

Chapter 6 moves into more sacramental—and sacrificial—terrain. It is a frequently overlooked fact that the argument of *Corpus Mysticum* turns upon the sacrifice of Christ. It is by sharing in this sacrifice that "the Eucharist makes the church." De Lubac draws upon Augustine of Hippo's theology of true sacrifice, which opens a vista to understanding Christ's sacrifice as the inmost reality of the church's existence. The eucharistic sacrifice is at once identical to Christ's sacrifice on the cross and a sign of the eschatological sacrifice of the whole Christ (head and body), which is charity.

xxvi   Introduction

Part Four, "Salvation Consummated: Eschatology and the Theology of History," continues the consideration of salvation history from the preceding discussion and sets the stage for a final synthetic statement. Chapter 7 is concerned with de Lubac's writings on Joachim of Fiora. Joachim and his posterity anticipate an intra-historical development that surpasses Christ, whether an age of the Spirit, of Absolute *Geist*, a worker's paradise, or a thousand-year *Reich*. Once more, all of these options are soteriologically deficient. The paschal mystery of Christ is the unsurpassable act of revelation and salvation, and eschatology will not leave Christ or his saving act behind but will rather be their full flowering and consummation. All that is provisional will pass away, and the whole Christ will be presented to God in a supreme act of worship. This is the finality toward which humanity and all of history is ordered. This anti-Joachimite impetus is discernible across de Lubac's œuvre, including the works on spiritual exegesis, the church, and the sacraments.

Chapter 8 turns to de Lubac's writings on Teilhard de Chardin and moves the Christological meaning of history into its broadest cosmic scope. De Lubac's interpretation of Teilhard parallels the theology of history articulated in Teilhard's writings on spiritual exegesis and the anti-Joachimite writings. Christ has introduced a genuine novelty into history, but one that embraces and fulfills what has come before. Within the writings of and about Teilhard, we discover an important trope that allows for an integration of de Lubac's œuvre: that of history's outcome as a cosmic sacrifice.

The coda, *"Mysterium Crucis,"* takes its name from the concluding meditation of *Catholicisme*, in which de Lubac considers humanity's passage into eternal life in God through participation in the mystery of Christ's cross and draws together the disparate threads that have emerged from this survey of de Lubac's major works, articulating a synthetic vision of their inner coherence and unity. The trope of cosmic sacrifice provides the integrating motif whereby this synthesis is able to occur. Here an exploration of the 1965 article "Mystique et Mystère" sets the stage for a resumé of the Lubacian corpus, read as centered upon the one sacrifice of Jesus Christ and humanity's incorporation into the life of the Trinity through it and as it. This reprise is left for the coda in recognition that while mysticism was central to de Lubac, most of his works were *about* something else. Having surveyed them on their own terms, with an eye toward their soteriological concerns, we are able to see in "Mystique et Mystère" the means of integrating the vision.

Throughout de Lubac's œuvre, theological loci interpenetrate and inform each other because central to his thought was an account of humanity's incorporation into Christ, leading to its assimilation into the divine life. This was the animating principle of his thought, which expressed itself throughout his work. And now, at last, it can be given a synthetic presentation. Though they are never systematically elaborated, de Lubac has continual recourse to the following complex of ideas.

Salvation is achieved by humanity's passage through Christ into the life of the Trinity. We share in the triune life by sharing in Christ's identity as members of his body. We come to share in the divine life through charity, which is God's very nature and which, within God, takes the form of an infinitely generous gift. We are brought into salvation by Christ's sacrifice on the cross, which has charity as its inmost content. This charity informs the life of Christ's body, the church, and the life of his individual members. His saving sacrifice is the fulcrum and the meaning of history, and history's fulfillment will likewise be this same sacrifice as the body of Christ is offered, in union with its head, to the Father as a supreme act of loving worship. This is the same sacrifice by which we were saved, and it is ultimately *as* this sacrifice that we are saved, entering into the loving beatitude of the Holy Trinity.

PART ONE

Salvation Desired

Nature, Grace, and Competing Humanisms

CHAPTER ONE

Saving Grace

Soteriology in the Works on Nature and Grace

There is probably no area of Henri de Lubac's theology that has resulted in so much controversy as his works on the supernatural. In a moment we shall attend to this controversy, which is exhaustively documented elsewhere, in a somewhat cursory fashion. But this chapter is about a rather distinct issue that is frequently obscured in the welter of literature discussing the adequacy of de Lubac's historical and/or speculative positions. De Lubac's works on nature and grace are primarily concerned with offering an account of humanity's salvation through Christ. Moreover, this soteriology has distinctly trinitarian contours, as human beatitude is ultimately achieved through incorporation into and envelopment by the Holy Trinity, an incorporation that occurs precisely through a share in the Son.[1] While de Lubac has much else to say about the relation between the natural order and its supernatural dénouement, his writings on the supernatural are animated by this vision. As the subsequent chapters will demonstrate, this Christological-trinitarian soteriology extends beyond the writings on nature and grace and indeed pervades the entire Lubacian corpus. When de Lubac writes about nature and grace, he is focused upon saving grace.

The *Surnaturel* Controversy

The publication of Henri de Lubac's *Surnaturel* in 1946 was a watershed moment in contemporary Catholic theology that altered the course of de

Lubac's life and career.[2] Presented as a historical study, particularly of the thought of Augustine of Hippo and Thomas Aquinas, *Surnaturel* advances the now famous thesis that humanity has a natural desire for the beatific vision.[3] By positing this *natural* desire for a *supernatural* end, de Lubac provoked the ire of neo-scholastic Thomists, who argued that this thesis undercut the gratuity of grace and redemption. Indeed, the controversy over *Surnaturel* led to a period of about eight years during which de Lubac was prohibited from teaching theology but continued to research and publish.[4] His works on Buddhism were produced during this time.[5] De Lubac had begun the work that became these books in the 1930s in order to prepare himself to teach the history of religions at Lyons. In the 1950s, with theology off limits, he published them.[6] And his *Meditation sur l'église* (1953) reads as a cri de cœur from one who never wanted to be anything more than a loyal son of the church, yet found himself on its margins. Although the book was substantially written before the controversy and, according to de Lubac, bore no particular relationship to it,[7] it may still have played some role in his "rehabilitation." In 1958, four of his works (the works on Buddhism, *Sur les Chemins de Dieu*, and *Méditation sur l'église*) were presented to Pope Pius XII. The next year, de Lubac was once again permitted to teach theology.[8]

In the fog of controversy, it is somewhat difficult to assess precisely what happened that led to de Lubac's silencing. Pope Pius XII's encyclical *Humani generis* warns against those who would undermine the gratuity of the supernatural, especially those who would suggest that "God . . . cannot create intellectual beings without ordering and calling them to the beatific vision."[9] Many understood this to be a direct condemnation of de Lubac and the thesis of *Surnaturel*, a position still endorsed by notable scholars.[10] However, de Lubac always maintained that *Humani generis* could not possibly have been directed against him, as (1) he never said anything of the sort with regard to God's inability to create intellectual creatures who are not ordained to the beatific vision, and, more crucially, (2) the pope adopted one of de Lubac's turns of phrase in the encyclical itself, thereby giving at least a tacit approval to de Lubac's work.[11] Nevertheless, *Humani generis* provoked enough anxiety among de Lubac's Jesuit superiors that they removed him from active teaching. De Lubac's reminiscences of the event display his bewilderment and pain: "During the whole affair . . . an affair that would last so many years, I was never questioned, I never had a single conversation about the root of the matter with any authority of the Church in Rome or the Society. No one ever communicated to me any precise charge."[12]

The literature on the nature-grace debate, and de Lubac's role in it, is vast. At the outset, I must note that the purpose of this chapter is not evaluative. The question is not whether de Lubac's formulation of the relationship between nature and grace is correct, whether it is fully adequate, nor whether his interpretation of Aquinas or Augustine is historically accurate.[13] All of these are worthy enough questions, but they clarify neither the soteriological center of de Lubac's thought nor the interconnectedness of its constituent elements—the central focus of this study.

After the publication of *Surnaturel*, de Lubac returned to the thematics of nature and grace in three additional monographs. *Augustinisme et théologie moderne* (1965) and *Le mystère du surnaturel* (1965) essentially develop the basic thesis from *Surnaturel* and clarify de Lubac's intention in the face of the criticisms it received.[14] *Augustinisme et théologie moderne* in particular is an expansion of the first part of the original *Surnaturel*.[15] *Petit catéchèse sur nature et grâce* (1980), among the last of his books, presents de Lubac's most mature statement on the matter. These works span almost the entirety of de Lubac's career, demonstrating that the relation between nature and grace was an abiding concern for him. Through these works, both consistency and development are discernible. My treatment of the works on nature and grace operates with two assumptions. First, de Lubac did not engage in revisionist history or "retconning" of his previous views. When he says that the later works should be understood as clarifications of what he intended in *Surnaturel*, he should be believed.[16] Second, the mature works should be prioritized in interpreting his thought. Over the decades, de Lubac gained clarity regarding his own commitments and priorities, and his later positions should be respected as more definitive than his earlier ones.

As we shall see, the trajectory evident in de Lubac's works on the supernatural is toward a greater Christological and redemptive focus and concern.[17] De Lubac's own retrospective criticism of *Surnaturel* suggests that he should have been clearer that he was following the practice of the scholastic discussions about which he was writing, abstracting from the concreteness of Jesus Christ, and that he should have paid more attention to "the transformation, or rather turning around, of the desire for God under the action of grace," beyond being "only just pointed out with a few words in the conclusion."[18] In the preface to *The Mystery of the Supernatural*, de Lubac notes the circumscribed character of the work, "He [de Lubac] has considered neither the mediating role of the incarnate Word, nor the entry of the adopted creature into the relations of the Trinity."[19] These issues are all bracketed in order to address the more formal problem that lay at the heart of the debate.[20] As we recognize this bracketing, we must also recognize that de Lubac is clear in stating that the reality he is addressing *is indeed* mediated by the incarnate Son of God and consists of the creature's integration into the life of the Trinity. Further, de Lubac notes that the "*séparatiste*" thesis that he sought to counteract is problematic precisely because within it "everything that comes from Christ, everything that should lead to him, is pushed so far into the background as to look like disappearing for good."[21]

While it was not absent from even the earliest works on nature and grace,[22] by the time de Lubac published his last word on the matter, there was no ambiguity regarding his understanding that the supernatural, at least in concrete terms, referred to and resulted from the saving work of Jesus Christ. Salvation answers to a deep exigence of human nature.[23] Because of how God has ordered the creation, especially humanity's place within that creation, the proper fulfillment of human beings is supernatural elevation into the divine life.

Surnaturel and Augustinianism

While *Surnaturel* drives toward its ultimate thesis that human nature, as spiritual, is constituted by its openness to and desire for the beatific vision, the book opens with treatments of Baianism and Jansenism, and it is in de Lubac's engagements with these heretically denatured Augustinianisms that his soteriological concern becomes especially evident. Michael Baius and Cornelius Jansen both purported to be heirs of an Augustinian understanding of humanity and grace. In contrast, de Lubac suggests that their teachings are radicalizations of Augustinianism, and therefore distortions of it.[24] Essentially, according to de Lubac, Baius and Jansen commit equal and opposite errors in radicalizing Augustine's doctrine of grace.[25] Baius shares with Augustine a revulsion at the notion that God would leave humanity to its own devices and without divine aid, yet he conceives of that aid not as a gratuitous gift, as Augustine construed it, but as something owed to the creature, which can be demanded of God.[26] In this way, Baius neglects the supernatural virtue of charity, "which is the principle of humanity's supernatural vocation," which "envelops the whole economy of salvation."[27]

Jansen's position is more complex. He understands that humanity can make no demands upon God. However, he views grace as entirely redemptive and remedial, so needed only after humanity's fall into sin. Prelapsarian Adam would have needed some measure of divine aid, but this measure would have been rather small indeed, only a sufficient grace (*adiutorium sine qua non*), not an efficient grace that actually brings about its effect (*adiutorium quo*).[28] So minimal was this aid that, had Adam persevered in innocence, his merits would have been merely human merit, and he would have had ground for boasting in himself and his own achievement.[29] For postlapsarian humanity, though, sufficient grace is now insufficient; only efficient grace truly suffices. Yet it does so in such a way that now *none* of humanity's merits are genuinely human.[30] In this way, grace more or less replaces the free activity of human beings.

De Lubac argues that at this juncture Jansen has fundamentally misread Augustine by making the anti-Pelagian writings the whole measure of his thought. When one looks more widely at Augustine's corpus, it is apparent that he saw grace as more than merely remedial. Humanity is, at all times, dependent upon God, requiring not only "grace," but supernatural elevation if the *cor inquietum* is to find its rest in God.[31] Put another way, even unfallen humanity would still need "salvation," because our beatitude can be attained only by a supernatural gift. At this juncture, it is worth noting that the language of nature and grace tends toward a certain ambiguity, because the debate touches upon two related matters, which are not reducible to one another: the supernatural order and grace.[32] To some extent, de Lubac is attentive to this distinction, as we have seen, though he does not differentiate between the matters rigorously enough to avoid all ambiguity. I suspect that a significant reason for this imprecision is the basically Augustinian character of de Lubac's thought (and the fact that Baianism and Jansenism cast themselves as Augustinianisms). Augustine, after all, lived and wrote before the theorem of the supernatural was developed.[33]

By the time he wrote the *Petite catéchèse*, de Lubac was quite explicit that these were two distinct, though related, problematics.[34] Brigitte Cholvy has attempted a systematic presentation of de Lubac's eventual position on the distinction between "grace" and "the supernatural," according to which the latter term refers to humanity's vocation or finality, while the former refers particularly to our coming to share in the divine life. God freely gives us being (nature) and ordains us to our end in him (supernatural), but our actually coming to share in the life of God (grace) involves our free acceptance of his invitation.[35]

Returning to the earlier works, if Baius loses the discontinuity between nature and grace, Jansen has lost sight of their continuity.[36] Missing from both of their conceptions of grace was the crucial dimension of "the novelty of Christ," which, as we shall see, animates so many areas of de Lubac's thought.[37] For Baius and Jansen both, the Old and New Testaments are essentially on the same plane, with the result that Christ's grace in the New Testament is only remedial, restoring what was lost. Hence, while "Augustine showed the completion of nature in its supernaturalization . . . Baius naturalizes the supernatural. He transforms a spiritual doctrine into a thesis of ontology."[38]

This is crucial, for it demonstrates that de Lubac's concern, even as early as *Surnaturel*, is not with developing an ontology (or even a non-ontology). This contrasts somewhat with the more ontological approaches to de Lubac's oeuvre. For instance, in *The Suspended Middle* John Milbank rightly notes that *Surnaturel* concerns itself with questions of grace and deification, phrasing the matter rather elegantly: "That which is wholly done for us by God, namely deification by grace, is yet also our highest act and as such properly our own—even that which is most properly our own."[39] From there, though, Milbank's preoccupations with the heretical character of the "secular order" tend to lead him from this soteriological concentration into considerations of ontology.[40] Instead, de Lubac's concern is soteriological.

While Augustine's teaching has ontological implications, they are not the center. This center is occupied by salvation in Christ: a "participation in the filiation of the Word . . . [which] introduces the creature into the bosom of the divine life."[41] This theme continues, lying at the origins of the term *supernatural*, which de Lubac traces through a consideration of patristic writings on theosis. The Son enjoys by nature a divine filiation and makes us "participants" in it "by his incarnation," raising us to a reality beyond our nature.[42] Indeed, the supernatural is "not only . . . above nature's . . . exigencies and forces . . . [but also] above even its perfection."[43] The human being is "destined to divine union, to participation in the trinitarian life in the 'beatific vision.' The supernatural is essentially the vision of God. . . . But by extension, all that which has a relation to that end."[44] To be sure, de Lubac is concerned with ontological implications. The theory of "pure nature," originally a sort of hypothetical designed to provide clarity to the question of what is, properly, our own attainment and for what we depend upon divine aid, devolves into a *system* of pure nature.[45] Then the state of pure nature transitions into being considered "*un* ordre *purement naturel*,"[46] which, in turn, funds a system of nature and grace separated from each other, leading toward "*laïcisation*."[47] Wherein the supernatural becomes simply a "*sur-nature*."[48] Nevertheless, these ontological implications matter precisely because of their soteriological import.

The supernatural refers, then, to divinization, which is conceived of as supernatural for two reasons, "Because it is divine and because it is gratuitous, and these two reasons make nothing but one in the end, the absolutely gratuitous necessarily coincides with the divine."[49] All this clarifies that when we speak of a supernatural order, or of a supernatural vocation, what is in view is precisely human salvation: the calling of humanity to share in the life of God through Christ.

The Spirit's Élan and Grace's Gratuity

In this connection, we must attend to the place of spirit in de Lubac's theological anthropology, for it is central to his conception of humanity's ordination to the Trinity's life.[50] De Lubac's most sustained consideration of the human spirit is found in the essay "Tripartite Anthropology," which takes as its starting point the Pauline statement in First Thessalonians 5:23: "May the God of peace himself sanctify you entirely; and may your spirit and soul and body be kept sound and blameless at the coming of our Lord Jesus Christ."[51] The remainder of the essay traces the consistent witness of the theological tradition to this threefold theological anthropology, from these biblical origins through the patristic and medieval periods and finally to our own day, when more rationalist tendencies predominate and spirit has been collapsed into mind, soul, or intellect. We shall return to this elision in chapter 3's consideration of de Lubac's theological epistemology. For now, what really matters is the relation between the human spirit and its ordination to God.

In the conclusion to *Surnaturel* de Lubac writes of the "paradox of the human spirit," which "is not only the double of a nature; it is itself nature. Before being a thinking spirit, it is a spiritual nature. An irresoluble duality as much as an indissoluble union. Image of God, but drawn from nothing. Thus, before it loves God, and in order to be able to love him, it desires. Made for God, the spirit is drawn by him. . . . The spirit then is desire for God."[52] Hence, fundamental to human nature, prior to all acts of thought or will, is spirit or the desire for God. As a created spirit, humanity is open to, desires union with, and is drawn toward God from its most abyssal depths.[53]

Yet this raises the question of the gratuity of grace. If the human spirit requires union with God for its fulfillment, are we not in the same position as Baius with his demands upon God for grace? It was, of course, to avoid this ostensible implication that the hypothesis of a pure nature without supernatural finality was proposed, a hypothesis that eventually became an entire system of pure nature.[54] In contrast, de Lubac opposes both the notion of pure nature and the idea that the spirit's desire for God could make demands upon God, or somehow undermine the gratuity of grace. He approaches this through several avenues.

The mention of humanity's creation in the image of God above raises one such pathway, which is itself an important dimension of de Lubac's thought: the distinction between the image (*l'image*) and the likeness (*ressemblance*) of God in humanity. Though historical critical exegesis tends to view this pairing from Genesis 1:28 as Hebrew parallelism, and so as referring to the same reality, de Lubac follows an older patristic approach that distinguished between them. In this case, *image* refers to our spiritual nature, which desires and is drawn toward union with God, while *likeness* refers to the actual attainment of union with God. The two are related, but not identical. One must pass from one to the other, and to do so requires divine assistance.[55] There is a disproportion between them, which admits of no natural passage.

The historical sections of *Surnaturel* establish that the supernatural order is a matter of divinizing grace, hinting at it in terms of sharing the

Son's filiation and entering the Trinity's life. In the book's conclusion, de Lubac throws back the curtain and turns from historical reconstruction to a speculative vision that draws these threads together into a vision of humanity's ultimate incorporation into the divine life.[56] In so doing, he provides a basis for his contention that grace remains gratuitous, even if it is required for human nature's fulfillment. We are called to love God, but before we can love him, and, indeed, so that we can love him, we desire him.[57] This desire is fulfilled in charity, and the "supernatural order . . . is the order of pure charity" because "God himself is charity."[58] Humanity is, by essence, called to share in God's life, which is love, leading Cholvy to speak of a "metaphysics of love."[59] This calling, like our creation itself, is a gift freely given. It is in us, but not from us. Its origin lies in God, who has created us and called us to himself and "in crowning our merits crowns his own gifts."[60] In essence, we need God because he makes us to need him.[61] This vision culminates with a vision of gift and sacrifice:

> Identically, beatitude is service, vision is adoration, liberty is dependence, possession is ecstasy. When one defines our supernatural end by possession, liberty, vision, beatitude, one defines nothing but an aspect. One does not envisage it except from the *anthropocentric* point of view, that which is moreover natural enough, because one occupies himself with the end of man. In itself, that point of view is not the principal one, if it is true that God, who has created the world by pure generosity, has however created it for himself and for his glory. . . . The entire world reaches its end thanks to the spiritual being, who receives it in himself to relate it to its creator. The spirit gives the world to God in giving itself to him in an act of total remission. This act only attains its perfection, that is to say it is only fulfilled in its entire purity, in the supernatural order, which is the order of pure charity. Nothing is lacking from the fullness of the "sacrifice of praise." Such is the essential aspect, the *theocentric aspect*. . . . [Humanity owes to God] service, adoration, love such as they are realized among the blessed. The entire sacrifice of praise. . . . God, being himself charity and disinterestedness, does not envisage our service except as a blessed participation in his life.[62]

Cholvy suggests that though Jesus Christ is not explicitly mentioned in this passage, it ought to be read Christologically. God calls humanity to a certain dispossession, a self-lessness, that participates in the selflessness of the God who is love. Christ is the "spiritual being" in whom this disposition is perfectly realized, and in the process he brings along the rest of the world, us included, offering them to the Father in an act of total remission.[63]

The fulfillment of our being is to give ourselves away completely, interior to the God whose life is gift. The supernatural order of charity is both the answer to our innate longing for God and a participation in God's very nature as love. Considered in this frame, no demand is conceivable. God, who is himself perfectly free and generous, gives freely and generously. A gift cannot be demanded, even if it is desired. To think otherwise would be to mistake entirely the nature of the gift and the nature of God.

In *The Mystery of the Supernatural* de Lubac clarifies that while a state of pure nature may indeed be a hypothetical possibility, no such state has ever actually existed. Human beings, as we actually exist, have always been ordained for a supernatural finality, one that consists in rather more than either the remediation of fallen sinfulness[64] or a mere "addition [*ajoutée*]" to who we are. It requires, instead, our "consent to a more total sacrifice," namely, a transcendence in excess of all of our native capacities,[65] echoing the speculative vision encountered at the end of *Surnaturel*.

Our failure to recognize the radical quality of this self-transcendence leads to either a truncated account of the supernatural vocation as merely reparative or additive or to a self-enclosed account of the natural order in possession of its own integrity without reference to God—a position that we shall see underwrites the various atheist humanisms against which de Lubac contends—or both.[66] This merely additive account of the supernatural winds up conceiving of supernatural realities as merely natural, and so as a sort of repristinated (or recrudesced) Baianism.[67] Or it can be dispensed with entirely, leaving humanity free to forge its own moral path without reference to or assistance from God, a return to Pelagianism.[68] Atheist humanisms, with which we shall deal in chapter 2, wind up pursuing the courses charted by the renewed Pelagianism and Baianism, though obviously unwittingly.

Ironically, while the system of pure nature leads to these deleterious effects, it does so without actually safeguarding the gratuity of grace because it proceeds without reference to the actual world order established by God. A hypothesis of pure nature can tell us that God was not obliged to offer grace to some other version of humanity that does not actually exist and never has, but it cannot affirm that within the world, the actual human being that *I* am, has received grace as a free gift.[69] Instead, in order to truly safeguard grace's gratuity, we must be able to demonstrate "that the supernatural end can *in no case* be the object of any requirement or debt, even by a being who here and now has no other end."[70] In other words, salvation must be gracious also for those who are called to it!

In contrast, de Lubac's account of grace's freedom is developed in an analogy with the freedom of the creation. God is under no obligation to create. And, should God determine to create, he is under no obligation to create beings called into friendship with and beatitude in him. Yet he does create, and indeed creates human beings so that they may share in his life. No debt or demand is involved here.[71] Further, our openness to and desire for God is not the same as our attaining to God. Desire is distinct from its fulfillment.[72] It is only by the action of grace upon humanity that our natural love is transformed into charity. Nevertheless, because God himself is charity, only charity can truly fulfill this longing.[73] Yet our desire for God remains a plea, not a demand. Rather than our nature making demands upon grace, the reverse obtains: "It is the supernatural which, so to say, must summon up nature before nature can be in a position to receive it."[74] This is the hinge upon which de Lubac's theology of nature and grace, as well as his theological anthropology, pivots: to understand *what* human nature is, we must consider the *purpose* for which it exists (its finality).[75] God has created us for the purpose of sharing in his eternal blessedness.[76] No account of human nature that fails to account for this is adequate to the data of reality.

This desire for God, which itself comes as a gift from God and can be satisfied only by God's gift, is universal. Nevertheless, de Lubac assiduously maintains the specifically Christian character of this desire. The precise contours of what it is that would fulfill this desire can be known only through Christian revelation. Pagan antiquity had some notion of what it sought, but never dreamed of such a radical fulfillment as occurs in Christ.[77] Its paradoxical character defies the strictures of rationalism but is rather resolved only by faith.[78] The revelation of God in Christ has disclosed the precise form of our natural desire's fulfillment:[79]

> The Platonist *epistrophe* has been succeeded by the Christian *metanoia*, something very different and far more fundamental. The "beatific vision" is no longer the contemplation of a spectacle, but an intimate participation in the vision the Son has of the Father in the bosom of the Trinity. Revelation, by making us know in his Son the God of love, the personal and trinitarian God, the creating and saving God, the God "who was made man to make us God," has changed everything.[80]

In the end, we see that de Lubac must break out from his self-imposed strictures of formal ontology in order to adequately express the reality under consideration, which is not a matter of metaphysical principles, nor of orders, secular or otherwise, but rather of the coming of humanity to share in the divine life through the Son's redeeming act.

Grace and Redemption

In view of de Lubac's retrospective self-criticism that in *Surnaturel* he should have paid greater attention to the concretely Christological character of the supernatural and his methodological bracketing of Christology in *The Mystery of the Supernatural*, it is rather striking that both works still manage to explicitly state that humanity's ultimate vocation is incorporation into the Trinity interior to the Son. The concretely soteriological character of the supernatural order is all the clearer in de Lubac's most mature articulation of the matter, *A Brief Catechesis on Nature and Grace*. Here he clarifies that the supernatural refers to "not so much God or the order of divine things considered in itself, in its pure transcendence, as, in a general and as yet indeterminate manner, the divine order considered in its relationship of opposition to, and of union with the human order," which includes such notions as "revelation, mystery, divine Incarnation, redemption . . . [and] salvation."[81] Here the supernatural is no longer a question of abstract finalities and the orders established (or not) by them but is instead highly concrete: it is the meeting place of God and humanity in the God-Man, Jesus Christ.

Understood in this light, the supernatural is not so much an order[82] as it is God's act of divinizing humanity.[83] The "perfect model" of this divinization is the divine life of the trinitarian persons and their "circumincession."[84] Once more, the notion of being brought by grace to share in the life of the Trinity, particularly the mutuality of the trinitarian relationships, comes to the fore. Supernatural divinization does not introduce a new nature but rather transforms our nature by assimilating it into the trinitarian relations.[85]

Faced with the realization of our radical dependence upon grace for attaining our proper end, we are led to a deepened humility and the undoing of all hubris.[86] The atheist humanisms' hubris is found precisely in a loss of such humility, which results from a willful forgetfulness of God and our status as creatures.[87] In connection with the idea of humility, de Lubac tantalizingly suggests that its true model is in a divine and trinitarian humility, whereby God, "Although sovereignly free in his transcendence, makes himself partially immanent in his creatures by that *kenosis*, that 'excentration,' that 'movement of descent' which is the Word's Incarnation."[88] De Lubac goes even further to suggest that the kenosis displayed in the Son's mission somehow "reproduce[s]" his eternal procession, making it "possible to speak of a still more radical humility on God's part, a humility native to his eternal being and consisting in the excentration (ecstasy) of each Person sharing himself completely with the other two."[89] While he does not develop the thought at length, this gestures toward a notion of the cross, by which we are brought to share in the trinitarian relations, as itself expressive of those relations. This is particularly pertinent when we recall that de Lubac's vision of humanity's ultimate beatitude is sacrificial.[90] The telos and the means by which it is attained share an identity of content.

In the *Brief Catechesis*, de Lubac notes that much of the debate on the matter, including in his own writing, has tended to focus on abstract categories that do not do full justice to the biblical and Christian nature of the reality under discussion.[91] *Grace* is a word with a double meaning. On the one hand, it refers to the freely given calling to and gift of an elevation beyond our nature. But it also refers to the divine favor freely given in the face of human sinfulness; "Grace is also mercy and pardon."[92] Once more we are returned to the imprecision that attends speaking in terms of nature and grace. Nevertheless, this imprecision can be fortuitous because it keeps us grounded in the actually existing order rather than counterfactual states (whether of pure nature or of unfallen humanity). The human vocation to share in God's life is one and concrete.

Because humanity as it actually exists is sinful, grace is also redemption, and the supernatural affects us not merely by elevating us, but by overcoming enmity, by our radical conversion.[93] Hence, "If the union of nature and the supernatural was brought about in principle by the mystery of the Incarnation, the union of nature and grace can be fully accomplished only through the mystery of the redemption."[94] This mystery is "a darksome drama . . . a bloody drama, the climax of which is Calvary. . . . But [one with] . . . a luminous conclusion. . . . For the sacrifice of Christ abolished definitively the powerless interventions of man who had always sought for expiation and pardon; it is capable of bringing salvation to all."[95]

This leads us to a realism that recognizes our inability to manufacture a perfect humanity at the level of either the individual or society.[96] This, once more, stands in marked contrast to the outlook of atheist humanisms and also underlies de Lubac's rejection of theologies of liberation as soteriologically inadequate.[97] I would contend that liberation theology, properly understood, does uphold the transcendent and eschatological reserve that de Lubac fears is lost, but again, the task here is not evaluative, so I put that matter to the side.[98] The mystery of the supernatural, then, finds its center and culmination in the salvation achieved by Jesus Christ. Human beings are both creatures and sinners. They are called to share in the divine life, and actually brought into it through the sacrifice of Christ.[99]

De Lubac's insistence on the novelty of Christ also lies behind his vociferous objections to the theology of Edward Schillebeeckx, which in turn clarify the precise nature of his position on the supernatural. De Lubac's Vatican Council notebooks chronicle his growing concern over Schillebeeckx, from a handful of passing references in the first volume of the journals to finding him "likable" at the launch of the journal *Concilium*, for which de Lubac served on the editorial board, and some brief correspondence with him,[100] to a concern that he had betrayed the gospel.[101] The theological positions articulated by Schillebeeckx both in public talks and in published works worried de Lubac, particularly the notion that the world had always been Christian and that Christian revelation accomplished no more than a movement from being implicitly Christian to being explicitly so. It was this that de Lubac judged a "betrayal of the Gospel."[102] De Lubac sought out and expressed his concerns to Karl Rahner.[103] Initially placated by Rahner's reassurances, de Lubac eventually decided that he had to resign his position on the *Concilium* board.[104]

In an essay appended to *Brief Catechesis on Nature and Grace*, de Lubac explains in some depth his reservations regarding the Dutch Dominican. In volume 3 of his work, *Approches théologiques*, Schillebeeckx appealed to the conciliar documents to identify the church as the sacrament of the world, a sign of the salvation God is achieving in the world, beyond the church.[105] De Lubac objected to this attribution on several grounds. Textually, it misquoted the documents of Vatican II, which never refer to the church in this manner.[106] Terminologically, it appeals to only one of the conciliar aspects of sacramentality, signification, leaving off the instrumentality of the church as sacrament of salvation.[107] Theologically, and this is the crucial point, it obscures the Christocentricity of salvation, as grace becomes normatively operative on a basis other than the proclamation of Christ carried out in the church.[108] For Schillebeeckx the church was witness and sign of a communion already achieved in the world among humanity and between humanity and God.[109]

The formulation of Schillebeeckx tends more toward a desacralized immanentism that forgets the instrumentality of the church in the realization of this salvation.[110] In the process, it risks losing sight of the constitutive instrumentality of Christ as well. The world is simply a *"christianisme implicite,"* such that church and world are both properly Christian and form complementary expressions of Christianity.[111] There is, further, no essential difference between the Old and New Testaments.[112] Yet, if all this is the case: if the world and the church are equally Christian, if nothing essential changes with the coming of Christ, we are left with the question of whether or not Christ makes any difference at all.[113] And by urging the question on these grounds, a crucial dimension of de Lubac's theology of the supernatural emerges, for it clarifies that his vision is not one of a nature that is always already graced.

One might expect that de Lubac's eschewal of the hypothesis of pure nature, and his commitment to a theological anthropology according to which humanity has never had any finality other than union with

God, would ally him with a vision like that of Schillebeeckx, which sees grace operative throughout the creation, giving all a share in God. And yet this commitment to pervasive grace does not suffice to give a properly Christian conception, in de Lubac's view. Instead, it is little more than an "*intégrisme inverse*,"[114] which ignores the decisiveness of Christ's saving act; the Christian novelty is the fulcrum upon which all else turns for him. There is no simple passage from nature to grace, from image to likeness, from desire to its fulfillment. Only by virtue of Christ's newness is this disproportion overcome. Anything that does not afford the paschal mystery this central role is judged inadequate by de Lubac's lights.

Conclusion: The Supernatural as Deifying Grace

The only finality that the human race has ever actually had is a calling to enter into the divine life shared by the Father, the Son, and the Holy Spirit. This is the proper fulfillment of humanity, at least of every human being who has ever actually existed. In the concrete order of things as it actually exists, this finality can be attained only through the act of redemption accomplished by Christ upon the cross, because, in addition to being called to share in the divine life, human beings have fallen into sin and need to be rescued from it. De Lubac affirmed that deification would have been our proper end even apart from sin. The order of salvation is not purely remedial, although, within the only world order that has ever existed, it has taken this form. This is the meaning of the supernatural: our being brought to share in God's life through the cross and resurrection of the incarnate Son. Intriguingly, at key junctures de Lubac casts this divinization in trinitarian terms, a point to which we shall return.

Within the debate on the supernatural, much is made of de Lubac's opposition to the notion of pure nature. Noting in the first place that this opposition was not absolute,[115] we must bear in mind not just this opposition, but specifically the concerns that grounded it. The most telling of these was that it made the salvation achieved by Jesus Christ something ancillary to what it means to be human. In this way, it abridged the genuine soteriological novelty of Christianity, either by making grace something merely additive or by reducing it to the proportions of nature so that it is more of the same. Such reductions render plausible an account of humanity left to its own devices, intelligible with no reference to God. Such a self-sufficient humanity is precisely what was posited and championed by the atheistic humanists with whom the next chapter is largely concerned.

CHAPTER TWO

Authentic Humanism as Salvation

The last chapter demonstrated that de Lubac's writings on the supernatural, while most definitely preoccupied with soteriology, also regularly gestured toward his concerns with secular and atheistic thought. By at best bracketing and often denying the singular and supernatural finality of humanity, secular and atheistic programs could—according to de Lubac—only ever result in distorted understandings of human flourishing. As actual human history has borne out, these distortions have often not only fallen short of their lofty goals but also resulted in death-dealing inhumanity. Meanwhile, the partisans of pure nature found themselves, in de Lubac's view, hamstrung and unable to mount a specifically Christian response.[1] In response to these perverse and deadly "humanisms," de Lubac proposed a social vision of salvation that also provided the basis for an alternative humanism grounded in the supernatural order and, in particular, informed by the theological virtue of charity, by which humanity comes to share in the life of the God who is love.

This chapter considers these alternative humanisms, and especially the soteriological visions that undergird each. As we shall see, it is not that de Lubac was concerned with salvation, while atheistic humanists had other desiderata. Rather, the atheistic humanists put forth their own alternative salvations, sometimes to the point of establishing rival ecclesiologies, clerics, and theologies of sainthood. De Lubac's response to these non-Christian humanisms was especially concerned with their soteriological deficiencies. Further, while there is a distinct difference between them in terms of subject matter and tone, there are also significant parallels between de Lubac's works on atheism and his works on Buddhism, both of which turn upon this perceived soteriological deficiency.

Atheist Humanisms (and Anti-humanisms)

In the foregoing material, we have already made certain gestures toward the phenomenon of atheist humanism. The Christian vision of humanity as created by God and ordained to share in the divine life provides the basis for an authentic humanism, one in which human dignity is championed and preserved precisely in its dependence upon God.[2] In contrast, the modern atheist movements with which de Lubac was familiar came to see God as a principle of limitation rather than of liberation; only by casting off the yoke of the divine could true human flourishing and authenticity be attained.[3]

In this way, the movement of atheist humanism purported to offer an alternative soteriology to that of the Christianity it understood itself to have surpassed. Ironically, though, the outcome of this atheistic salvation is a hellish anti-human humanism, as de Lubac clearly witnessed during the Vichy years. Time and again, the promise of human freedom and flourishing is contradicted by oppression and dehumanizing circumstances. It should come as no surprise that, cut off from our transcendent ground in God, we lose our commitment to human dignity. Nor should it surprise us when the denial of the one in whom alone we can attain beatitude, and upon whose grace we depend in order to attain it, leads to misery and ruination rather than bliss.[4]

Atheist humanism lacks the realism provided by the Christian doctrine of sin, and as a result sets out, in hubris, to do the impossible, to perfect humanity by human strength.[5] Such an endeavor would have been futile even for an unfallen humanity, for there remains a radical disproportion between nature and the supernatural, and the passage from image to likeness depends upon the gift of God. Sin compounds, with distortion of our nature and disruption of our relationship with God, what was already the case metaphysically: our ultimate happiness cannot be attained by our efforts alone but requires the novelty of Christ.[6]

The Promethean aspirations of atheistic humanism are seen especially clearly in Nietzsche, who, positioning himself as an atheist mystic,[7] attacks Christianity root and branch, especially the ideas of dependence and of the cross, seeking instead to establish the Will to Power.[8] This enthronement of individual will leads to a direct repudiation of charity, cutting humanity off from the only means by which blessedness can come.[9] Nietzsche's mysticism gestures toward something basic to humanity, according to de Lubac. Human beings can live their lives in denial of God or anything beyond their positivist reason and observation, but they cannot efface the divine image nor their basic orientation toward its fulfillment in the divine likeness. A vital élan remains basic to humanity, which will reassert itself in one way or another. Hence, the renewal of mythical forms in atheistic movements, or mystical sensibilities like Nietzsche's or Bergson's.[10] Opposed to this resurgence of a mythical consciousness, de Lubac gestures toward the Christian notion of mystery, which responds to the same human exigency, but offers something distinctly different. "Myth and mystery may both be said to engender a *mystique*," but these are of opposite quality.[11] Christian mysticism, which amounts to an interiorization of the Christian mystery, actually answers to the ineffaceable dynamism of human nature, while the mythical mysticism ultimately falters and fails. When set against the backdrop circumstances of its writing, especially during the Vichy regime of World War II, we see the deleterious results of this tendency; the atheist humanists are not negatively deprived of beatitude but rather positively instate atrocities.[12]

The parodic character of atheist humanism and its attempt to provide an alternative soteriology is perhaps even clearer in Auguste Comte, who went so far as to develop his own church, sanctoral calendar, and rites, with a class of scientist-clerics.[13] For Comte, Christianity was a step along the way of human maturation, an evolution from primitive fetishism to a true religion in positivism.[14] Comte, then, represents something more than just an atheism, because for him God was not even really worth the trouble of denying.[15] Comte viewed Christianity as inherently and problematically antisocial; he thought Jesus put too much emphasis on the dignity of the person at the expense of a collectivist ideal.[16] Seen in this light, Catholicism represented to him a genuine advance, because he saw it as consisting in an unwitting repudiation of Christianity and its gospel.[17] This led Comte to attempt to make common cause with the Catholic Church against the religion of Jesus, an overture that, to his great surprise, was rebuffed.[18] Comte's surprise betrays how little he understood the Catholicism with which he sought to ally. Nevertheless, de Lubac believed that Comte's positivism had done great harm in sapping much of the spiritual vitality from the Catholic faith. As de Lubac wrote: "The faith that used to be a living adherence to the Mystery of Christ

Authentic Humanism as Salvation   23

then came to be no more than attachment to a social program, itself twisted and diverted from its purpose. Without any apparent crisis, under a surface that sometimes seemed the reverse of apostasy, that faith has slowly been drained of its substance."[19]

In this repudiation of Comte's positivism, de Lubac also denounces Action Française.[20] One of its organizers, Charles Maurras, had, like Comte, sought collaboration with the Catholic Church in an endeavor to reverse course on French liberalism and return to the monarchist past, though de Lubac's connections remain restrained and more or less relegated to footnotes.[21] Reflecting later, in *At the Service of the Church*, de Lubac operates with a similar reserve: "*Drame*, particularly the part devoted to Auguste Comte, did not at all please the followers of Maurras. Yet I know that in his prison, Charles Maurras had read me, pen in hand, and that in several places he had noted that what I saw was correct."[22] In this somewhat tacit criticism, we can discern an important connection to the theology of the supernatural. It was precisely the system of pure nature's endorsement of prescinding from humanity's supernatural end that made the Action Française so insidious.

Though the Catholic Church did eventually condemn Action Française, this condemnation was a long time in coming. Twelve years before Pius XI's condemnation, Pius X had called Maurras's books "*damnabiles, non damnandus* (worthy of condemnation, but not condemned)," a judgment which Nolte believes "clearly meant that the church regarded Action Française as a valuable although impure means to an end which it did not want to relinquish until it had served its purpose."[23] Despite the recognition that something was badly wrong, the condemnation was slow, in part because, when it came to the "natural order," Action Française seemed to have things right, erring only when it came to the supernatural order.[24] Such an understanding assumes both that the natural and supernatural orders may be detached from each other and that the supernatural order is merely super-added to nature. Ironically, it was by dispensing with a vision of humanity as essentially ordered to salvation that plausibility was lent to a system that not only repudiated the church's vision of salvation but also sought to establish a rival and alternative soteriology.

Similarly, in its pure form, Marxism aspires to provide both salvation and a unified mystical body, only without Christ.[25] The humanistic quest for a utopia, especially when this utopia is cast in terms of the outcome of some inevitable historical progress, and all the more especially when Christianity is something to be transcended, is a rival eschatology, and hence a rival soteriology, and even a rival ecclesiology. In opposing atheist humanism, de Lubac seeks a reassertion of the doctrine of supernatural grace. But—and this is crucial to recognize—he does not suggest this as some rival order, opposed to the secular order, but rather suggests a renewed commitment to the proclamation of salvation achieved by the gospel of Christ. To attempt to counter anti-humanist humanism by an alternative politics is to re-inscribe the same mistake made by the atheist humanists, namely, to assume that our problem is a result of poor organization. Instead, the parody of salvation offered by atheist humanism can be countered only by a reassertion of genuine salvation.[26]

It happens that a genuine Christian vision of salvation does indeed provide an alternative vision of society, ordered on different principles, but these are a consequence of salvation, not the reverse. Moreover, this salvation is, ultimately, a divine rather than a human achievement. It cannot be attained by us or our efforts. It comes as a new birth, as a kingdom that is received rather than built.[27] No matter what our attainments and progress, true human flourishing will occur only through "the renewal of the Paschal Mystery."[28] Once more the Christian newness is the determinative criterion for de Lubac.

In this connection, the enigmatic figure of Pierre-Joseph Proudhon stands in some continuity and also considerable contrast. Like the atheist humanists, Proudhon sought to offer an alternative soteriology, going so far as to state that "socialism is the doctrine of universal reconciliation."[29] Like the dialecticians, Feuerbach, and Comte, Proudhon believed that religion's time had come and gone, having been surpassed by progress.[30] Like Nietzsche, Proudhon was not content to merely deny the existence of God but positioned himself as an "anti-Theist." And yet, the character of his anti-theism is considerably distinct from Nietzsche's. Because, while Proudhon opposed God, he did not believe that he could deny him.[31] The ubiquity of religion precluded this possibility for him.[32] The problem was not that God did not exist but that God was evil, holding back humanity from its proper vocation of revolutionary justice.[33]

This commitment to revolution also puts Proudhon at odds not only with the religious, but with his irreligious confrères, whose efforts he dismissed as utopian half-measures.[34] Indeed, Proudhon inverts the atheist humanists. Rather than seeking to replace God with humanity as the object of adoration, he decries humanism as a false religion and instead professes an anti-humanism.[35]

Turning against religion, Proudhon insists that the notions of providence and charity must be opposed because they serve as justifications and props for the unjust status quo. This is a major part of why he opposes God as evil: the use to which the idea of God is put harms humanity.[36] In this regard, de Lubac recognizes that Proudhon's devotion to Justice approaches the Christian's devotion to Christ[37] and that the notion of Justice as the Absolute can indeed be affirmed by a Thomist, who recognizes the divine simplicity: God is indeed Justice.[38] Though Proudhon sought to articulate a pure immanentism, he remained haunted by transcendence.[39] Indeed, he could not avoid speculating about whether "'humanity's end' would not be, on the contrary, 'its definitive reconciliation with God, and its passing from time to eternity.'"[40] With this speculation, Proudhon stands at the threshold of the Christian hope. De Lubac's engagement with him aims at making clear that his lofty ambitions are ultimately fulfilled in Christ and his salvation.[41]

Catholicisme: Funding a Christian Humanism

De Lubac's first book, *Catholicisme*, reads as a manifesto, not only for his subsequent works but also for an alternative Christian humanism or "*humanisme* converti."[42] This is particularly evident in the original French subtitle: *Les aspects sociaux du dogme*. De Lubac sought to explain Christian dogma not in its totality, but "only in certain of its aspects," particularly those that had a bearing on humanity's common life and destiny.[43] De Lubac recognized in his contemporaries' humanistic ambitions some of the "deepest yearnings" of his generation.[44] Among the reasons for the rise of collectivist ideologies like Marxism was the loss of a truly Christian collectivism.[45] This claim is crucial, for it lays at least part of the blame on Christian deficiencies that have helped to give rise to the pretensions of atheist humanism; with the church's "fraternal community" lost, humanity is left "isolated, uprooted, 'disconcerted'... asphyxiated." Under such circumstances, something else must come in to fill the void.[46]

Therefore, while "the Catholic cannot adopt this program [of humanism] as it stands, . . . [neither] can he simply reject it as a disastrous illusion."[47] Echoing Blondel, de Lubac believed that humanity's transcendent longings should lead us to affirm and hold fast to our transcendent ground, God.[48]

The central thesis of *Catholicisme* is well known: humanity's salvation in Christ presupposes a prior and fundamental unity for the human race. Sin disrupts this primordial unity, and through his incarnation, death, and resurrection, Christ assumes our nature and restores it in its totality, including the restoration of its unity.[49] In a crucial passage, de Lubac writes:

> The Word did not merely take a human body; his Incarnation was not a simple *corporatio*, but, as St. Hilary says, a *concorporatio*. He incorporated himself in our humanity, and incorporated it in himself. . . . In [assuming] a human nature, it is *human nature* that he united to himself, that he enclosed in himself, and it is the later, whole and entire, that in some sort he uses as a body. . . . Whole and entire he will bear it then to Calvary, whole and entire he will raise it from the dead, whole and entire he will save it.[50]

This restored unity finds its expression in the catholic universality of the church, wherein all that is truly human is integrated into one body,[51] a reality realized and effected by the sacraments, whose effect is not primarily individual, but social.[52] Just as the redemption results in the restoration of humanity's lost unity, the consummation shall be social.[53] The beatific vision occurs in the "well-ordered society" of the "kingdom of God,"[54] and the unity of the heavenly city is ultimately trinitarian, which is to say a differentiated unity, capable of embracing all the diversity of the *catholica*.[55]

In contrast to the soteriological pretentions of atheist humanism's collectivism and the soteriological impoverishment of an individualistic Catholicism, de Lubac saw the possibility of a fully Christian humanism in the renewal of a theology of the mystical body of Christ,[56] which avoids both "a cosmopolitan individualism" and "a kind of unitary socialism" because "the good of the community, or universal common good, coincides in the final analysis, in a perfect way with the personal good of each."[57] An authentic humanism, then, will recognize this distinctive

Authentic Humanism as Salvation   27

telos of humanity, and anticipate it here and now, respecting the inviolable dignity and inseparable unity of all human beings. Respect for the supernatural character of human fulfillment will recognize that all of our social efforts can be only provisional, only anticipations of the final dénouement.[58] This rules out two equal but opposite pretensions: that of a (Pelagian) attempt to bring about the perfect society before the eschaton and that of an indifferentism that allows social forms contrary to humanity's proper end to continue unchallenged and uncorrected. This first Pelagian option was discerned in the "social humanism which is the present phase of man's hopeless endeavor to save himself by his own efforts" and which Christianity "refutes by bringing salvation."[59]

The second error stems from the "naturalist trends of modern thought, on the one hand, and the confusions of a bastard Augustinianism," on the other, leading to a lost understanding of the integral relationship between nature and grace.[60] The system of pure nature led to a consideration of our nature as entirely self-contained, comprehensible without reference to its supernatural finality. And then, "after such a complete separation, what misgivings could the supernatural give to naturalism? . . . The most confirmed secularists found in it [the system of pure nature], in spite of itself, an ally."[61] Because the supernatural order is the proper consummation of our nature, "There is nothing good, which Catholicism cannot claim for its own."[62] All of the riches of human achievement find their place within and lead toward (though they cannot, of themselves, attain) humanity's supernatural finality.[63] This being the case, Catholicism is not merely *a* religion or system, not even "the only true religion" or "the only system that works." Instead, "it is the form that humanity must put on in order to finally be itself."[64]

This is the conclusion of de Lubac's theology of the supernatural. And it stands in ironic contrast with the integralist vision, delivering what integralism sought to provide: a fully unified account of human flourishing. Because humanity is always ordered toward the beatific vision, all that is authentically human can be received and elevated. Because the supernatural fulfillment of our nature will be the fulfillment of our *nature* (which grace does not abolish, but perfects), all that is authentically human *must* be received and elevated. This is why salvation must take the form of an authentic humanism, because it is the proper fulfillment of humanity. And it is precisely in recognition of this that social action can be undertaken.[65]

Nevertheless, in contrast to integralism, while the church properly influences society's direction and structures, its proper mission is not concerned with these.[66] And while the church's teaching concerning salvation prepares for social engagement, "it cannot be a question of purely and simply transposing what the faith teaches us of the supernatural world into the natural order: that would be to transform a divine reality . . . into a vain ideology, a reckless secularization, about which one could well speak again of Christian truths gone mad."[67] On the one hand, the natural and the supernatural cannot be elided, which rules out the prospect of reverse-engineering the kingdom of heaven, or arriving in its precincts by Whiggish progress. On the other hand, though, they are not separate, and the supernatural order does indeed influence the natural, and so is hardly irrelevant to a properly functioning social order.[68] And all the while, one's collaborators "are not . . . merely our collaborators or our instruments for purely human tasks, but spiritual beings, made like us for God alone; and, as miserable, as closed, as dull as they may seem to us, at the very depths of each of them still burns at least a sacred spark, and all these sparks are destined to be joined for a salvation that God wishes to be fraternal."[69]

This brings us to the heart of recognizing the soteriological impetus of de Lubac's theology of the supernatural. It has ontological and political relevance, but neither of these is the intent, and to confuse the issue leads to an instrumentalization of grace for some other end, at once losing sight of grace's gratuity and its fundamental orientation toward humanity's divinization. Such a move, even if it rejects the system of pure nature, results in a bracketing of salvation every bit as grievous as those political philosophies predicated upon the hypothesis of pure nature (or on the rejection of any grace at all).

Fundamentally, this soteriological humanism is grounded in the supernatural gift of charity,[70] placing it in marked contrast with the vision of Proudhon, who opposed charity as a demotivating factor. As a theological virtue, charity lies beyond what humans can naturally achieve; it is the gift of God.[71] Nevertheless, and *contra* Proudhon, charity does inform genuinely human acts. Moreover, it is by this gift that human beings come to share in the divine life. As Blondel noted, the supernatural liberates human activity, and it is precisely in and as action that humanity attains to the divine.[72] Charity has its origin in God, because

God is love. As absolute being, God has no needs, and so loves in complete freedom and generosity, which de Lubac characterizes as "the exchange of a perfect Gift."[73]

This infinite generosity is then bestowed upon and echoed in redeemed humanity, enabling us to love all of humanity in imitation of God, who loves not isolated individuals, but the human race and individuals as part of that collective identity.[74] Indeed, de Lubac suggests that the thesis of *Catholicism* can be summed up in the "Augustinian formula *unus Christus amans seipsum* [one Christ loving himself]."[75] It is in Christ, then, that this charitable human unity is realized and given. "We are fully personal only interior to the Person of the Son, by whom and in whom we take part in the exchanges of the trinitarian life."[76]

It is particularly the redemptive act of Christ's death on the cross that insinuates this charity into humanity and by which humanity passes into the Trinity; this is the essence of the Christian novelty. In "The Light of Christ" (1949) de Lubac writes of Christ's sacrifice on the cross as the "great . . . Deed of Charity" that has transformed the world and humanity.[77] And in the conclusion to *Catholicism*, titled "*Mysterium Crucis*," he notes: "There is no smooth transition from a natural to a supernatural love," which means that this authentic humanism requires our radical conversion. "Humanity, whole and entire [tout entière] must die to itself in each of its members so as to live transfigured in God."[78] Yet this death has indeed already occurred definitively in Christ, who has already borne humanity "whole and entire [tout entière]" to the cross, already raised it "whole and entire [tout entière]" back to life, already "whole and entire [tout entière]" saved it.[79] "By Christ dying on the cross, the humanity which he bore entirely [toute] in himself renounces itself and dies," and in this way passes into eternal life in God,[80] a life that we have seen takes the form of gift and oblation.

Buddhism

De Lubac's turn to charity serves as a bridge to another set of writings engaged with non-Christian thought. In his works on Buddhism, de Lubac found a way to continue making theological contributions while working under the restrictions imposed in the wake of the *Surnaturel* controversy. His engagement with Buddhism reinforced his commitment to both the unique soteriological center of Christianity, especially to a notion of the Christian newness.[81] In his student years, de Lubac had been primed for this by a formative encounter with Pierre Rousselot's contribution to Joseph Huby's text on the history of religions, *Christus*, which impressed upon de Lubac the supernatural uniqueness of Christianity vis-à-vis the other religions.[82] Following in this vein, his *Aspects of Buddhism* presents a sympathetic yet trenchant critique of what de Lubac regarded as a soteriological deficiency in the tradition.

We must be careful not to mistake ourselves here. De Lubac held Buddhism in high regard, writing, "I consider it something like the greatest human feat, because of its originality and its multiform expansion across time and space as well as because of its spiritual depth."[83] Moreover, he makes it clear that his soteriological critique should not be understood as a "judgment . . . on individual souls," which lies solely within God's competency.[84] Instead, his concern has to do with the notions of charity and salvation that lie at the heart of Buddhism and Christianity, respectively. At the same time, much has changed since the 1950s, when de Lubac published these works, not least in Western understandings of Buddhism and in the fields of comparative religion and inter-religious dialogue. When de Lubac wrote these works, the field was dominated by Orientalism, and Vatican II's Decree on the Church's Relation to Non-Christian Religions, *Nostra aetate*, had not yet been published. In fact, these studies helped pave the way for the decree.[85] In light of these recognitions, I must once more note that my purpose is not evaluative. Whether de Lubac is accurate in his assessment of Buddhism is not the question at hand, nor is the propriety of his undertaking such an assessment to begin with. Rather, what matters for our purposes is uncovering the soteriological preoccupation that informed his engagement with Buddhism.

At first blush, one might expect a great deal of common ground between Buddhism, with its commitment to disinterestedness, and Christianity, with its prioritization of charity understood as a purely altruistic (i.e., disinterested) love. However, de Lubac contends that such a comparison is facile and that any similarity between the two concepts is superficial, stemming from a misunderstanding of what Christian charity properly is.[86]

Christian charity is preeminently the love displayed by Christ upon the cross as he gave his life for the life of the world. It is, then, grounded in concrete reality and in the particularities of a historical event.[87] In contrast, Buddhist charity is ahistorical and only tangentially connected to the figure of the Buddha.[88] It is, therefore, an ideal that proves to be "unrealizable."[89] It was precisely this that led de Lubac, in subsequent writings, to focus more on the Amidist tradition, which tends toward a more personalized devotion to the Buddha as such.[90] Moreover, within Buddhism the neighbor can never be loved for his or her own sake, but only ever for the negative purpose of detachment.[91] Hence, charity is only "provisional" for Buddhism.[92] In contrast, Christian charity endures eschatologically (1 Cor 13:13) and indeed "expresses the very Being of God," with the commandment to love one's neighbor as oneself related to and based upon the love of God.[93] Once more, as with the atheistic humanisms, we see de Lubac's insistence that apart from a foundation in God, commitment to human dignity winds up being vitiated.

In contrast, the work of Christian mission, grounded in charity, is genuinely motivated by the other, for "the Christian does not use the unbeliever whom he converts in view of realizing himself. . . . [Rather] his life is itself the gift, because to give is to participate in the divine life, which is gift. . . . The Christian offers his individuality to the divine charity . . . like the wood offers itself to the flame to allow it to burn."[94] Christian charity bears an intrinsic relation to its end, eternal life in God, whereas Buddhist love, "being provisional and not final, and remaining a means intrinsic to the end sought, vanishes inevitably when it is regarded from the point of view of absolute truth."[95]

The tradition of Amidism within Buddhism would seem to provide even further common ground with Christianity, with its particular devotion to the figure of Amida (or Amitābha), a heavenly Buddha, and the practice of invoking his vow as a means of attaining salvation. Amidism appears to provide an analogue to the Christian doctrines of merit and grace. By the merits of Amida's vow, and without consideration for their deserts, supplicants can be delivered despite their shortcomings and inadequacies.[96] Early Christian missionaries noted the similarity between the Amidist trajectory and the Lutheran teaching on justification by faith alone.[97]

However, because Amidism remains within the same broad confines of Buddhist "orthodoxy," this similarity is only superficial.[98] Within Amidism, as in "orthodox" Buddhism, karma and samsara, rather than a personal God, govern the universe, with the result that good and evil remain only relative terms.[99] Hence, the evil against which Buddhism must contend is not primarily moral evil, but rather the metaphysical evil of samsara. What is sought is not redemption, but release, an escape from this universe of inevitable suffering.[100]

Similarly, while both Buddhism and Christianity trade upon the image of a cosmic tree of life—the Bodhi tree in Buddhism and the cross in Christianity—there obtains a basic soteriological difference between the traditions. The Buddhist tree of life is a tree of knowledge, allowing for self-actualization and a shift in consciousness. The Christian cross, though, utterly reinvents things. It is a new wine that bursts the skins.[101] The cross of Jesus is novel and unique, bringing about the world's salvation in a way that no other tree has.[102] While the Buddha eventually passes away into obscurity, absorbed into the void of Dharma, Christ remains "the person of Jesus of Nazareth, Man and God to all eternity, the one author of salvation."[103] The center of all things for Christianity is not spatial, but rather "an event in time . . . Calvary."[104]

Christianity brings about more than a shift in consciousness. Conversion is more than renewed thinking; rather, it results from the unique act of Christ's death on the cross and presents a novelty, a definitive change in status. Far from a renunciation of the self, it is a commitment of the self. Christian salvation is not a matter of changed perspective. Rather, "one needs to be delivered from an evil which is only too real, and to triumph over a death which is only too real. That is why the principle of our salvation is not to be found in one privileged moment of enlightenment, Bodhi; the redemption of the world will come as the result of the Act which is consummated upon the Cross."[105]

In the end, Buddhism, even the seemingly more soteriologically focused Amidism, offers "an illumination, not a salvation."[106] This underscores the radicality of grace and of the supernatural order, which infinitely surpasses even the greatest of human achievements. Whatever spiritual riches there are to be found in Buddhism—and no doubt de Lubac recognized at least some of them—the decisive newness of Christianity is a difference that makes a difference. Jesus Christ brings not more of the same, but something radically novel: the salvation of the human race.[107]

Conclusion: True Humanism, Grounded in the Cross

Henri de Lubac's theology of the supernatural precludes any analysis of humanity that brackets or ignores our supernatural finality. Because human flourishing consists of salvation, to consider human beings apart from this telos is to misconstrue who and what we are. In the neo-scholastic system of pure nature and the tradition of atheist humanism, de Lubac encountered what he perceived as two sides of the same coin. Both endorsed a purely natural analysis of humanity, though for rather different reasons.

This is a phenomenon with a twofold irony. The first irony is that while atheistic humanism endeavors to liberate humanity through an alternative soteriology, it winds up imprisoning humanity in a deepened ruination. The second irony is that while de Lubac's opponents championed pure nature for the sake of defending the gratuity of grace, the thesis of pure nature does no such thing. It provides the condition of possibility for the pseudo-salvations of atheist humanism while *failing* to safeguard the gratuity of grace. In contrast, a vision of humanity grounded in our common vocation to salvation provides the basis for an authentically Christian humanism. Because of humanity's fundamental unity and social nature, salvation is a social reality that bears upon our relationship to God and to one another. The supernatural virtue of charity, by which human beings attain to God, also informs those acts by which we relate to one another and funds a concern for all.

Hence, while de Lubac's position on the supernatural has political and ontological implications, it is not motivated by either politics or ontology but rather by soteriology. This soteriological concern is also on display in his engagement with Buddhism. Basic to his commitments in the matter of the supernatural is de Lubac's conviction that Christ's redemption makes a decisive difference and that humanity's proper fulfillment and final flourishing flows from and depends upon Christ's act on the cross. The charity operative upon the cross is the same charity that constitutes the life of God, into which human beings are drawn through the cross. Christ's self-gift is expressive of the trinitarian self-gift and comes to include us within its donation, liberating us to make that same gift-of-self, and so to be one with God, who exists as self-donating love.

At the same time, by de Lubac's own admission, this crucicentrism is muted in many of his works on the relation between nature and grace, leaving the act of Christ on the cross and the meaning of redemption somewhat unspecified. It lies at the heart of his conception of the supernatural but remains notional, still in need of specific content. This content will begin to be provided in the next chapters, which consider, in turn, de Lubac's theological epistemology and understanding of revelation and the area of de Lubac's thought in which the nature of the Christian newness is most clearly on display: the theology of spiritual exegesis.

PART TWO

Salvation Disclosed

Revelation and Spiritual Exegesis

CHAPTER THREE

Knowing the Mystery

De Lubac's Paradoxical Theological Epistemology

Humanity has a natural desire for supernatural happiness in God. While this desire for the beatific vision is innate to humanity as spirit, our knowledge of it, de Lubac argues, depends upon divine revelation.[1] This paradoxical state of affairs, of a natural desire that can be fulfilled only supernaturally, and which is inscribed into our very being, but knowable only by revelation, lies at the heart of de Lubac's theological epistemology, which itself gives ample room for and relies upon the notion of paradox.[2]

De Lubac's appeal to paradox stems from several interconnected commitments that, taken in concert, allow us to fill out with greater depth the manner in which his thought is pervaded by a soteriological impetus. Our knowledge of God takes a paradoxical form because it is knowledge of a reality that utterly exceeds the capacities of our finite intellects, i.e., a mystery. It is the nature of this mystery that our apprehension of it goes beyond mere cognition. Rather, we are drawn and incorporated into it. This being drawn into the mystery is at once the fulfillment of the natural desire and the telos of knowledge of God. It is, moreover, the basic meaning of mysticism in de Lubac's mature thought. For de Lubac, both mysticism and theology are means of engaging with mystery. And the relation between them clarifies what is at stake in de Lubac's theological epistemology, namely, the ordering of all of human life, including theological inquiry, to our participation in the life of the Trinity through the saving act of the incarnate Christ.

Mysticism and the Constitution of Humanity

De Lubac's conception of Christian mysticism sheds considerable light on his theological anthropology, for it clarifies the nature of the fulfilment of the desire that constitutes human nature. As we noted in the introduction, de Lubac understood his entire project to be, in some measure, animated by a vision of Christian mysticism; though he was unable to complete his desired book on the topic, nor is any major work devoted to it as such. Nevertheless, his 1965 article "Mystique et Mystère" gives considerable insight into his conception of Christian mysticism. Essentially mysticism consists in "a certain effective union with the Divinity . . . the tri-personal God of Christian revelation, a union realized in Jesus Christ and by his grace."[3] Set against the backdrop of the previous chapters, this can be recognized as essentially the fulfillment of humanity's supernatural vocation and the human spirit's natural desire for that fulfillment.

De Lubac makes this connection even clearer when he delineates those features that comprise a specifically Christian mysticism over against the various natural mysticisms or those belonging to different religious traditions. A Christian mysticism is, in particular, a "mysticism of likeness," meaning that, by virtue of being created in the image of God, humanity is called to be conformed to his likeness through the beatific vision.[4] The distinction between image and likeness is crucial to de Lubac's theology of the supernatural, as *image* corresponds to our vocation to union with God, while *likeness* names its fulfillment. Between the two there is a radical disproportion, so that we could never attain to this goal without supernatural aid. De Lubac explains: "A mysticism of *only* the image would be an awareness of oneself, of the depth of one's being, without the gracious intervention of God by the gift of the mystery," while as a "mysticism of likeness, Christian mysticism is by that very fact oriented forward, towards a term, towards God who calls us and draws us to the end of the road."[5] Hence, it involves an anagogic dimension, as this movement toward God can never be fully completed within this life.

Understanding the matter thus, we can see that de Lubac's understanding of the image of God in humanity more or less corresponds to spirit within his conception of tripartite anthropology. Both name our basic openness toward and vocation to God. This is borne out in de Lubac's *The Discovery of God*, in which he writes, "God reveals himself continuously to man by imprinting his image upon him. That divine operation constitutes the very center of man. That is what makes him spirit."[6] Tellingly, de Lubac understands spirit to be the site of mysticism (*Le lieu de la mystique*).[7] It is here, in that aspect of our nature whereby we are open to and summoned to God, that mysticism, understood as the fulfillment of that summons, occurs.

The Thomistic Milieu

Within his discussion of the spirit as the site of mysticism, de Lubac provides some key distinctions that inform his theological epistemology. In order to understand it properly, though, we must set it against the backdrop of his intellectual milieu. In many ways the story of modern Catholic theology is one of reckoning with the shock to the system represented by the epistemological revolution inaugurated by René Descartes and further prosecuted by the likes of David Hume and especially Immanuel Kant. In the wake of Kant, no one could remain in their state of dogmatic slumber. The naïve assumption that we can simply know the real was banished, leaving a vacuum that was filled by the Scylla of rationalism, which made discursive reasoning the measure of all things, and the Charybdis of fideism, which retreated from rational activity for the ostensibly safer confines of an enclosed, self-referential system with no need of making external contact with the rest of the world.[8]

Catholic theology was not immune from these effects, and at the First Vatican Council the Constitution on the Catholic Faith, *Dei Filius*, condemned both fideism and rationalism.[9] According to *Dei Filius*, there is a twofold order of knowledge: that which is accessible to us by natural reason and that which is available by way of supernatural faith in divine revelation.[10] God, the Council taught, can be known in both manners: by supernatural revelation and by the light of natural reason.[11] Revelation had been given for two reasons: to provide clarity and certainty regarding those things that can be known naturally and because humanity's supernatural vocation exceeds the proportions of our natural reason.[12] Faith

40 *Salvation Disclosed*

and reason were intimately and integrally related, according to the Council, such that "reason, if it is enlightened by faith does indeed ... achieve by God's gift some understanding, and that most profitable, of the mysteries [which lie beyond its comprehension], whether by analogy from what it knows naturally, or from the connexion of these mysteries with one another [*mysteriororum ipsorum nexu inter se*] and with the final end of humanity."[13]

In this way, the constitution repristinated the classical ideal of theology as faith seeking understanding. The mysteries were believed by virtue of being divinely revealed, and their intelligibility was probed through various speculative frameworks. This distinction between revealed doctrine, which is received, and speculative enterprise, whereby the truth is not established but rather understood, is the basic method of the scholastic theology exemplified by Thomas Aquinas, but was practiced by other figures such as Duns Scotus and Bonaventure. In many ways, *Dei Filius* represents an implicit reinstatement of scholastic theology in a time of epistemological uncertainty.[14]

This endorsement of scholasticism became unmistakable a decade later, when Leo XIII issued his 1879 encyclical *Aeterni Patris*, which surveyed the fragmented landscape and commended a renewed scholasticism, especially a renewed commitment to the scholasticism of Thomas Aquinas, as the way forward.[15] Just as Thomas had been able to synthesize the diverse strands of the antecedent Christian tradition into one coherent system, so a renewed Thomism could bring about the unity needed within fragmented modernity, or so Leo reasoned.

This teaching set the stage both for the modernist controversy, which followed it as a somewhat unfortunate sequel,[16] and for de Lubac's own theological epistemology, which, as we shall see, received major touchstones from the Council's teaching and even adopted its own paradoxical idiom as a means of respecting *Dei Filius*'s parameters; it also operated within the renewed Thomistic ambit called for by *Aeterni Patris*.

In the decades following the call of Leo XIII's *Aeterni Patris*, there was indeed a renewal of Thomistic studies, as Thomistic principles formed the basis of clergy formation and theological curricula.[17] Yet these Thomistic principles tended to come in the form of the Twenty-Four Thomistic Theses that seminarians learned as their philosophical formation before advancing to properly theological study, rather than actually engaging with Aquinas himself.[18] The Thomistic theses covered various metaphysical principles that served as the substructure upon which theological reflection would eventually be built. They belonged to the order of knowledge accessible to natural reason, which would then be augmented by the truths of divine revelation but without any essential connection to those latter truths. The Thomistic theses represented the first principles from which one would reason in order to reach true conclusions in the theological realm. Such was the manualist tradition.

While manualism is frequently elided with neo-scholasticism, this is an unfortunate occurrence, for the two were not identical. The latter was far more intellectually rigorous and could be broadly construed as the attempt, from the nineteenth century onward, to reassert the scholastic enterprise in the face of modern philosophical currents, particularly Kantian and post-Kantian philosophy.[19] At the same time, it was through the manuals that most students of theology encountered neo-scholasticism, so their elision is not entirely without basis.[20]

Meanwhile, such manual Thomism proved inadequate for either meeting the challenges of modernity or providing the synthesis Leo desired. Turn-of-the-century France was marked by an atmosphere of unfettered confidence in scientific progress, positivism, and reductive rationalism, which sought to explain the world in mechanistic terms. Progress was moving humanity past religion, though a certain resurgence in the occult provided some continuing sense of mystery.[21] Meanwhile, through developments in the sciences, this mechanistic conception of the universe became destabilized and untenable, breaking up the alleged omnicompetence of science and reason.[22] Within this context, secular thinkers such as Henri Bergson attacked the supremacy of reason and the mechanized worldview that accompanied rationalist thought.

Bergson saw in scholastic thought and Kantianism alike the very rationalism that reduced the *élan vital* to mechanistic determinism.[23] Bergson garnered controversy and support, with adherents among secularists and Christians, liberals and Maurrasians. His ripostes against intellectualist hegemony, while not exactly friendly to the prevailing Catholic sentiment of the day, opened up a space for figures such as Charles Péguy, Jacques and Raïssa Maritain, and Étienne Gilson to embrace their Catholic faith unfettered by rationalist reductions.[24]

At the same time, and following the directives of *Aeterni Patris*, important studies of the thought of Thomas Aquinas appeared, and with them there emerged a picture rather different than what tended to pervade the manualist tradition.[25] Pierre Rousselot's *L'intellectualisme de saint Thomas* recovered the crucial distinction between *ratio* (discursive reason) and *intellectus* (understanding/intelligence) and realized that the latter was held in the higher regard by Thomas himself, while the former was the lowest of the intellect's operations.[26] Rousselot's turn to intelligence allowed him to articulate a new Thomistic realism that moved beyond the weaknesses of the conceptualism of his day, which sought to respond to Cartesian, Kantian, and Bergsonian critiques by a reassertion of a realism grounded in concepts, but remained susceptible to that same critique.[27] For Rousselot, the activity of the *ratio* aims at the rest of the satisfied *intellectus*.[28] This allows a shift in priorities from demonstration—the domain of the *ratio*—to intellectual contemplation, a point to which I shall return.

Étienne Gilson, Joseph Maréchal, Henri Bouillard, and Marie-Dominique Chenu all also engaged in serious historical study of Aquinas within his own intellectual milieu, with the result that the notion that there had been one uniform scholastic tradition of which Aquinas was the chief exemplar became untenable.[29] Within the scholastic period, a good deal of plurality obtained.[30] And so, from within the Thomistic tradition, and grounded upon Thomistic principles, the notion of a single unified scholasticism became increasingly unstable.[31]

On the one hand, this can be understood as the undoing of *Aeterni Patris*, which operated with the assumption that scholasticism was a single enterprise, essentially a science in the Aristotelian sense, which, as such, was capable of delivering timeless and immutable truths. On this understanding, Aquinas's uniqueness was his towering genius, which allowed him to provide the most comprehensive of syntheses, even though what he synthesized was something already fairly unified. These historical studies of Thomas, though, recovered his contingent and historical uniqueness as well, and recognized his differences with other figures, such as Bonaventure, as, in some cases, irreducible.

On the other hand, though, this undoing of the notion of scholasticism as a single unified artifact can be understood as the fulfillment of *Aeterni Patris*, which, when calling for a return to the wisdom of St. Thomas, clarified:

> If anything is taken up with too great subtlety by the Scholastic doctors, or too carelessly stated—if there be anything that ill agrees with the discoveries of a later age, or, in a word, improbable in whatever way—it does not enter Our mind to propose that for imitation to Our age.... [And] lest the false for the true or the corrupt for the pure be drunk in, be ye watchful that the doctrine of Thomas be drawn from his own fountains.[32]

In this way, the pope called for a return to Thomas himself, not just to Thomism, generically understood. As historical studies of Aquinas progressed, it became clear just how Suarezian or Banezian, rather than Thomistic, much of the prevailing "Thomism" of the age was. The pluralism that roiled the neo-scholastic synthesis was, in many ways, a recovery of authentic Thomism and authentic scholasticism. It was within this milieu that de Lubac received his formation and worked.[33]

A standard narrative understands the *ressourcement* movement in general, and Henri de Lubac in particular, to be a reaction against and repudiation of scholastic theology. In the wake of modernism, which unsuccessfully attempted to bring Catholic theology into a more fruitful dialogue with contemporary developments in philosophy and science, and particularly the conditioning role of historical particularity in theological reflection, a contingent of mainly French theologians, among them de Lubac, returned to the sources of Scripture, the church fathers, and the liturgy, and in so doing upset the neo-scholastic synthesis that had dominated Catholic theology since Vatican I and its sequel, *Aeterni Patris*. Initially resisted, the *ressourcement* theologians saw their vindication at Vatican II, which integrated their key insights into the mainstream of Catholicism. Or so the narrative runs.

Depending upon what one means by several of these terms, this narrative can be either more or less accurate, but even so it fails to adequately account for the complexity of the intellectual currents of the period. More crucially for our purposes, it fails to adequately account for de Lubac's own positions, convictions, and intentions. Attention to de Lubac's theological epistemology in particular disrupts this narrative in significant ways. While de Lubac should not be understood as a scholastic theologian per se, it is also not the case that his theology was a repudiation of scholasticism in any straightforward sense. In his account of human knowledge, especially knowledge of God, he attempted to operate within the parameters established by *Dei Filius* and *Aeterni Patris*, and he deliberately positioned himself as operating within the strictures of the "*philosophia perennis*," noting that it was the philosophy "which nourished me, and my thought continues to live in that climate."[34] In fact, in 1984 de Lubac's attention was drawn to an article suggesting that he sought "to reverse the encyclical *Aeterni Patris* by substituting a modern philosophy for Thomist philosophy."[35] He responded that "nothing could be more false."[36] Such sentiments cannot be relegated to some discrete isolated period, but rather, and with consistency, spanned de Lubac's lifetime, from private correspondence in the midst of his theological formation to published works before and after Vatican II and into his cardinalate.

While de Lubac was certainly not operating with a scholastic methodology in the sense of constructing a system built upon a rigidly defined philosophy, it can nevertheless be misleading to understand him as repudiating either scholasticism or *Dei Filius*, whether explicitly or tacitly. Indeed, he recognized that a departure from scholastic disciplines had brought about "in the young generations . . . a deficit in the precision of thought that is not without danger for theological rectitude."[37] And, while he recognized certain "compensations" that attended this shift, he still "note[d] a deficit, nevertheless, with regret."[38] The fault for that contemporary antipathy for scholasticism lay not with scholasticism nor with Aquinas, but with "a certain narrow and sectarian Thomism."[39] De Lubac's objections were not to intellectualism or to scholasticism, but to manualism and rationalism, a rationalism that was rejected by *Dei Filius*, and for which Rousselot believed he had found the antidote in Thomas's intellectualism.[40]

Beyond Intellectualism

While de Lubac was influenced by and appreciated the renewed intellectualism of Rousselot, he also deemed it insufficiently radical.[41] For instance, he believed that the distinction between *intellectus* and *ratio* is an "essentially 'scientific' (philosophical) theory, having little relation to the spiritual life" and falling short of the Pauline trichotomy of body, soul, and spirit.[42] In contrast, spirit/pneuma transcends and undergirds all other faculties, whether of intellect, reason, or will.[43]

Knowing the Mystery   45

And so, whereas Rousselot had written that the "intelligence is essentially the sense [sens] of the real, but it is the sense of the real only because it is the sense of the divine,"[44] de Lubac suggests instead that "intelligence is the *faculty* of being because *spirit* is the *capacity* for God."[45] Rousselot's intellectualism posited a humanity ordered toward the vision of God, but by locating this orientation in a single faculty, it fell short of the fundamental orientation envisioned by de Lubac. By locating this drive toward God in the spirit, which is prior to and undergirds the other faculties, a far more radical position is sketched, one that upholds the unity of all the faculties in humanity's basic orientation toward God.[46]

This allows de Lubac to insist that our knowledge and affirmation of God occurs at a level more profound than and prior to any other faculty or act.[47] All of the operations of knowledge and volition by which human beings might affirm (or deny) God are themselves dependent upon God because they are functions of our being spirit, created after God's image. Hence, "Our most natural and most spontaneous activity is no more than a response."[48] This signals that the initiative is always God's and that this is the case in the order of nature as much as it is in the order of grace. Humanity exists in a state of radical dependence upon God.

Important as the intellect is, it remains but one aspect of a creature that is holistically dependent upon and ordered to its creator.[49] Rather than being a faculty, or even an operation, spirit, for de Lubac, is fundamentally a drive or élan toward God. It is because we are spirit, that is, because we are oriented and drawn toward God, that we know (intellect) and love (will).[50] This being the case, the affirmation of God is itself prior to and the basis of our affirmation of anything else.[51] Therefore, no knowledge is, strictly speaking, neutral. Every act, conscious or otherwise, is affected by one's position vis-à-vis God. De Lubac, however, distinguishes between the times before and after any individual's "refusal or acceptance of grace":

> During the first period, ontological certitude is what it is, and there is no reason to declare it illegitimate or, rather, illusory. After the refusal, those epithets take on meaning—and need to be carefully analyzed. For although it may then be possible to describe the ontological certainty in question as illegitimate or illusory, that does not mean calling it illusory in itself—since the nature of the intelligence

has not changed—but because from then on it is vitally contradicted. . . . If he deliberately goes against his vocation as spirit, he inevitably introduces contradiction not only into his intelligence—which may continue to function as before—but into his very being, setting his intelligence and his life in contradiction.[52]

This, then, sets into proper perspective de Lubac's relationship to intellectualism. While he was clearly and explicitly not an intellectualist, neither would it be accurate to understand him as an anti-intellectualist. The reality *God* does not surpass our intellect because of any irrationality. Instead, "Infinite intelligibility—such is God."[53] In approaching God, we face not a dearth, but a surplus of meaning. It is for this reason that our concepts and pronouncements can only grope toward and attempt an approximation of God rather than being able to give full expression to his reality.[54]

This is borne out further in the essay "Théologie et ses sources: Reponse," published in 1946 as a response to criticisms of *ressourcement* by Marie-Michel Labourdette in his article "La théologie et ses sources" (1946). While technically anonymous, de Lubac was involved in its composition. The essay notes Labourdette's accusation of anti-intellectualism, but notes that the words used are *"plein d'équivoques"* and demands distinction. If by it one means "anti-intellectual," and so, "against intelligence," the authors would flatly deny the charge.[55] If, however, one means anti-intellectualist in the sense of being against intellectualism, further distinctions are in order. There is "in theology, a certain intellectualism against which we do not hesitate at all to take our stand." This intellectualism reduces revealed truth to a mere system from which one reasons while losing sight of the way the truths of revelation always exceed the mind's conceptual grasp.[56] If, though, intellectualism refers to a prizing of the "act of intelligence," following Rousselot, then the authors have no objection to it, but have rather learned from it.[57]

Yet, and crucially, de Lubac also saw himself as going *beyond* intellectualism. As he writes, "There is something more fundamental in the human mind: not outside, but at the very heart of intelligence," such that "genuine intellectualism is not a narcissism of the concept. It is not the love of the intelligence for its own sake, or a complacent delight in its products: it is the free and confident use of the intelligence in the search of the truth."[58] De Lubac, then, is not an anti-intellectualist, because he does not reject intellectualism. Rather, he aims to be more than an intellectualist, situating the intellect as interior to and dependent upon spirit, and so as fundamentally oriented toward God, but not as the exclusive locus of such orientation, rather as an expression of an even more fundamental drive.[59]

This consideration of the fundamental élan of the human spirit will return with greater force near the end of this chapter when I turn to a consideration of the relation between theology and mysticism. For now, though, it suffices to note that the constitution of the human being involves an ineffaceable drive toward God that undergirds all of our cognitive function and acts of knowing. As the outcome and satisfaction of this drive, mysticism has a significant bearing on our understanding of humanity's knowledge of God.

The Mystery Revealed and Apprehended

Thus far we have more or less confined our reflections to the sort of natural knowledge of God that is innate to human persons as created spirit. In so doing, we have not been able to entirely bracket supernatural revelation, and this for two reasons. First, as created spirit we are ordered and drawn to a supernatural end, which means that a consideration of humanity as spirit cannot remain within the confines of nature alone. Second, as we noted at the outset of this chapter, our knowledge of our ordination to God is dependent upon revelation. When we turn more explicitly to consider the knowledge of God as revealed, our understanding is considerably deepened and a distinctly soteriological account of theological epistemology emerges.

Like others of his generation, Henri de Lubac swore the antimodernist oath, and so affirmed the possibility of a natural knowledge of God.[60] While an oath imposed by ecclesiastical authority that one accepts knowledge of certain things on the basis of natural reason can only possibly be ambiguous,[61] still, as the last section traced, the affirmation of a natural knowledge of God is wholly consistent with de Lubac's theological commitments. His position on a supernatural finality for human nature leads to a theological anthropology that understands the

48 *Salvation Disclosed*

human spirit as openness to God,[62] and for this reason, the knowledge of God is inscribed in our nature, inescapably constituting us as what we are.

This is, essentially, the sort of natural knowledge of God as creator that the constitution *Dei Filius* insisted was available to natural reason. De Lubac posits that this natural knowledge is sufficient *"en principe."*[63] However, within our concrete existential condition, ontologically limited by finitude and morally vitiated by sin, there is a very real sense in which we are dependent upon supernatural revelation, beyond just the light of reason. Indeed, given our supernatural vocation, such knowledge is all the more essential to the realization of that very longing by which we responsively intuit and reach toward God.[64] In this way, de Lubac actually echoes *Dei Filius*, which taught that revelation was given to address both of these issues: our currently vitiated condition and God's gracious invitation of us into the divine life.[65] We face, then, a twofold disproportion, one ontological, as creatures cannot, by their efforts, attain to God, the other moral, because sinners require redemption to return to friendship with God.

Because of de Lubac's fundamental convictions regarding humanity's supernatural vocation, his emphasis falls far more on the God who reveals himself in grace, inviting "us to participate in the Life of God himself," than on the God we are able to affirm solely on the basis of natural reason.[66] By nature, we are led to affirm that there is a God, but through his revelation, we know that God is the Trinity and that he has destined us to share in the trinitarian life.[67] God, of course, would still be the triune God even if human beings never came to recognize this, indeed, even if human beings never existed, but this is a realization that would not have been available to us had God not first made it known. This revelation of God as Trinity is soteriological in two senses. First, it has salvation as its end: God reveals himself to us as Trinity so that we can be incorporated into the divine life shared by the Father, the Son, and the Holy Spirit. Second, and crucially, this revelation is soteriological in its content, as "the mystery of the Trinity is not revealed to us first of all in itself but in the Trinity's action outside itself, in its saving activity," though, of course, "the term of that saving action is indeed . . . the Trinity itself."[68]

It is through the revelation of the "economic" Trinity that we are led to affirm the reality of the "immanent" Trinity, because in order for God to have acted on our behalf as he has in Christ and the sending of the Holy Spirit, he must also antecedently be Father, Son, and Holy Spirit.[69] There is an important tension that must be observed and maintained in this regard. On the one hand, "Every act of revelation is . . . a revelation of the Trinity, [and] the entire revelation of the Trinity is a revelation through action, and all this action is directly concerned with man" because it aims at our redemption and elevation into the divine life.[70] Indeed, all of God's revelation touches upon our salvation.[71] The "original state" of doctrine, from which springs all of the "Christian newness," is "the redemptive Action; it is the gift that God makes of himself in his Son," such that "it is already a first abstraction . . . to separate . . . the gift and the revelation of the gift, the redemptive action and the knowledge of redemption, the mystery of act and the mystery as proposed to faith."[72] Nevertheless, we cannot simply reduce our doctrine of God to soteriology, such that we lose sight of Christ behind his saving benefits.[73] Our epistemological access to these truths of God is dependent upon and conditioned by the reality of salvation, but the God we know through our salvation is neither dependent upon nor conditioned by his saving acts.[74] At the same time, *as revealed*, the mysteries are inherently soteriological. While God is necessarily the Trinity, and while Christ would be the hypostasis he is even without the incarnation (or the creation), the revelation of these truths is entirely bound up with our salvation.

The content of revelation, then, is a complex of soteriologically oriented mysteries having to do with humanity's union with and assimilation to God the Trinity through the incarnate Word. While we can distinguish between the elements of this complex, so far as revelation goes, we must recognize that they are a unity because they are revealed in the singular act of redemption, which was for the sake of our incorporation into the divine life. The recognition of a nexus of the mysteries with each other and our final end is essentially an acknowledgment of this fundamental unity. As we recognized in the introduction, de Lubac, along with a significant portion of twentieth-century Catholicism, came to recognize this unity and especially a Christological-soteriological concentration of the mystery.

50   *Salvation Disclosed*

The mystery revealed is revealed for the sake of our assimilation to it. It is revealed so that this mystery might be received. Our apprehension of the mystery plays out in two primary manners: theology (*théologie*) and mysticism (*mystique*). Theology is an intellectual endeavor whereby one reflects upon the meaning of the mystery, pursuing, so far as possible, its intelligibility. Mysticism, as we have delineated above, is a spiritual movement whereby we are drawn into and have the mystery reproduced within ourselves. As we shall see, these two modes of apprehension, while distinct, are intimately related to each other, and it is precisely in discerning their relation that the soteriological impulse undergirding de Lubac's theological epistemology becomes clear.

Bertrand Dumas identifies "two typically Lubacian manners of resorting to a theological presentation capable of nourishing the mystical élan: paradox and the spiritual understanding [l'intelligence spirituelle] of Scripture."[75] We shall consider these each in turn.

Paradox and Mystery

The mysteries are all "aspects of a global and unique truth": salvation in Jesus Christ.[76] Yet, while this unity of the truth inheres in the "substance," it is not always perceptible to the human intellect because, as noted before, it exceeds the proportions of that intellect.[77] This leads, then, to a peculiarity of de Lubac's approach to theological language, the use of paradox. I began this chapter by noting the centrality of paradox to de Lubac's theological outlook. The elements we have sketched thus far demonstrate the particular fittingness of paradox within his theological epistemology. Given that we are dealing with mysteries beyond the capacity of the human intellect—and indeed, mysteries that aim at a level of the human being beyond the intellect—it makes sense that they will not be subject to full intellectual comprehension.

De Lubac's affinity for paradox may be discerned in his aphoristic collections, *Paradoxes* (1945), *Nouveaux Paradoxes* (1955), and the posthumously published *Autres Paradoxes* (1994), along with his ecclesiological work *Paradoxe et mystère de l'église* (1967).[78] In addition, we can note the paradoxical affirmation that lies at the heart of his theology of the supernatural: that humanity has a natural desire for a supernatural destiny.[79] It also asserts itself in what we might call the decline narratives

Knowing the Mystery 51

found in *Corpus mysticum* (1944) and *Exégèse médiévale* (1959–64). In both of these works, de Lubac traces a development in which a quest for increasing clarity leads to a decreased comfort with polyvalence, ambiguity, and paradox. De Lubac does not dispute the genuine gains that have come from dialectical precision. Indeed, he recognizes, somewhat wistfully, that these developments were, in some measure, necessary, due to challenges to the faith that had arisen.[80]

Nor does this mean that de Lubac simply eschewed dialectic, though we must set our consideration within the context of his rejection of rationalism. We noted above that de Lubac cannot properly be accused of anti-intellectualism. He sought to surpass intellectualism, but not necessarily to reject it. Building upon Rousselot's retrieved distinction between *intellectus* and *ratio*, we should note that the supplanting of paradox by dialectic traced in *Corpus mysticum* is not, properly speaking, intellectualism, but rather rationalism, an epistemological outlook that de Lubac explicitly rejected.

Such rationalism is what lay behind the conclusions theology of the manuals, and "Apologétique et théologie" was an early expression of de Lubac's concern regarding it. Swafford describes the lecture as the "epistemological expression" of de Lubac's theology of nature and grace.[81] De Lubac suggests that the time has come to move from the then-prevailing model of apologetics, which sought to demonstrate the truths of the faith, or at least to function as *preambulae fidei*, in favor of a fundamental theology that instead explains the faith.[82] This, essentially, represents a preferring of the *intellectus* over the *ratio*. Rather than reasoning one's way to the faith, or even to faith's threshold, one ought to grasp the intelligibility of the faith. De Lubac is clear that the "unavowed rationalism, which had been reinforced for a century by the invasion of positivist tendencies," was reducing faith to a syllogistic enterprise.[83]

For all this, though, dialectic remained an important and indispensable tool. The difference between the philosopher and the mystic does not lie in dialectic, for they both use it.[84] Indeed, "Dialectic is a powerful weapon because it corresponds to one of the essential processes of the mind."[85] The problem comes "when it tries to engender thought, instead of organizing it," for then "its soul is a blind necessity."[86] The recognition that our affirmation of God is not due to reasoning does not render rational argumentation regarding his existence pointless. Rather, with God we encounter a reality beyond the *ratio*'s capacity.[87] Because the idea of God is, indeed, an idea, "it certainly is subjected, like all other ideas, to dialectic."[88] At the same time, though, "Far from corresponding to a phase in human dialectic, it is, on the contrary, dialectic which plays the intermediary role, linking in its process a reality already perceived and a mystery surmised, without ceasing to be sustained in its movement by a presence."[89]

By contrast, paradox signals a willingness to suspend dialectic, recognizing its merely intermediate position. While a "most fruitful" knowledge and understanding of the mysteries is available to reason, guided and enlightened by faith, "even when logic has constrained us to affirm that he exists, his mystery remains inviolate. Our reason does not penetrate to him. Dialectic and representation cannot cross the threshold. But beneath dialectic and all representation, our spirit already affirms Him who, attained by the mediation of dialectic and representation, is beyond all representation and all dialectic."[90] Paradox marks the proper mode of expression for the mystery of God, which exists beyond the grasp of dialectical precision.

De Lubac writes: "Paradox is the reverse of what, properly perceived, would be synthesis. But the proper view always eludes us. . . . Paradox is the search or wait for synthesis. It is the provisional expression of a view which remains incomplete, but whose orientation is ever towards fulness."[91] Paradox, then, seeks to probe the divine mysteries, but with the recognition that "dogma is a vast domain which theology will never wholly exploit. There is always infinitely more in Dogma . . . than in this 'human science of revelation,' in this product of analysis and rational elaboration which theology always is."[92] As Wagner notes, "Paradox is ceaselessly desirous of an ultimate synthesis."[93] Yet this desire remains respectful of the mystery, as Swafford explains:

> The category of paradox allows the theologian to embrace the fullness of the ontological "mystery" of faith, in all its integral unity. On the other hand, without the deliberate employment of paradox, human reason naturally tends to emphasize one or other aspect of a given mystery, attempting to alleviate tension between various dimensions of a particular mystery of faith. . . . Accordingly, the category of paradox allows one to move beyond the conceptual frailty of

Knowing the Mystery   53

our finite intellectual faculties in order to behold the mystery as it truly is in itself, in all its unified integrity.[94]

Or, as Dumas puts it, "Generator of a fecund tradition by this simultaneous enunciation of contraries, Lubacian paradox is found to be both a theological and a spiritual path by which the Mystery is respected in its profound nature of mystery and call to surpass."[95]

In some ways, paradox serves a function similar to speculation within scholastic theology, yet with a crucial difference that stems from the contours of de Lubac's theological epistemology and the theological anthropology that informs it.[96] Both seek to penetrate as far as possible into a mystery that exceeds one's faculties in order to approach, as nearly as possible, its full significance. Yet speculation is primarily an intellectual endeavor, while paradox recognizes humanity as fundamentally spirit and aims at contemplation. By it one dwells in and upon the mystery.[97] While it is not at all accurate to characterize de Lubac as anti-scholastic, and while, as we have seen and will continue to see, a speculative vision does indeed inform his thought, this is a key distinction.

Spiritual Intelligence/Contemplation

With this notion of contemplation of and dwelling in the mystery, we are brought to the second of the Lubacian categories identified by Dumas: spiritual intelligence. Dumas demonstrates that as de Lubac's thought matured, his notion of spiritual intelligence became increasingly tied to Scripture. This will be the focus of the next chapter, so for now I prescind from the material role of Scripture in spiritual intelligence and instead consider its meaning more formally. De Lubac uses the terms *intelligence spirituelle* and *intelligence de la foi* more or less interchangeably. For simplicity, I shall tend to use *spiritual intelligence* in my discussion.

Outside de Lubac's writings on spiritual interpretation of Scripture, to which we shall turn in the next chapter, the clearest presentation on the nature of spiritual intelligence is the chapter "From Symbolism to Dialectic" in *Corpus Mysticum*.[98] As I noted above, this chapter traces the rise of dialectic and a concomitant discomfort and dissatisfaction with the ambiguity of symbolism, the very ambiguity that paradox manifests and upholds. This development represented something of a sea change in human thought, with the result that "this Christian rationalism could no longer envisage the understanding of mysteries outside their demonstration."[99]

This rationalistic demonstration supplanted a more "mystical" grasp of the truth.[100] Returning to the concerns of "Apologétique et théologie," this is a move whereby "apology for dogma succeeded the understanding of faith."[101] Augustine is held forth as an exemplar of this mystical contemplation, which was by no means a "renunciation of the exercise of intelligence" but rather an instance of faith seeking understanding.[102] The mystery disclosed in dogma, while "obscure to our carnal faculties . . . is in itself radiant with a secret intelligibility" that summons our questions and bids inquiry as "we glimpse a deep luminosity in the background" and "seek and obtain an ever-greater understanding."[103] Spiritual intelligence, then, is essentially a mode of faith seeking understanding.

There are echoes of intellectualism in de Lubac's position on spiritual intelligence. Indeed, how could it be otherwise when we are dealing with spiritual *intelligence*, which grasps the real and attains to truth?[104] Rousselot had claimed that God is supreme and absolute intelligence, while the human intellect reflects the divine intellect, albeit discursively rather than as the infinite and simple pure act that God is.[105] In *Corpus Mysticum*, de Lubac insists that humanity, created in the image of the Logos, "shared an intimate relationship that the activity of reasoning had the aim of bringing to perfection. Starting from Nature, starting from History, or Scripture, or the Liturgy, starting from everything, the mind had the same orientation towards spiritual understanding."[106] For Rousselot, the activity of the *ratio* aims at the rest of the satisfied *intellectus*, a dynamism that we see echoed here.[107] For de Lubac, though—and this is a crucial distinction—this was a dynamism not merely among the faculties, but of the whole human person, who as spirit is constituted by a dynamic openness and propulsion toward God.

This, then, at once recalls the note of spirit as élan and points to another important feature of de Lubac's notion of spiritual intelligence, its anagogical character.[108] I shall return to the matter of anagogy in the next chapter, in connection with the anagogical sense of Scripture. For now, though, suffice it to say that there is a dynamism at play in spiritual intelligence by which one is drawn upward and into God.

As Dumas puts it, "The intelligence of faith is not theology, but a movement of the whole human being toward God, which thus combines the (mystical) desire to see God and the (theological) resources of rational science."[109] We are brought, then, to the relation between mysticism and theology. Theology seeks to understand the mystery; it is an intellectual exercise. Mysticism seeks to enter into the mystery, to have it be reproduced within oneself, and it corresponds to the spirit, which is the site of mysticism. As we have seen, the two structural features of de Lubac's theology, paradox and spiritual understanding, both invite a contemplative mode of engagement with the mystery whereby one dwells with and beholds the mystery to the end of being drawn deeper into it. These structural features of theology, then, promote mysticism. This is confirmed by Dumas's careful study, which demonstrates that, as de Lubac's thought matured, he came to understand *théologie* as interior to *mystique* and to place them both in a relationship of dependence upon *Mystère*.[110]

In other words, as de Lubac's thought matured, his position on mysticism came to express his prior anthropological and epistemological commitment to the primacy of spirit. Theology and mysticism are not opposed, nor in a hierarchical relationship, but rather in a relationship of inclusion. Theology is itself interior to and included within mysticism, and it is especially the spirit that is the site of mysticism, wherein one truly and profoundly encounters the mystery of God.[111] This, in turn, bears out the central thesis of this study, that de Lubac's major works demonstrate and are unified by a soteriological preoccupation. The task of theology unfolds within the reality of mysticism, whereby human beings are drawn into the life of God through the redemptive work of the incarnate Christ.

Knowledge of God as Salvation

In light of the foregoing, then, we can conclude that for de Lubac, not only is our knowledge of God ordered to salvation, but the dynamic movement of our knowledge of God is itself salvation. Within the twofold order of knowledge described by *Dei Filius*, truths can be known by natural reason and by divine faith. Faith, then, is the form of knowing God of which we are capable (1) by supernatural grace and (2) this side of the beatific vision. In the light of glory we shall see God as he is, and faith will give way to sight. Even then, though, we will not fully comprehend the divine essence. And until vision replaces faith, faith is the means by which we acquire supernatural knowledge of God.

De Lubac understands faith in far more dynamic and personalist terms than as mere assent. This may be illustrated by his analysis of the presence or absence of the preposition *in* in the credo's articles. The believer confesses belief *in* God, but not *in* the church. The church is an article of faith, even the context within which faith is received, nurtured, and confessed, but it is not an object of faith.[112] In contrast, faith does not just lead us to affirm God but actually thrusts us into God.[113] This follows naturally from the character of revelation. The revelation of the Trinity occurs through the work of redemption, and "the Trinity is revealed to us only to the extent in which it makes possible our elevation and our redemption through the work of salvation."[114] Because God is revealed precisely in the saving act, and for the purpose of salvation, it follows that faith in what is revealed (i.e., the saving acts, which are meant to elevate us to share in God) brings us into communion with the Trinity.[115] This occurs in a twofold movement of the "development of dogma and deepening of the mystery."[116] It is by this latter movement of deepening the mystery that the saving mystery is entered into by and interiorized for the Christian.[117] Such knowledge of God does not remain exterior to us, but rather comes to characterize us at the most profound of levels. The mystery of salvation, which we grasp by faith, comes to be reproduced in us. In the following chapters, we shall gain further clarity about the nature of this saving mystery and how it is that we come to share in it.

Dogma and practice, then, are a unity, because the whole of dogma is summed up in Christ, who is charity incarnate, whose redemptive act is a great deed of charity and draws forth from us the response of charity, which brings us to share in God, whose nature is love.[118] Understood in this way, faith is "that movement which, upon hearing the Word, freely ratifies the destiny inscribed in our very being by the Creator; in other words, the resumption and transformation of the secret movement essential to every creature through the dynamism of faith."[119] The knowledge of God is inscribed in the depths of our being by nature. The return to God through faith takes us further than and perfects, but does not do away with or abridge, this most fundamental élan. The knowledge of God is a graced response to his primordial call.

With this notion of faith as a journey of return to God, de Lubac retrieves and re-expresses one of the most central soteriological motifs of Augustine of Hippo, who understood the return to God to occur not through local motion, but through a volitional purification driven by faith's humility. By consenting to faith rather than direct vision, redeemed humanity was properly humbled, enabled to set its loves in the proper order, and so return to the source of true beatitude, God.[120] For Augustine, as for de Lubac, the purpose of God's revelation was to guide and carry us along this journey, a journey in which Christ is both the homeland we seek and the way by which we return.[121]

Conclusion: *Sur les chemins de Dieu*

By making this return in faith, hope, and charity, the Christian actually already participates in God, because God is charity.[122] This movement, then, both perfects our natural love and represents a supernatural novum. This participation in God is distinctly trinitarian, because salvation is the common and inseparable work of the Trinity, such that "everything comes *from* the Father, *through* the Son, *in* the Spirit."[123] Moreover, "The only way to a real encounter with God is the Living Way which is called Jesus Christ," a theolegoumenon that underlines the title of *Sur les chemins de Dieu* (on the paths of God).[124] It is through Jesus Christ that one is brought back and returns to God. And this way into God is a journey that will continue throughout eternity, for true and proper theology "is the movement of faith, adoration, and ecstasy in God. That theology will never end because God is inexhaustible."[125] It is this inexhaustible delight in God—the beatific vision, which is the outcome of salvation, into which we enter through the crucified and risen Christ—that is the fundamental content and purpose of de Lubac's theological epistemology. As Dumas puts it, this leads to "a theological intelligence that is truly theological, thus paschal."[126] It is precisely this mystery that is reproduced within the faithful through the knowledge of God.

As it stands, our accounts of revelation and of knowing God remain somewhat formal. The following chapter further specifies the nature and purpose of revelation as well as the movement of passing into God through Christ, and does so by attending to the material content of revelation, particularly of sacred Scripture, and of the Christian church's engagement with it through the practice of spiritual exegesis.

CHAPTER FOUR

Spiritual Exegesis and/as Salvation

While *Surnaturel* was the storm center of de Lubac's career, his writings on spiritual exegesis encapsulate his theological vision as does no other locus within his œuvre.[1] As Joseph Flipper notes, de Lubac devoted more volumes to spiritual exegesis than to any other topic, including the theology of the supernatural,[2] and Susan Wood has ably demonstrated that a good deal of the unity perceived in de Lubac's thought emerges as a result of his "immersion in the patristic and medieval practice of spiritual exegesis."[3] This is because de Lubac's treatment of the four senses of Scripture, particularly in what he dubbed their doctrinal form, is far more than simply a method for biblical interpretation. It provides a heuristic structure for a theology of history that can serve as a scaffolding for understanding his thought as a whole.[4] Indeed, this theology of history is centered upon the relationship between the Old and New Testaments, understood less as the collections of books bearing those designations and more as economies for God's covenants.[5] Hence, the theology of spiritual exegesis also pivots upon the peoples generated and placed into relationship with God through those economies, and so also impinges upon ecclesiology.[6]

De Lubac's engagement with the four senses of Scripture provides a structure that reproduces itself in nearly every other area of his thought.[7] This structure turns upon the relation between the Old and New Testaments, particularly upon the category of the "Christian newness,"[8] which we have already discerned in his writings on the supernatural. Indeed, the theology of spiritual exegesis provides perhaps the clearest window into the nature of this Christian newness by precisely specifying the nature of the continuity and discontinuity between the Old and New Testaments.

Similarly, there is a strong connection between de Lubac's interest in Christian mysticism and the theology of spiritual exegesis. As he notes in "Mysticism and Mystery": "Since Christian mysticism develops through the action of the mystery received in faith, and the mystery is the Incarnation of the Word of God revealed in Scripture, Christian mysticism is essentially an understanding of the holy Books. The mystery is their meaning; mysticism is getting to know that meaning."[9] As Bertrand Dumas has shown, as de Lubac's thought matured, he increasingly saw Christian mysticism as rooted in such engagement with Scripture. The central category of spiritual intelligence that we considered in the previous chapter came to be increasingly seen as the spiritual intelligence *of Scripture*, which takes on concrete form through a consideration of the fourfold sense of Scripture.[10] All of these factors, taken in concert, considerably advance the central contention of this study: that de Lubac's theology coalesces around a soteriological preoccupation.

As we shall see, at the core of spiritual exegesis is a theology of salvation in Christ, and this is the case for a couple of reasons. First, because Christ's redemptive act is the central content of Scripture as disclosed through spiritual interpretation. The two testaments pivot upon the cross, which effects the transition from the one to the other. Second, because the process of spiritual exegesis is itself a reproduction of this transition, and so is itself conversion to Christ, and thus salvation.

Because spiritual exegesis concerns itself with God's revelation in Sacred Scripture, it is to be expected that this locus would impinge upon other areas of theology that receive their content and parameters from this revelation. For this reason, it is rather difficult to consider spiritual exegesis in isolation from other areas of de Lubac's thought. Hence, this chapter will make note of the connections that exist between this material and what lies behind and ahead while keeping its focus on spiritual exegesis itself and reserving fuller discussion for the appropriate time.

Spiritual Exegesis as *Ressourcement*, Not Methodology

De Lubac's writings on spiritual exegesis reflect, perhaps as does no other area of his thought, the priorities and sensibility of *ressourcement* and, at the same time, serve to clarify what *ressourcement* was and was not for de Lubac. Like so many of de Lubac's works, the works on spiritual exegesis are couched as historical studies, reflecting the *ressourcement* turn to the foundations of Scripture, the church fathers, and the liturgy. This is not to suggest that de Lubac had no agenda beyond pure historical reconstruction. He was clearly enamored with the exegetical procedures of the patristic and medieval figures whom he surveyed, but, as we shall see, his agenda was not simple repristination. Instead, the past held forth an alternative vision of the church's relation to Scripture, a road not taken of sorts,[11] but not one that invites our passage. There was no possibility of returning by that same path in any straightforward way—history's flow is irreversible.[12] Nevertheless, one could look to the past and draw inspiration for an alternative present and future. Cholvy describes it well: "To present questions, the Tradition can bring not solutions, but clarifications, and it permits us to resituate positions that are only recent."[13]

De Lubac sought a respect for Scripture as a living Word, as revelation from God, not a mere historical artifact. His neo-scholastic contemporaries, so concerned with drawing proper conclusions, were, it seemed, eager to move beyond the revelation of Scripture in order to produce a purer truth, refined from its ore.[14] Recalling the previous chapter's distinction between rationalism and intellectualism, rather than pursuing an understanding of the Scriptures, a conclusions theology adopted them as first principles from which to reason. In contrast, and going beyond mere intellectualism, the fathers and medieval scholastics had inhabited and were permeated by Scripture. Theirs was an existentially involved and transformative encounter, a spiritual intelligence. It is in this sense that the writings on spiritual exegesis represent a *ressourcement* turn to Scripture, not in the sense of actually doing spiritual exegesis, but in its conviction that sacred Scripture lay at the very heart of theology and could not simply be overpassed or transcended.[15]

These writings, though, were as much, if not more, a turn to patristics as to Scripture. They grew, initially, out of de Lubac's study of Origen, a pursuit that was almost *de rigeur* for his generation.[16] The 1930s and 1940s saw the important publications on this once outre and heterodox figure by Jean Daniélou and Hans Urs von Balthasar.[17] De Lubac's own study on Origen, *Histoire et esprit*, appeared in 1950, but he relates having been at work gathering its material for the previous twenty years.[18] As he set out in his study of Origenian exegesis, de Lubac soon discovered that what he was engaged in was "no longer . . . a matter solely of exegesis. It was a whole manner of thinking, a whole world view. . . . A whole interpretation of Christianity of which Origen . . . was less the author than the witness."[19] This recognition launched him into the further studies that comprise *Exégèse médiévale*'s four volumes, in which he makes it clear that he is not engaged in "an allegorical or spiritual study of Scripture" but rather in "an historical and literal study of ancient commentators on Scripture."[20] The focus, then, is on the theology of the fathers more than on the contents of Scripture, per se.

Finally, the writings on spiritual exegesis have a strong connection with that third font of *ressourcement*, the liturgy. As de Lubac surveys what once was, and its disappearance, it is in the church liturgy's appropriation of biblical imagery in witness of Christ, and its juxtaposition of biblical texts according to the pattern of promise and fulfillment, that he sees the enduring contribution of spiritual exegesis.[21] For this reason, at the end of his lengthy study on Origen, de Lubac asks, "What remains of this vast doctrine, which emerges again before our eyes like a dream palace through the mist of the distant past? Depending on our perspective in approaching it, we would respond: Not much, or, on the contrary: Everything essential,"[22] because "spiritual exegesis has long since accomplished an essential part of its task."[23]

This is crucial to recognize, for to the extent that we read de Lubac's writings on spiritual exegesis as though he is advocating for a return to pre-modern exegetical methodology, we will miss his point. As Kevin Hughes notes: "If de Lubac is making a historical claim [about the fourfold sense], it is a bad one. But let me suggest that de Lubac's judgement itself is theological. That is, his process of reconstructing the fourfold sense from the scattered, fragmentary witness of so many ancient and medieval figures is founded on a Catholic theological understanding of tradition as an organic whole."[24] De Lubac is clear in his recognition that, in many ways, the time for spiritual exegesis has passed. Modern historical critical exegesis is not so omnicompetent as it would like to claim, but we cannot simply turn back the clock and ignore the gains that it has brought.[25] Instead, de Lubac concerns himself with the doctrinal core that is disclosed by and motivated the spiritual interpretation of patristic and medieval exegetes. To lose their methodology is no great loss. It had its liabilities, not least its tendencies toward excessive and untethered inference. To lose this doctrinal core, though, would be to lose the heart of Christianity, which is disclosed in the four senses of Scripture: the mystery of Christ.

Lewis Ayres notes that de Lubac's vision of spiritual exegesis turns upon a moral pedagogy and that de Lubac lamented the separation of such a spirituality from exegesis and theology.[26] We might say, then, that de Lubac desired a return to the spirituality, but not necessarily the methodology of spiritual exegesis. And with this recognition we have reached the crux of what motivated de Lubac's *ressourcement*: not a more ancient way of doing things, but rather a dwelling upon the mystery of Christ and his redemption, a contemplation that draws the contemplative, through Christ, to share in the life of the Trinity.[27] This is precisely the meaning of spiritual intelligence that we saw was central to de Lubac's theological epistemology in chapter 3 and that characterizes the account of mysticism that pervades his œuvre as a whole.[28] De Lubac did not seek to reinstate procedures whose time had passed; this would be to reduce our engagement with the mystery to a matter of technique, a triumph of rationalism, which seeks to domesticate the mystery, rendering it not so mysterious after all. Instead, he sought to recapture a vision that had been obscured.

Passing Over into Christ: The Four Senses of Scripture and their Doctrinal Form

Scripture's four senses are summed up in an ancient "distich," which served as a mnemonic device:

> The letter teaches events, allegory what you should believe,
> Morality teaches what you should do, anagogy what mark you
>   should be aiming for.[29]

This rhyme (it does rhyme in Latin) identifies Scripture's senses, each with its own telos as the literal, the allegorical, the moral (tropological), and the anagogical. Of course, understandings of the multiple senses of Scripture were never uniform in either the patristic or the medieval eras,[30] and de Lubac was well aware of this. Some authors spoke of three senses, others of four.[31] Some related the senses to each other differently than did others. So the distillation of the "four senses" of Scripture (literal, allegorical, tropological, and anagogical) represents an abstraction in order to demonstrate the doctrinal motive force that underlay patristic exegesis.[32] This, once more, indicates that de Lubac's agenda was not to advocate for a return to patristic exegetical methodology. Such a return would be impossible, because there never was any *one* form of patristic exegesis. Instead, a common doctrinal structure is discernible in the senses of Scripture. It is this doctrine that interests de Lubac,[33] for in it he finds a key for ascertaining how premodern theologians understood the mystery of redemption by Christ.[34]

Counterintuitively, the best way to appreciate and understand the meaning of the fourfold sense of Scripture is to first reduce it to two members, a reduction that de Lubac referred to as their "doctrinal form." The doctrinal form's two members are the literal sense and the spiritual or allegorical sense, which correspond to the Old and New Testaments, respectively.[35] The "letter" refers not to the biblical text, but to the historical events recorded in the Old Testament, an affirmation borne out by the fact that non-historical texts, like the Proverbs, particularly those that employ figurative language, "have no literal sense," while the "spirit" refers to the letter's fulfillment by Christ in the New Testament.[36] Indeed, the designations "Old Testament" and "New Testament" do not refer primarily to biblical texts as such, but rather to covenantal economies. This is evidenced by the fact that certain passages located within the "New Testament" canon belong to the "Old Testament," a matter of some import and to which we shall return. The spiritual sense of Scripture, then, is the new meaning bestowed upon the Old Testament by Christ. This is significant, because Christ's fulfillment of the Old Testament is not in the mode of predictions coming to pass but is rather a transformative act on Christ's part.[37]

In this connection we must acknowledge that many of the patristic sources upon which de Lubac draws and whose words he approvingly reproduces utilize deeply anti-Jewish rhetoric in their account of the transition from the Old Testament to the New.[38] On the one hand, we can and should distinguish between theological anti-Judaism and racist anti-semitism and recognize that de Lubac worked in solidarity with and defense of his Jewish contemporaries during World War II, at great personal risk.[39] On the other hand, we must not only not excuse but also oppose such rhetoric and seek to express the central insight of the Christian novelty and Christ's fulfillment of the letter in non-supersessionist terms.

It is important to recognize that the spiritual and literal senses are not in a competitive or adversarial relationship.[40] No violence is done to the letter by the spirit's transformation of it. Instead, the letter is upheld in all its historical particularity even as a new meaning is given to it.[41] Flipper characterizes this Christological transformation of the Old Testament as a "retroactive causality."[42] There is a genuine novelty that results from Christ's action, but this novelty is itself intrinsic to the letter. It remains what it was but is made something new all the same. In other words, had Christ not come, the allegorical sense would never have been discovered in the Old Testament's figures; it would have been an unnatural imposition with no foundation in the letter.[43] However, Christ has indeed come, and through his decisive act of exegesis, the Old Testament has always, in fact, been about him.[44]

Here we can discern a formal parallel with de Lubac's theology of the supernatural. Humanity, as created spirit bearing the image of God, has a genuine orientation toward its fulfillment in the likeness of God. And yet between this natural desire and its supernatural fulfillment there is a radical disproportion. Created spirit cannot attain its own fulfillment by its own resources, but it is nevertheless constituted by its ordination to that fulfillment. This is the fundamental shape of the Christian novelty that so captivated de Lubac.

This doctrinal reduction of the spiritual senses allows for theological reception of the fruits of historical critical research while also finding in Christ the meaning of the Old Testament. Because of the spiritual sense's novelty, we can benefit from historical reconstructions of the biblical authors' situations and horizons, even as we recognize in the Scriptures a meaning that transcends those horizons. This transition bears witness to the Christian novelty: Christ has made all things new. This is the difference between seeing spiritual exegesis through the lens of methodological advocacy and seeing it through the lens of doctrinal structure. Advocacy would require establishing that such and such exegetical method was the one used by Origen or Cyril or whomever, as well as a call to go and do likewise. If the concern is doctrinal, though, we can simply note the way in which Christ transforms the meaning of the Old Testament even as he preserves it in himself.

De Lubac wrote, "The informed theologian ... accepts the progress that has been made by scientific knowledge and he takes care not to perpetuate all the forms by which faith in the divinity of Scripture was once freely expressed, [nevertheless] he recognizes unequivocally that the existence of a twofold sense, literal and spiritual, is an ineluctable given of the tradition."[45] As a matter of fact, de Lubac was consistently critical of the methodological particularities of his patristic and medieval interlocutors.[46] What he opposed was not a departure from their method, but instead (1) the historical conceit that premodern interpreters were mere naïfs, waiting in darkness until they could sit at the feet of the Enlightenment, and (2) the loss of the spirituality that drove their interpretation.[47]

At this juncture, spirituality is crucial, for while de Lubac does not encourage a return to premodern exegetical *methods*, he does advocate for their exegetical *outlook*. The passage from Old Testament to New Testament is a matter not only of transforming Scripture's meaning, but also of transforming its reader. For ancient Christianity, biblical interpretation was a paideia, the queen of the arts, itself encompassing the whole of theology.[48] To grasp the spiritual meaning of the literal sense was to "pass over into Christ," and so be converted.[49]

This is the first of the ways that salvation provides the crucial content for the theology of spiritual exegesis: the two are isomorphic. Properly understood, spiritual exegesis is not so much a matter of interpreting texts as it is a matter of engaging with the Christ who communicates himself in those texts, and to whom they bear witness. This, moreover, is why a departure from patristic exegetical methodology is not fatally problematic, because such a saving encounter with Christ can occur in other modes than biblical interpretation, but a departure from the doctrinal sense is fatal because it amounts to a departure from this saving encounter *tout court*.

With this transformation in Christ, we have the pith of the doctrine de Lubac excavates from his patristic and medieval interlocutors: the Old Testament (history) testifies to and finds its meaning in Christ (spirit), who is its Lord and directs it in accordance with the newness of his salvation. The other two senses of Scripture add depth, but not content, to this doctrinal structure.[50] In addition to the binary of letter (history) and spirit (allegory), the senses of tropology and anagogy unfold as dimensions of the spiritual/allegorical sense.

Tropology turns especially on morality and the ascetical life, while anagogy consummates the whole, and does so in a twofold manner. As we saw in chapter 3, a certain anagogic dynamism pervades de Lubac's theological epistemology, as we are swept up and drawn into the mystery, passing from image to likeness. The first consummation of the anagogical sense, then, refers to the completion of tropology and mysticism, the full assimilation into the mystery disclosed and contemplated in Scripture. Anagogy is also the eschatological sense of Scripture, referring to the consummation of all things.[51] As we shall see, particularly in chapters 7 and 8, these two modes of fulfillment are intimately related.

The movement from history to allegory involves a genuine novelty, a radical conversion, a leap across a caesura. "The passage from allegory to tropology [and also to anagogy] involves no such jump," according to de Lubac. "After the historical sense, all those that can still be counted belong to one and the same spiritual sense."[52] Tropology and anagogy are not new senses of Scripture, but rather the clarification and flowering of allegory. They are themselves interior to the allegorical sense.[53] Significantly, locating tropology and anagogy within allegory marks out both the moral progress of one's Christian life and the eschatological consummation of all things as interior to Christ. Growth in holiness does not take one beyond Christ but is a journey within Christ. The alternative would be an implicit Pelagianism in which one's own virtues derive from a source other than Christ and his grace.

All this lies behind de Lubac's preference for the fourfold division of Scripture (history, allegory, tropology, anagogy) to another, also common, threefold structure (history, tropology, allegory).[54] The threefold arrangement fairly easily, though not unambiguously, maps onto that tripartite anthropology according to which the human spirit is a privileged site of the encounter with God.[55] However, it also risks a downgrading of the central place of the mystery within Christianity. It provides "a kind of anatomy and physiology of the soul that, in principle at least, was not presupposing revelation ... [while the former provides] a salvation history of the soul in function of the salvation of mankind by Christ, or a call to the salvation of the soul in the common salvation of the Church."[56] Depending on whether tropology "precedes or follows the

Spiritual Exegesis and/as Salvation   67

allegorical sense, that is to say, according to whether it is unrelated to it or dependent on it," one's account of morality can either lack anything "specifically Christian" or it can have "christological, ecclesial, and sacramental complexion . . . wholly Christian, in its content no less than in its form, in its end results no less than in its deeply rooted foundations."[57]

Hence, the fourfold/twofold doctrinal sense keeps the mystery foregrounded, insisting that, for all our progress, we can never progress further than the mystery of Christ. Moreover, it cuts both ways. As we have just noted, locating tropology within allegory ensures that the mystery's centrality is upheld. Additionally, though, it indicates that the reception of the mystery by tropology is itself a dimension of the mystery, not some extrinsic addition to it.[58] This recalls the observation of the previous chapter that, precisely by virtue of the nature of the mystery that is revealed, our reception of the mystery is involved, because God has revealed himself precisely for the purpose and in the act of drawing us into his own life and including us in it.

Similarly, the future hope is not a hope beyond Christ's fulfillment of history but the consummation of a fulfillment that has already occurred within history. The alternative would be a Joachimite surpassing of Christ by some further development, a point to which we shall return in chapter 7.[59] In either case, the arrangement would be a displacing of Christ as the definitive and constitutive source of salvation and the content of revelation. The Christian newness, then, is not only a *novum*, but a *novissimum*—to evoke the classical characterization of eschatology as the *novissima*—the state wherein no more novelty is possible, not because newness is in the past but because the superlatively new has come.[60]

In this connection, we are able to discern an important distinction between scholarly trajectories on de Lubac. In this eschatological differentiation anagogy unfolds as the consummation of allegory in such a way that the twofold fulfillment of history by Christ is, in point of fact, the same reality, thereby granting to history a sacramental structure in de Lubac's thought. This sacramentality is best discerned in the relationship between allegory and anagogy, and so is a historically dynamic sacramentality.[61] Hans Boersma's account of a "sacramental hermeneutic" in service of a more general sacramental ontology locates the sacramentality in the relation between the Old and New Testaments.[62] This is not wrong, per se,[63] since there is an identity of substance between allegory

68   *Salvation Disclosed*

and anagogy, but insofar as it misses the historical dynamism of de Lubac's thought, it gives only an incomplete picture. To develop the sacramental analogy further, it stops upon reaching the intermediate level of the *res et sacramentum* (thing and sign), not recognizing that it is itself still the sign of the ultimate reality, the *res tantum* (thing only).[64]

The Cross as the Meaning of Scripture

De Lubac's theology of spiritual exegesis provides us with a coherent theology of history, centered upon Christ. In chapters 6, 7, and 8 we shall return to this theology of history, whose structure is most clearly visible in the relation between the senses of Scripture. Our present concern, though, is to see how the fourfold sense of Scripture is constituted by salvation. As we have seen, this is the case in terms of process: at its heart, spiritual exegesis turns upon the passage into Christ, which occurs both in the transformation of the Old Testament into the New and in the transformation of Scripture's reader. This conversion to Christ is precisely salvation. Additionally, the content of the fourfold sense is constituted by salvation because it pivots upon Christ's redemptive act.

The doctrinal form of the fourfold sense "plants the Cross of Christ at the center of everything. . . . Time and space, heaven and earth, angels and [humans], the Old Testament and the New, the physical universe and the moral universe, nature and grace: everything is encompassed, bound together, formed, 'structured,' and unified by this Cross, even as everything is dominated by it."[65] With these words de Lubac signals that, to his mind, all things find their meaning in Christ's death on the cross. The relationship between the two testaments, the centerpiece of the doctrinal form of the fourfold sense of Scripture, hinges upon the cross. The relationship between nature and the supernatural is concentrated in the cross.[66] The universe's very intelligibility derives from the cross. In one stroke, de Lubac has centered all of our preceding considerations, from nature and grace to theological epistemology, on the cross.

De Lubac's insistence that the cross is the pivot upon which all things turn is not limited to isolated statements here and there, but rather begins in his programmatic *Catholicisme*, which insists: "If theology, according to a much-used equivalent expression perpetuated by St. Thomas at the beginning of the Summa, is the science of the Scriptures, then in truth it may be said that the whole of theology is *Theologia Crucis*, that is *Theologia a Cruce*. For it is the Cross which disperses the cloud which until then was hiding the truth,"[67] and then runs throughout the five volumes on spiritual interpretation.[68] Of particular significance is de Lubac's identification of the cross with the great act of exegesis by which Christ bestows his meaning upon the Old Testament:

> We can, however, speak in less general terms. Jesus is a scriptural exegete par excellence in the act by which he fulfills his mission, at that solemn hour for which he has come: in his sacrificial action, at the hour of his death on the cross. . . . In pronouncing the words "It is finished" on that gibbet which is a symbolic representation of the last letter of the Hebrew alphabet, Jesus imparts to all of Scripture its fulfillment. . . . His Cross is the sole and universal key. By this sacrament of the Cross, he unites the two Testaments into a single body of doctrine, intermingling the ancient precepts with the grace of the Gospel. . . . Just as "universal recapitulation" has been accomplished by the sacrifice of Jesus, so, similarly, we find that the ancient Scriptures have been definitively opened and condensed.[69]

Indeed, the *"substance"* of the New Testament, that is to say, the allegorical sense, which is also to say the meaning of history, is the "*Mystère du Christ*" and his redemption, including his life, death, resurrection, and ascension.[70] Hence, the very hinge upon which de Lubac's understanding of spiritual exegesis turns is the saving cross—understood as a synecdoche for the entire redemptive act of the paschal mystery. It is *this* mystery that is internalized and reproduced in the lives of the faithful.

Recalling that the Old and New Testaments refer not so much to canonical texts that bear those names as to the two economies that they represent lends further support for the idea that it is by Christ's sacrifice that the transition from the Old to the New has been accomplished. De Lubac explains that the events of Christ's life recorded in the Gospels up to the events of his passion are "anterior" to the New Testament and hence belong to the Old:

> Because if one can date the New Testament from the moment of the incarnation, that is insofar as one can see it as already preparing for the redemptive Act in view of which it is accomplished . . . the

New Covenant was founded by him at the Last Supper; the veil that still hid its true nature was not fully removed until his death followed by his resurrection and ascension, and until then his disciples and he himself observed the Jewish law according to its letter.[71]

Even in those writings that belong to the New Testament canon, the events that precede Christ's sacrifice are part of the Old Testament economy.[72]

It is particularly by "the unique Sacrifice, and the unique Priest, and the unique Victim . . . the perfect holocaust . . . the holocaust that God will never disdain, the one who remains always before his face," that "the great passage has been accomplished" that facilitates both the transition from the Old Testament to the New and the passage of humanity into the life of the Holy Trinity.[73] The trinitarian dimension is significant here, for it appears in a section where de Lubac writes about Christ as the *"verbum abbreviatum."* His argument concerning Christ as the abbreviated word turns upon the affirmation that there is but one Word of God, the one eternally uttered by the Father: the Divine Word who was in the beginning with God (John 1:1).[74] It is precisely "in Him [that] the 'many words' of the biblical writers become 'one Word' forever. Without Him . . . the bond is undone: once again the Word [Parole] of God is fragmented into 'human words'; words that are multiple, not merely numerous, but essentially multiple, and without any possible unity."[75] And so it is that the Word made flesh is the temporal expression of the "eternally uttered Word."[76]

Hence, the incarnate Christ, especially in his redemptive act, is an expression, within the confines of history, of the eternal relationship of the Son to the Father. He gathers up the figures of the Old Testament, making them his figures, making them expressive of the Word that he eternally is and that he now temporally enacts. A good many of those figures, of course, were the temple/tabernacle sacrifices performed according to the Levitical law. This will be particularly significant when we turn to the Eucharist in chapter 6. For now, though, we see that what Christ does in time—which is concentrated, so to speak, in his sacrifice on the cross—he does as an expression of his eternal relationship with God as his Son and Word. Moreover, within the course of this discussion, de Lubac binds together the trinitarian life, the sacrifice of Christ, and the coming of humanity to dwell with God, a passage into God that

Spiritual Exegesis and/as Salvation   71

is precisely spiritual exegesis. In this way, he reprises the themes of sacrifice and trinitarian incorporation evident in his theology of the supernatural, his vision of authentic humanism, and his theology of revelation.[77]

While there are passages in which de Lubac speaks as if the incarnation is the content of the allegorical sense, one should not differentiate too strongly between these and the others that I have highlighted, which speak of the passion as the spirit's fulfillment of the letter.[78] While Noel O'Sullivan ably demonstrates that de Lubac's Christology proceeded along more "Scotist" lines, so that the incarnation would have occurred even apart from the Fall, two points serve to keep my emphasis here intact.[79] First, even in an unfallen world in which redemption were not necessary, the incarnation would have occurred for the purpose of humanity's supernatural elevation to the divine life, which is the most basic content of "salvation" and the purpose of the redemptive passion. Second, as we saw in chapters 1 and 3, de Lubac was vigorously committed to thinking in terms of the concrete order that actually exists. In this actually existing world order, the incarnation was for the purpose of the redemptive act.

De Lubac's understanding of Christ's saving passion as the constitutive meaning of the allegorical sense of Scripture (and, hence, of history) takes on a particularly interesting flavor when we recognize that allegory refers not just to the historical Jesus, but also to the mystery of Christ and the church, who together "are just one great mystery."[80] Indeed, according to de Lubac, "The whole mystery of Scripture, the whole object of *allegoria*, resides in this [the unity of Christ and the church]."[81] The *totus Christus*, head and members, is the content of Scripture's spiritual meaning.[82] The architectural symbols of spiritual exegesis turn largely upon the body of Christ, which is also the new temple in which God dwells.[83] The Johannine Jesus identifies the temple with his (historical) body, while the Pauline and Petrine epistles mark out the church (ecclesial body) as the new temple. The principle that the content of allegory is the mystery of Christ and the church allows us to affirm both of these temple images without positing a tension between them. These two bodies of Christ are, indeed, one.[84] And in this connection, we must recall that the temple was not merely a dwelling place for God, but also the place where sacrifices were offered to God. This is a cultic and sacrificial image. In fact, according to de Lubac, "The cross of Christ is a *machina* that Christ himself wanted to construct to the end of restoring and gathering all things."[85] This building, Christ's body, so closely associated with the cross, eventually reaches up into the trinitarian life: "All of the Christian's faith comes from the Trinity and goes to the Trinity. Finally, at the summit of it all, shines the Cross."[86]

Similarly, "The tropological sense does not presuppose only the Mystery of the Christ, but also that of the Church, which is, as we have seen, inseparable from it. The tropological sense presupposes, or rather, expresses the mystery: for if the souls are Christian only within the Church, the reverse holds."[87] For this reason, the moral purification depicted in the tropological sense occurs interior to the body of Christ.[88] Indeed, this ecclesially located purification shares an identity with the mystery of Christ's passion, which is the chief content of the church's liturgy.

> However varied are the circumstances of the church's history or of the life of each of its members, this Mystery always reproduces itself, essentially the same, because the Lamb of God does not cease for a single day to remove each of our sins by his sacrifice. . . . This Pasch does not cease to reproduce itself in reality, as at the first day. God renews it within the soul, and it must contribute to its conclusion.[89]

The historical event of the passion, its "external face[,] is in the past, as are all things that belong to time—Christ, having entered into his glory, suffers no more, dies no more—but its internal face remains. . . . We are here at the heart of Pauline morality."[90] In other words, the Christian moral life and Christ's death on the cross have their inmost reality in common. The moral life reproduces in the individual Christian the reality of Christ's sacrifice on the cross.[91] This is the meaning of tropology.

The further spiritual senses of Scripture, which intensify and develop allegory, also have Christ's sacrifice as their most basic content:

> Every allegory is concentrated within the paschal mystery; but we must still say, with St. Ambrose: "Every year the pasch of Jesus Christ, i.e., the crossing of souls, is celebrated. . . . In other words, if it is true that nothing is superior to the Mystery of Christ, one ought not forget that this Mystery, which was prefigured in the Old

Testament, is realized again, is being actualized, is being completed within the Christian soul.[92]

While du Lubac believes that allegory "consist[s] entirely in the Mystery of Christ, this mystery finds itself interiorized within tropology . . . in virtue of the cross of Christ."[93] Similarly, anagogy considers the church:

> The first and the second coming of Christ are included within the last. . . . For it is in each of the members of his mystical body that Christ, at the end of time, completes the work of the Father. . . . Thus the goal and the path to it are interwoven, so to speak, with the same material. . . . The eschatological reality attained by anagogy is the eternal reality within which every other has its consummation. . . . It constitutes the "fullness of Christ."[94]

This realization accounts for why "Christ signifies himself," or is said to be "transferred to the Church," because "the Church will be the plenitude of Christ."[95] Christ, who *is* the fulfillment, is also a figure of a greater fulfillment, the whole Christ. And yet he is this figure in such a way as to share a genuine identity with that greater reality. He is the head of the body, and the body is his own fullness.

Conclusion: The Cross as Scripture's Meaning

Henri de Lubac's theology of spiritual exegesis, which does not provide a blueprint for actually engaging in the practice of spiritual interpretation of Scripture, provides a scaffolding that structures the other areas of his thought. Rather than being a manifesto for how to read the Bible, the writings on spiritual exegesis provide a concentrated account of the Christian newness, that soteriological novelty introduced by and centered upon the figure of Jesus Christ, which was especially enacted upon the cross. This Christian newness is continuous with what had come before: the spirit does not abridge or repudiate the letter, but rather elevates, transforms, and preserves it, just as grace does not abolish, but rather perfects nature. At the same time, it is radically discontinuous. There is no natural progression from the Old Testament to the New:

Christ's fulfillment is not passive, but active, and apart from his intervention, the spiritual meaning of allegory would be a violent imposition upon the letter rather than its proper consummation. Human nature achieves its supernatural elevation to the divine life not by its own striving, by evolutionary process, nor by social engineering, but solely by God's gracious gift in Christ.

The Christian newness, which constitutes both the fulfillment of the natural desire for the supernatural and the fulfillment of the letter by the spirit, is, then, the basic content of revelation. What tends to remain formal and abstract in the writings on the supernatural becomes concrete and specific in the writings on spiritual exegesis. Yet in both cases it is the same reality under consideration, God's gift of salvation through Christ's redemptive act. Knowledge of this gift can be conceptually distinguished from its reception and the gift itself, but in reality they are all of a piece. To know God is to be drawn into his life. To grasp the spiritual meaning of Scripture is to pass over into Christ. And this passage into God, through Christ, is identical with the saving act of the cross: this is the pivotal content of the allegorical sense, which unfolds itself within the Christian's moral life (tropology) and reaches its ultimate fulfillment at history's consummation (anagogy). Crucially, these latter two spiritual senses are interior to allegory. Hence, the transformative realization of salvation and its eschatological fulfillment both occur within Christ.

With this notion of salvation unfolding and being realized interior to Christ, we are brought to the threshold of ecclesiology, for the church is Christ's body and the context within which salvation occurs. We have just seen that the meaning of allegory is not solely Christological, but also ecclesiological: it is the mystery of Christ and the church that is disclosed by spiritual exegesis because by his redemptive act Christ brought about the union between himself and his body. As we have already seen, de Lubac understands the salvation Christ achieves to be social and ecclesial. It is in the church that the salvation disclosed by revelation is realized. It is to the church, then, that we must next attend.

PART THREE

Salvation Realized
Ecclesiology and Sacraments

CHAPTER FIVE

Church as the Community of Salvation

With ecclesiology we approach the center of Henri de Lubac's theological vision.[1] He wrote more about the church than he did even about Christ,[2] and it is in ecclesiology that the mysteries of the faith converge, and in the church that salvation is realized.[3] As we saw in the previous chapter, the mysteries of Christ and of the church are one, for Christ has come to save, and has done so by uniting humanity to himself. This is *the* mystery, in the Pauline sense of the term: salvation, particularly salvation as the unity of humanity in Christ (e.g., Eph. 3:3–4; Col. 1:26–27). This unity between Christ and the church is particularly expressed in the Pauline trope of the church as the body of Christ, which has also been variously expressed as the *totus Christus*, or whole Christ, and eventually as the mystical body of Christ.

While the mystery of the church exceeds any one image, a recognition reflected in Vatican II's Dogmatic Constitution on the Church, *Lumen gentium*,[4] de Lubac gave a particular centrality to the image of the church and privileged it as the body of Christ, which he believed was "best fitted for integrating the elements of that doctrine [of the church]."[5] Once more this sensibility is reflected in *Lumen gentium*, which, while deploying a variety of biblical images for the church—the people of God, a vineyard, a sheepfold, and so forth—marks out the image of the church as the body of Christ as enjoying a certain centrality.[6] Indeed, of all the images of the church found in the Constitution, only that of the body of Christ is developed at any length. For these reasons, while I will attend to other images of the church in passing, most of the accent of my own treatment of de Lubac's ecclesiology will be focused upon the image of the church as Christ's body.[7]

77

By focusing our consideration on the language of the body of Christ, we are also naturally brought into a consideration of de Lubac's sacramental theology, which should be treated together with ecclesiology rather than separately. De Lubac, after all, was committed to a social and ecclesial understanding of the sacraments.[8] Moreover, a recovery of the connection between the church and the Eucharist was the central contribution of *Corpus Mysticum*. De Lubac believed that the sacraments are incomprehensible apart from ecclesiology. Complementarily, a discussion of the church that sidelines or omits the sacraments fails to reckon with the full reality of the church, which attains its fullest expression in the eucharistic celebration. After all, de Lubac wrote, "The Eucharist makes the church."[9] As we shall see in the course of the discussion, this oft-quoted phrase is particularly expressive of the church's soteriological center. The Eucharist makes the church because it expresses and realizes the mystery of salvation: Christ's sacrifice upon the cross and the church's participation in it. This participation in Christ's sacrifice is both the reality that lies at the heart of the church's existence and the destiny to which the church is called.

Salvation as Social (*Catholicisme* Reprised)

Most fundamentally, de Lubac's ecclesiology derives from the social account of salvation articulated in *Catholicisme*. In his words, the "supernatural unity" of Christ's mystical body "supposes a prior natural unity . . . of the human race."[10] In view of this natural unity, the salvation of the human race will necessarily be social.[11] We cannot be saved in isolation from each other without violating our nature, which would hardly be a salvation at all. Christ's bearing of human nature, "whole and entire [tout entière]" from his incarnation through the cross and into his risen life, re-establishes this primordial unity, effects its passage from death to life, and elevates it to supernatural dignity.[12] Because Christ's bearing of humanity is "whole and entire," he himself is our salvation, and salvation consists in our union with Christ, which is necessarily a union with one another.[13] With these anthropological and soteriological affirmations we are brought to the threshold of ecclesiology, for this is the fundamental meaning of the church.

Étienne Guibert captures the theological essence of de Lubac's ecclesiology well in considering the church part of a double gift of Christ. By his redemptive act, Christ has given the gift of what Guibert calls "the total and definitive act of revelation, which calls us to faith, and the gift of the church as society and body."[14] As he explains, the response of faith and of incorporation into the church are not simply "super-added conditions" but are instead "really necessary to salvation," the condition of the possibility of receiving the gift of divine life interior to our own life.[15] Eternal life is given in the person of Christ and is doubly received by the act of faith and within the church, which is Christ's body and through which one begins to share in the very life of the Trinity.[16] "Being the body of Christ," Guibert explains, "entry into this body is participation in eternal life. This eternal life being the intimacy of the Father, and of the Son, and of the Holy Spirit, the participation in these trinitarian relations, in the person of the Son, renews the relational life of humanity."[17] Finally and critically, though, these two gifts are really one; the free response of faith and incorporation into the church are mutually interior and reciprocally implicating. By them we come to share in the divine life through Christ's singular redemptive sacrifice.[18] By this saving act he gathers humanity into one in order to bring us to share in the life of the Trinity. We shall explore the sacrificial dimensions of this ecclesiology more fully in the next chapter.

The Church's Dependence upon Christ

Within this more theological understanding of the church, it is the church's relation to Christ that is paramount, a reality reflected in the patristic image of the church as the moon, borrowing and reflecting the light of the Sun (Christ) rather than possessing any light of its own.[19] Without being explicitly lunar, this understanding is operative in *Lumen gentium*'s opening paragraph, which states that Christ is the light of the nations—a truth that de Lubac considered worth continual reiteration, however redundant its assertion might appear, and whose effacement he lamented. The Constitution also states that this light is radiant on the countenance of the church, which exists as a sort of sacrament (*veluti sacramentum*) of the saving unity of humanity among its members and with God.[20]

This sacramental language owes much to de Lubac, who in *Cathol-icisme* had written that "if Christ is the sacrament of God, the Church is for us the sacrament of Christ; she represents him, in the full and ancient meaning of the term: she really makes him present."[21] This notion of the church's sacramentality does important work for de Lubac.[22] It upholds, at once, the real identity between the church and Christ while also maintaining a real distinction between them. Sacraments are effective signs, and therefore are distinct from the realities that they signify, even as they mysteriously and effectively bring that reality about. By identifying the church as the sacrament of Christ, or the sacrament of salvation, de Lubac insists that the church is really and intrinsically related to salvation in Christ, but without thereby enclosing salvation within the church, as though it could reach no further. The church is utterly dependent upon Christ, but Christ is not limited by the church.

This is not, though, to say that Christ is in no way dependent upon the church. Insofar as the church is summed up in Mary (a point to which I shall return below), its member par excellence, there is a certain dependence of Christ upon the church. Mary, the Mother of God, gave birth to, nurtured, and raised Jesus. However, even this dependence of Christ upon Mary is conditioned by a greater and asymmetrical dependence of Mary upon Christ.[23] He is her creator and her redeemer. The fiat by which Mary consented to be the Mother of God, and so allowed the incarnation to occur, could be given in all its freedom because of her immaculate conception, which was a special grace to her merited by Christ's redemptive act on the cross. It was only by a free act on his part that Christ came to be dependent upon Mary, and even that dependence occured within her dependence upon him.

The church's sacramentality also points to another important feature of de Lubac's ecclesiological vision, namely, the church's provisionality and unsurpassability. On the one hand, he writes, the pilgrim "church is destined to pass away. It is a sign and sacrament: now signs and sacraments will be resorbed in the reality that they announce. It is a means: a divine means, a necessary means, but provisional like every means."[24] Because the church is a sacramental reality, a sign of something else, "it must be traversed, and not halfway, but totally."[25] This passing through the church occurs not only completely, but also consistently. There is no end to this motion.[26] Of what, though, is the church a sign? Of Christ, obviously, but not simply of the historical Jesus (nor even the Christ of faith, should one be inclined to find such distinctions helpful), but of the mystical body, or *totus Christus*, the entire company of the redeemed in union with Christ.[27] Keeping this in mind serves to clarify the other end of the dialectic, for inasmuch as the church is provisional, it is also unsurpassable.[28]

The church's unsurpassability expresses itself in two complementary ways. On the one hand, the church's passing away is not so much a loss or discarding of its identity or being as it is a passing over into its own fullness, what de Lubac calls a "manifestation of sacramentality's own proper truth . . . a glorious epiphany and a consummation."[29] With the coming of the eschaton, the church will undergo a radical transformation analogous to the transformation undergone by the human body at the resurrection. But just as the resurrected body will be the same body that previously lived, only now made glorious, the transformed church will be just as much its proper self, and perhaps even more so. Those elements of the church that will pass away—its visible and institutional structures, the hierarchy, the sacraments—will not be lost. Rather the *res* that informed these *sacramenta* will be fully disclosed, unhindered by the limitations of the signs that previously had given it expression.[30]

The second way that this unsurpassability is expressed is closely related to the first. The sacramentality of the church is not just some arbitrary sign that can be discarded or altered to suit our inclinations:

> It is found in an essential relation to our present condition, which no longer fits in the time of pure figures, but which does not yet entail the full possession of the "truth."[31] . . . It can never be dismissed as having ceased to be useful. This diaphanous milieu, which one must always traverse and traverse totally, one has never however, finished traversing it. It is always in its traversal that one attains that of which it is the sign. It can never be outdated, nor its boundaries crossed.[32]

With this we are brought to a major preoccupation of de Lubac's ecclesiology: there is a fundamental continuity to the church across all the stages of its existence.[33] True to the Nicene mark of unity, the church is fundamentally one. This is not merely an "ecumenical" statement regarding apparent ecclesial plurality but is a theological statement, corollary to the social character of salvation. The pilgrim church is one with the

82   *Salvation Realized*

eschatologically complete church. The church militant, suffering, and triumphant are not three churches but one church, existing in three different states. Whatever transformations it might undergo, it retains a fundamental identity as the community of salvation.[34]

Ecclesial Antecedence: *De Trinitate et Ex Hominibus*

The church's dependence upon Christ finds further expression in a structural dynamic. The pilgrim church exists in two dimensions that coincide to maintain both an over-againstness and an identity vis-à-vis the faithful. The church is *de Trinitate* and, as such, calls together the faithful, giving them and nourishing new life. It sanctifies and baptizes. But it is just as truly *ex hominibus*, and so is called together, receiving new life. The church is *sanctified* and *baptized*.[35] This distinction is, more or less, the classic distinction between the *ecclesia docens* (teaching church) and the *ecclesia discens* (learning church). It also bears some affinity with, but does not map precisely onto, the distinction between the church as *congregatio fidelium* (gathering of the faithful) and the church as a hierarchically ordered institution. The institutional dimension of the hierarchy does give expression to this over-againstness, but that over-againstness cannot be reduced to the hierarchy and, further, the members of the hierarchy are themselves first called to new life by and in the church.[36]

The church, then, is at once antecedent to and composed of its members. It has no existence apart from them and yet is more than just the sum of its parts.[37] In this regard, the Virgin Mary plays a central role in de Lubac's ecclesiology.[38] She is at once *Sponsa Dei* and *Mater Dei*, at once the preeminent saint and the mother of the faithful, the child of the church par excellence, but also the preeminent expression of the church's motherhood. As de Lubac puts it, "The Catholic faith concerning the Blessed Virgin symbolically sums up, in its privileged case, the doctrine of human cooperation in the Redemption, thus offering as well the synthesis or mother-idea of the dogma of the church. So one could say again that the one and the other must hold or collapse together."[39] Just as the hierarchy gives expression to but is not identical to the church's antecedence to the faithful, so it is with the Blessed Virgin. In her the church's sanctity is encapsulated, and yet she, too, is redeemed by Christ rather

Church as the Community of Salvation 83

than being a redeemer. She, like the church, is the chaste spouse and fruitful mother. As de Lubac writes:

> Mary was presented in the Temple, in offering herself completely to her God she offered the church with herself. When the Word, taking flesh within her, poured his treasures upon her, he married and satisfied his church in the person of his mother. Mary's *Fiat* accepted the full realization of the promises, for herself personally, but also for all collectively, and it is in the name of all that this *Fiat* was awaited.[40]

The redemption that was perfectly and preeminently realized in the Blessed Virgin eventually came to be realized in the rest of the faithful, who, in union with her Son, are also her children. While there is an at least implicit gender essentialism operative here, which can and should be critically interrogated,[41] the essential point—that of the church's antecedence to the faithful—need not be expressed in gendered terms. De Lubac held traditional views on gender, but these were assumptions in the background of his ecclesiological reflections rather than the positive point he was trying to make. I shall not retroactively correct his thought, even as I insist that its reception on this score should involve a more critical interrogation of gender identity informed by current understandings drawn from the social and hard sciences.

Mary encapsulates the maternity of the church, by which new life is brought forth and nourished in the faithful. Through the Word and sacraments, which derive from Jesus's death and resurrection, Christians are given new birth and then carried along in the bosom of mother church.[42] While this maternal character bears a special relation to the hierarchy, the church is not identical to the hierarchy, and maternity characterizes the entire church.[43] All of those who are gathered back to God by Christ are church and are mother, and within each Christian soul, Christ is born.[44]

The maternity of the church is given a privileged expression in the paternity of the clergy, through whom the Word of God continues to be handed on so that new life continues to be borne in the ecclesial womb.[45] The clergy are servants for the sake of the people of God, to whom they administer the sacraments through which the faithful come to share in the trinitarian relationships and, indeed, in the "internal life of the Divinity."[46] The entire purpose of the church, and of the clergy, is to bring about this new life in the bosom of God. And for this reason the paternity of the clergy is entirely dependent upon Christ and derivative from the paternity of God the Father.[47]

There is also a particular connection between the church's maternity and the magisterium, one that further underscores the church's soteriological substance. While the church's teaching office is often thought of as providing boundaries—which, of course, it does—it is also the case that the magisterium is itself bounded. The church's teaching office is, at least in principle, limited by the content and contours of revelation. In a work on ecclesiology or theological authority, it would be important to analyze the precise mechanics, dynamics, and power relations of magisterial authority to provide some account of the various levels of authority by which the church might be said to teach something and to question to what extent the church's actual exercise of this power conforms to its principles.[48] Because our goal here is an understanding of de Lubac's conception of the church, particularly the way in which it informs the soteriological unity of his œuvre, these matters, important as they are, can and must be left to the side.

Prescinding from all but the most relevant questions regarding theological authority, then, we can recall the soteriological content and purpose of revelation. God reveals himself so that we might be drawn into the life of the Trinity, and he reveals himself precisely in those acts by which he draws and invites us into this life: the paschal mystery of Christ's life, death, resurrection, and bestowal of the Holy Spirit. This redemptive act, the Christian mystery, de Lubac states, is the "original state of doctrine" and "the Whole of Dogma."[49] Indeed, Dumas argues that "while inscribed in different problematics, Lubacian 'Dogma' signifies the same thing as 'Mystery.'"[50] However, of course, there is a necessary distinction between "Dogma in its first state—the Christ, gesture of God's love in the world—and dogmas, these formulations issuing from human intelligence guided by the Spirit of Truth."[51] In other words, in the mystery of Christ "the whole of Dogma" has been given, inaugurating the twofold movement described in chapter 3, that of developing dogma and deepening mystery.[52] The church's magisterium is the servant of this Dogma. And this, once more, gives expression to both the church's

Church as the Community of Salvation   85

soteriological substance and its dependence upon Christ. What authority the church possesses derives entirely and receives its content and boundaries from the Christ's saving mystery, which is, in fact, the inner theological content of the church itself.

With this in mind, we are in a position to consider de Lubac's own relationship with ecclesiastical authority. As we saw in chapter 1, during the controversies surrounding *Surnaturel* and *Humani generis*, de Lubac endured suspicion and censure from church authorities. A commonplace narrative regards *ressourcement* as a reaction against "neo-scholasticism," a label that includes not only neo-scholasticism, properly speaking, but also scholastic theology in general and the post–Vatican I milieu, including the modernist controversy and authoritarian attitudes.[53] According to this narrative, the late nineteenth and early twentieth centuries witnessed the consolidation and centralization of ecclesial power and authority, against which *ressourcement* struggled until Vatican II's turn toward openness and collegiality. While this narrative certainly makes sense of the struggle for Catholic self-definition after Vatican II, it sheds little light on de Lubac himself, who, despite his own travails with the hierarchy, consistently wrote about the importance of submission to the magisterium and lamented the erosion of doctrinal authority.

In *The Splendor of the Church*, written during the period when de Lubac was forbidden from teaching theology, he explains the dispositions of the "*ecclésiastique*," or *vir ecclesiasticus*, who "will always accept the teaching of the Magisterium as the absolute norm" and whose obedience springs from love.[54] During, and especially after, the Second Vatican Council, de Lubac displayed increasing distress at the forms *aggiornamento* was taking, a tendency he called that of the "para-council." While he was pleased with the conciliar documents, especially the four constitutions, he feared what Chantraine and Lemaire refer to as "a certain *intelligentsia* 'for whom all dogma is practically rejected, which uncritically accepts all the suggestions coming from anti-Christian milieus. . . . For them, the Council is but a first step, still too timid, down the path of a general liquidation.'"[55] Of particular note is de Lubac's refusal to sign the "Déclaration sur la liberté et la fonction des théologiens dans l'Église," published by the journal *Concilium* in 1969. This declaration— which was signed by such figures as Karl Rahner, Yves Congar, and Joseph Ratzinger—de Lubac refused to join, judging it to lack an ecclesial spirit.[56] His desire was never to be liberated from ecclesiastical authority, which he saw as a gift to be embraced, but rather to more authentically inhabit the riches of the theological tradition. In this regard, a reminiscence from his years of formation displays his dispositions:

> I had this blessed impression that there are far fewer things condemned than one says sometimes, and that in any case, they are the sort of things and ideas that we would not try out; thought moves well across theology, which opens to it quite vast horizons, it can even without danger abandon itself to some boldness, provided that in all its steps, it respects certain sure norms. . . . [Here de Lubac lists these norms, which have to do mainly with divine transcendence and freedom.] With these, and on the condition that one never forget one's condition as a sinner, I believe one can, without further embarrassment, spread one's wings.[57]

Even after his own ordeal with the hierarchy, de Lubac maintained this essential viewpoint, refusing to seek liberty from the magisterium's ostensible constraints.

Another episode from de Lubac's formation is telling. Around 1928 there seems to have been some concern among the Jesuit superiors regarding a "*groupe Lubac*,"[58] which prompted Victor Fontoynont to look into the matter. In his report to the superior general,[59] Fontoynont relates several matters of some interest. He recognizes that the scientific and philosophical outlook has changed since the thirteenth and sixteenth centuries and that, accordingly, there ought to be some sort of updating of scholastic theology to reflect this new context. He contrasts this updated scholasticism with the "formalist eclecticism, cut off from any relationship to life . . . which was honored at Jersey . . . and which tends to deny the name 'scholastic' to any manner of thought that does not imitate its own."[60] While Fontoynont did indeed recognize that there were anti-scholastic sentiments among some of the Jesuits in formation, and indeed notes that "it is inevitable that many spirits should clash with what is unassimilable and unwelcoming in that which many give as being *the* scholasticism and *the* sure doctrine, and so are repulsed from these towards others,"[61] he also suggests to the provincial that "to suppress the influence of Fr. de Lubac, would be to suppress precisely a moderating influence," and that "this goes far beyond the question of 'progressivism' and 'conservatism.'"[62]

Among other things, Fontoynont's report signals that de Lubac did not and does not fit neatly within the ideological binaries that have come to characterize much post-conciliar theology. His commitment to *ressourcement* was a commitment to a radical grounding in the Christian mystery. This commitment informed his own filial submission to the church's magisterium, which he understood to be expressive of and charged with guiding the faithful deeper into this mystery. While this hardly gives us a complete theology of the magisterium, to say nothing of resolving the critical questions that must be asked vis-à-vis the actual exercise of magisterial authority, it does serve to demonstrate how intertwined de Lubac's attitude toward the magisterium is with his understanding of the church's nature as the community of salvation.

The hierarchy of the church is ordered to the salvation of humanity, which occurs as, through the sacraments, the faithful are brought into the trinitarian life. When the end comes, the hierarchy, along with all of the visible and institutional dimensions of the church, will pass away, absorbed into the reality that they effectively signify here and now (in this case, Christ's redemptive work and the trinitarian mystery). However, this does not render the hierarchy superfluous or dispensable. "The Church we call our Mother is not some ideal and unreal Church but this hierarchical Church herself; not the Church as we might dream her but the Church as she exists in fact, here and now."[63] While the institutional and hierarchical dimensions of the church must be distinguished from and even subordinated to its theological and soteriological substance, they cannot be separated. As *Lumen gentium* explains, the mystical body of Christ or the community of salvation, and the hierarchically structured society form "one complex reality."[64] Hence, while de Lubac recognized the importance of moving away from a hierarchology in ecclesiology, he did not suggest that an account of the church that ignored or dispensed with the hierarchy could be adequate. In "a 'Church' without structure, invisible and diffuse . . . the Christian faith would . . . be emptied of its content."[65]

The church's sacraments accomplish humanity's incorporation into the body of Christ, which de Lubac explains to be a concorporation with Christ.[66] This amounts to a reproduction of the Christian mystery within the church, corporately, and the faithful, individually. This recalls especially our discussion of the tropological sense of Scripture in chapter 4, which is at once ecclesial and personal and is especially concerned with the outworking of the mystery disclosed in the allegorical sense within the concrete lives of the faithful. It is the nature of this mystery that it be received, internalized, and reproduced in the lives of those to whom it is given. This is, once more, the basic meaning of Christian mysticism. As de Lubac writes:

> If mystical life at its summit consists of an actual union with the Divinity, such a union could be possible only through a supernatural grace whose normal setting is the Church and whose normal conditions are the life of faith and the sacraments. . . . It follows, then, that Christian mysticism is still, is necessarily an ecclesial mysticism, since the Incarnation achieves first of all in the Church the marriage of the Word and humanity.[67]

As Guibert has shown, it is especially through the *mysterium crucis* that this regathering of humanity occurs,[68] as Christ bears humanity *tout entière* through his paschal mystery,[69] which not only achieves but constitutes our salvation.

Our salvation occurs insofar as we are united with Christ, a union that is inseparable from our union with one another. Hence, baptism's first effect, its indelible character, is our entry into the visible church, while its final effect is our spiritual regeneration, a share in the mystical body of Christ.[70] Similarly, reconciliation restores our ruptured unity with God and the people of God.[71] This notion of salvation as incorporation reaches its clearest expression in the sacrament of the Eucharist, which also provides a framework for us to better grasp the soteriological center of de Lubac's ecclesiology.[72] This is a consideration that will carry us (more or less indirectly) through the remainder of this chapter as well as (directly) through the next.

The Church as Particular and Universal

In particular, the priesthood is ordered to the offering of the Eucharist, by which, as we shall shortly see, the church as the community of salvation is realized. Upon their ordinations to the priesthood, and for some time thereafter, de Lubac's letters to his friends frequently return to the theme of offering the Mass in union with Christ and his sacrifice.[73] In one notable example, he reflects, "It seems to me that this prayer [to be united with Christ in his sacrifice], very simple, comprehends everything; and that moreover, the spiritual transformation in Jesus Christ is the sole path by which we can be conducted into an understanding of his mystery."[74]

It is in this eucharistic ordering that the relationship between the particular church and the universal church is clearest. The New Testament speaks of the church in the singular and the churches in the plural, giving expression to the notion that there are both local and universal dimensions to the reality called church.[75] These local dimensions have tended to be expressed by the terms *local church* and *particular church*, which generally have been treated as synonyms. However, to avoid confusion, de Lubac forges a more precise distinction between them, using the term *particular church* to refer to "the church presided over by a bishop."[76] A particular church is the gathering of the faithful around their bishop for teaching and the Eucharist.[77] While the particular church is also local, it is fundamentally a theological reality determined by the mystery of faith—bishop, community, altar—rather than a matter of culture or location. In contrast, the local church is characterized by such ethnographic features. De Lubac gives the example of the Latin American Episcopal Conferences (CELAM) to illustrate the local church.[78] There is something irreducible about the particular church and contingent about the local church.[79]

The particular church is the concrete expression of the universal church, and the two are mutually interior to one another. For this reason, the universal church is not a mere "federative" grouping of otherwise distinct particular churches, nor are the particular churches branch offices or franchises of the universal church; they are wholly the church in their particular places.[80] Ingredient to this ecclesiological vision is the unity of the episcopacy. The episcopal office is one, and the Eucharist is one.[81] And so, by virtue of the bishop, the particular church is made universal and its Eucharist shares in the one Eucharist of the one church. In times past, this reality was expressed by the practice of the *fermentum*, by which a fragment of host from one bishop's Eucharist was carried to another's (or, in some cases, from the diocesan bishop's Mass to those of his presbyters).[82] Such realities as the episcopal college give expression to this interplay of the particular and the universal church. While collegiality was a distinct emphasis of Vatican II, de Lubac refused to see this as a break from previous tradition, stressing its continuity and complementarity with Vatican I's emphasis on the Roman primacy.[83]

Far from eroding the episcopal college, the bishop of Rome is the guarantor of that college's unity. The church's authentic freedom from worldly pressures is safeguarded in the person of the pope, whose universal jurisdiction moves the episcopate beyond any purely local considerations.[84] Yes, he is the bishop of a particular church—that of Rome—but his solicitude and jurisdiction extend to all churches. While all bishops are properly concerned for the universal church, each bishop's jurisdiction extends no further than his particular church, and so remains enmeshed within local concerns. The pope, though, is able to transcend this.[85] And in this way Rome provides a gathering center point that prevents the church from degenerating into a chauvinism of the local, marked by interminable and irresolvable squabbling.[86] De Lubac had little patience with the post-conciliar impulse to exert the "rights" of the local churches over against Rome's primacy, thereby eroding their connection with the center of unity.[87] While some viewed this tendency as a renewed Gallicanism, de Lubac acerbically suggested that this "would perhaps do it too much honor," for at least Gallicanism "was endowed with a doctrinal apparatus, it comprised a tradition, it was attached to venerable usages, it expressed itself in a culture that was not only ecclesiastical but human, perhaps too narrow, but solid, attested by so many remarkable works and so many illustrious names. Here, on the contrary, one is faced with an adolescent reaction, a crude and rootless ideology, a withdrawal without grandeur."[88]

This, de Lubac deemed, was just the inversion of the "curialist" impulse, which he also opposed.[89] This latter point is significant, for it clarifies that de Lubac was not simply advocating for increased centralization. He noted that some measure of decentralization would be appropriate so long as it did not weaken the bonds of unity.[90] Admittedly, such a centralization did characterize the papacies of John Paul II, a dear friend of de Lubac's whose election as pope gave him great hope as he lamented the para-council's ascendency, and Benedict XVI, both of whom, like de Lubac, emphasized a hermeneutic of continuity for the implementation of Vatican II. However, de Lubac's clear emphasis on the particular church and his opposition to curialism ought to mitigate against seeing him as in favor of Roman consolidation, *tout simple*. In either case, de Lubac understood Vatican II's teaching on episcopal collegiality and its emphasis on the local and particular church as a completion, rather than a correction, of Vatican I's teaching on the papacy.[91]

Pontifical Conclusion

It comes as no surprise to note that de Lubac favored the so-called hermeneutic of continuity over against a "hermeneutic of rupture" when it came to Vatican II. These two opposing tendencies with regard to conciliar interpretation and implementation are often associated with the journals *Communio* and *Concilium*, respectively. De Lubac's disengagement from *Concilium* (discussed in chapter 1 and revisited in the present chapter) and his involvement with *Communio*, founded to provide an alternative voice to that of *Concilium*, are well known.[92] What is perhaps less clear is the light that this sheds on de Lubac's preconciliar outlook and agenda. We need a hermeneutic of continuity for de Lubac himself. Though before the Council, he was perhaps seen as a renegade or liberal, and after it as a conservative, his reaction to the para-council should not be interpreted as an about face on his part. He always respected ecclesiastical authority. When censured, even despite his perplexity and his conviction that he had done no wrong, he accepted the restrictions. In his turn to the sources, his aim was not to break free from hierarchical or doctrinal restraints—he lamented their erosion—but to recover the authentic tradition of the church.

This authentic tradition, though, was never placed in an adversarial relationship to the contemporary church. Yes, de Lubac viewed certain theological tendencies as misguided, even dangerous (see his opposition to the hypothesis pure nature and to *Action français*), but these were not authentic teachings of the magisterium, which is precisely what his historical studies sought to uncover. He was quite clear that authentic *ressourcement* could not be placed in opposition to the church's teaching office in the contemporary day and age.[93] To take refuge in a bygone era in this way would be to "reject the fruit and blossom of the live branch . . .

[in which case] it is, as far as you are concerned, a dead one."[94] The decline narratives he advanced, particularly in *Corpus Mysticum* and *Medieval Exegesis* were not straightforward falls from grace, or failures, but rather occurred in response to new questions. To some extent, these developments had to occur. A naïve return to a time before the questions had been asked was impossible and undesirable even if it could occur, and so de Lubac sought to return to these sources, not in order to thwart subsequent developments, but to enrich the present context.

The para-council, though, threw off all constraint, whether from the contemporary magisterium or the prior tradition.[95] And if such para-conciliar figures should appeal to *ressourcement* as justification for their flights from authority, that only serves to show that de Lubac's *ressourcement* proceeded along different lines and for different reasons. Indeed, as Susan Wood has noted, his concern for the tendencies that would eventually be dubbed para-conciliar are found in pre-conciliar texts. In *Méditation sur l'église* (1953) he warned against a *"sacramentalisme inversé"* that claimed to discover the ultimate reality of the truths of the faith by interiorizing them, not in the sense of integrating them fully into one's being, but in the sense of absorbing them into immanent realities.[96] De Lubac attributed this tendency to a Hegelian/Comtean dialectic that saw Christianity as ultimately surpassed in humanity, a theme we have already seen in chapter 2's treatment of atheistic humanism and to which we shall return in chapter 7's consideration of Joachim of Fiora's spiritual posterity. When de Lubac opposed the para-council, seeing in it the other side of the immanentism he had opposed in the guises of atheistic humanism and integralism, he clearly displayed the consistency of his agenda: to make clear the relationship of all things to the salvation of Christ.[97]

Crucially, it is the Eucharist that binds all of these other considerations together. The hierarchy is ordered to the offering of the Eucharist. It is in the Eucharist that the church's identity as the body of Christ and the community of salvation is realized. And it is the Eucharist that most adequately clarifies the relationship between the particular churches and the universal church. The Eucharist can only possibly be celebrated by particular churches. Because there is no sacramental order beyond the bishop, there is no office according to which a universal Eucharist could be celebrated. Even the pope is, sacramentally, only a bishop. He cele-

Church as the Community of Salvation   93

brates the Masses he does as the bishop of Rome and only for the particular community gathered around him. Due to his universal jurisdiction, this may take place in particular churches other than the church in Rome, but even so, those celebrations are only ever particular and local. So it is only in the particular church that the universal church can be realized. Nevertheless, the reality at the heart of the particular church's Eucharist, the mystery of salvation in Christ, is a universal reality. Salvation is the union of all with all in Christ, and this necessarily extends beyond the particular church. With this turn to the Eucharist, we enter upon one of the most distinctive contributions of de Lubac's ecclesiology.

CHAPTER SIX

Corpus mysticum verumque

The Eucharist forms a natural bridge between the previous chapter's consideration of the church as the community of salvation and this chapter's consideration of the body of Christ, making the conclusion of chapter 5 doubly pontifical (focused upon the papacy's relation to the episcopate and on bridge-building).[1] The eucharistic character of de Lubac's ecclesiology and the ecclesiological character of his understanding of the Eucharist are well known.[2] The well-worn dictum "the Eucharist makes the church" has become a baseline truism for ecclesiology, though not always with any particular attention to how or why this is the case. De Lubac's major work on the relationship between the church and the Eucharist famously turns upon the history of its titular phrase, *corpus mysticum*, and its relation to another, *corpus verum*. This study notes that the term "body of Christ" has a threefold referent: to the body born of the Virgin, hung on the cross, buried in the tomb, raised from the dead, and now seated at the Father's right hand (the historical body); the body present on Christian altars under the species of bread and wine (the sacramental body); and the body of the redeemed, united by their head (the ecclesial body).[3] Significantly, these are not three bodies of Christ, for there is but one Christ. Rather, they are three modes of Christ's body, all of which are truly the body of the one Christ.[4]

More significantly, de Lubac's survey of patristic and medieval sources demonstrates that over time the referents of the terms "mystical body" and "true body" were reversed.[5] Originally, the "mystical body" was the sacramental body, the body present in mystery, which reflects the way that *mysterium* and *sacramentum* both translated the Greek μυστήριον,[6]

94

while the "true body" of Christ was the church, which gathered around and fed on this mystical body.[7] The patristic notion of ecclesial communion was intimately bound up with eucharistic communion.[8] To be in communion with someone was to receive Christ's body and blood with them, and vice versa. This intimate connection between the church's communion and sacramental communion was expressed in ritual practices such as the *fermentum*, in which a portion of the host consecrated at the bishop's Eucharist would be sent to the other parishes of his diocese and/or to a brother bishop in his diocese, showing that the church and its Eucharist are both one. Though eventually a cleavage emerged between these two forms of Christ's body,[9] in the earliest days of the church it was not so. As de Lubac wrote: "Fundamentally, they are not so much used to describe two successive objects as two simultaneous things that make one whole. For the body of Christ that is the Church is in no way *other* than the body and the blood of the mystery."[10]

Eventually, controversies surrounding the real presence of Christ in the sacrament shifted the emphasis: now "true body" was used to refer to the sacramental body in an effort to avoid the notion that Christ's eucharistic presence was a mere fancy or an empty signifier, while the church came to be seen as the mystical body.[11] Now, of course, *mysticum* had come to lose its association with the mysteries of the church's cult and so suggested something more along the lines of *ethereal*. The result was a downgrading of the centrality of the church in eucharistic doctrine. While the notion of the church as the body of Christ never fully disappeared, and while the Eucharist's *res ultima* remained the union of head and members in the whole Christ, the intrinsic relationship between the church as the body of Christ and the Eucharist as the body of Christ was occluded.[12]

De Lubac, though, sought to retrieve the unity of the threefold body of Christ, and this unity is particularly disclosive of the soteriological vision that pervades his theology. Yet, if we were to read *Corpus Mysticum* as if its primary lesson were terminological, we would rather shallowly miss the point. We are not invited to conclude that the real tragedy occurred when we started calling the church the "mystical" body, so theologians ought to be sure to not use this designation when talking about the church. De Lubac recognized that the term "mystical body" *did* come to describe the church and that time cannot be reversed in such matters.

96   *Salvation Realized*

Indeed, his post–*Corpus Mysticum* writings refer to the church as the mystical body.[13] By contrast, this chapter will serve to clarify the threefold body's soteriological import by considering in what way the Eucharist makes the church. As we shall see, it is most especially as Christ's sacrifice that the Eucharist's ecclesiurgic character is on display.

The Church's Sacrificial Center

In order to fully appreciate de Lubac's contribution here, though, we must set his account of the church and the Eucharist within the economy of salvation, for the patristic doctrine of the threefold body is neither purely horizontal/social nor static but is both historically dynamic and ordered toward union with God. The term *mystical* carried two primary senses in the patristic period, which, as we shall see, are intimately linked. As we have seen, it could refer to ceremony and ritual, such that, in de Lubac's words, "everything that touches upon the mystery of the altar is broadly and almost without differentiation qualified as mystical."[14] It could also connote hiddenness, with a range of meaning that de Lubac referred to as "scriptural" in the sense of coherence with the practice of spiritual exegesis.[15] It is this latter sense that locates the discussion of *Corpus Mysticum* within the economy of salvation, though it is the former sense that winds up providing much of the latter's content.

Hence, at the outset we can observe a certain terminological parallel with the pair *mysterium/sacramentum* in *Corpus Mysticum* and in *Medieval Exegesis*. *Mysterium* refers to the inner reality (or *res*) that the *sacramentum* at once signifies and hides. This is at once the relationship between (a) the sacramental species and the body and blood of Christ[16] and (b) the Old and the New Testaments.[17] Hence, the term *sacramentum* corresponds broadly to the Old Testament, and *mysterium* refers to the New Testament. The true and hidden meaning of the Scriptures is the mystery of Christ. According to de Lubac, "The *sacramentum* would therefore play the role of container, or envelope with regard to the *mysterium* hidden within it."[18] Donath Hersick observes that the distinction between these two terms, which were initially synonymous, lies in the fact that the *sacramentum* is also a sign, allowing for the development, observed by de Lubac, of the idea of the *sacramentum* containing the *mysterium*.[19]

A further distinction will be quite important for the remainder of our considerations. Generally, de Lucac writes, a mystery has to do more with "an action than a thing," such that we *do* the mysteries and *receive* the sacrament.[20] The mystery "is synthetic and dynamic. It bears less on the apparent sign or rather on the hidden reality than on both at once: on their rapport, their union, their mutual implication."[21] This active and dynamic sense of mystical/*mysterium* bears a special connection to its cultic dimensions, especially to the notion of the Eucharist as a sacrifice. De Lubac's survey of patristic usage covers terms like *mystical host, mystical oblation*, and *mystical sacrifice,* with the accent always on the action.[22] So the first referent of the phrase *mystical body* is to the liturgical action of the church as it celebrates the sacred mysteries.

Sacrificial Memorial

Sacrifice plays a crucial yet largely unexplored role in the argument of *Corpus Mysticum.*[23] Even when turning from the realm of ceremonial to that of the scriptural range of *mystical's* meaning, de Lubac urges his readers that "it will be necessary to forget, however convenient and well-founded it may be, the separation placed in so many modern treatises between 'the Eucharist as sacrifice' and 'the Eucharist as sacrament.' Because the sacrament cannot be understood without the sacrifice."[24] This is not just a passing statement, either, but winds up providing the pivotal meaning to the "scriptural" discussion of the *corpus mysticum.*

The statement that we cannot understand the sacrament without understanding the sacrifice occurs within a discussion of the Eucharist as "Memorial, Anticipation, [and] Presence," and it is specifically because the sacrament is a memorial of Christ's sacrifice on Calvary that it cannot be understood apart from a consideration of sacrifice.[25] This lends greater specificity to the identity of the mystical (sacramental) body of Christ. As de Lubac states:

> No longer simply, as in the first case, *"corpus in mysterio"* [the body in mystery], but *"corpus in mysterio passionis"* [the body in the mystery of the passion]. It will be the body as the object of a mystical oblation, itself entirely relative to that oblation that Christ made of himself at the end of his earthly life; the body engaged in a mystical

action, the ritual echo indefinitely multiplied in the time and the space of the unique Action from which it borrows its meaning.[26]

Hence, the sacramental body's identity fully derives from its relationship to Christ's sacrifice on the cross. The *mystery* that gives it its character as a *corpus mysticum* is the paschal mystery of Christ's death and resurrection.[27]

Indeed, de Lubac says, despite the subsequent centuries' handwringing about real presence, "the essential perspective of these [patristic] texts is not that of a presence or of an object, but that of an *action and of a sacrifice*."[28] Given the narrative traced in *Corpus Mysticum*, this is a particularly salient point. After all, de Lubac is concerned with showing how an undue preoccupation with the real presence (which, of course, he would never deny!) led to an occlusion of an original insight into the relationship between the sacrament and the church. And here he notes that the patristic accent was upon sacrifice more than upon presence qua presence. In other words, a recovery of the sacrificial character of the Eucharist is not ancillary to the retrieval to which de Lubac invites us, but essential.

Sacrifice, then, is central to the patristic discussion of the Eucharist, and this sacrificial center is clarified, in large measure, by considering it in the context of the relationship between the two testaments. Indeed, de Lubac observes, just as the patristic accent is on "an action and a sacrifice ... the vocabulary relative to this action and this sacrifice is driven in great part by the vocabulary relative to the two Testaments."[29] The fathers understood Christ's sacrifice as the fulfillment of the sacrifices of the Old Testament.[30] It is this fulfillment that is memorialized in the church's Eucharist, which, as the memorial of Calvary, is also understood as fulfilling the Old Testament's sacrificial economy. It is in the Eucharist that the pure offering is made from the rising of the sun to its setting (Mal. 1:11). The memorial dimension of the Eucharist is thoroughly bound up with the notion of sacrifice.

Sacrificial Anticipation

As we turn from the Eucharist's memorial dimension to consider its other aspects, we do not leave behind the notion of sacrifice. By his cross and resurrection, Christ has brought about the fulfillment of the Old Testament, but this fulfillment occurs on a differentiated terrain. History continues beyond Calvary. The Eucharist is not simply backward-looking. "It is a sacrament of memory but also a sacrament of hope," de Lubac writes,[31] anticipating a future consummation. These two perspectives underly the Pauline "When you eat this bread and drink this cup, you proclaim the Lord's death [memorial] until he comes again [anticipation]" (1 Cor. 1:26). De Lubac suggests that it is especially here, in the Eucharist's anticipatory dimension, that "our two spheres, both the 'ceremonial' and the 'scriptural,' become enmeshed."[32]

Susan Wood clarifies that "within the dynamic of memorial, presence, and anticipation, there is a double sacramentality. In the first, the bread and wine become the sacrament of Christ's sacramental eucharistic presence. In the second, Christ's sacramental presence under the species of bread and wine becomes the sacrament of final completion of all in Christ."[33] What, though, is this anticipated consummation prefigured in the sacrament? De Lubac provides several interlocking answers to this question, because the Eucharist is a sacrament of the ecclesial body of Christ:

> It is the effective sign of the fraternal charity which binds its members . . . it is the effective sign of the peace and unity for which Christ died and towards which we are reaching, moved by his Spirit. . . . It therefore signifies us to ourselves—*our own mystery, a figure of ourselves*—in what we have already begun to be through baptism . . . but above all in what we ought to become: this is the sacrament of unity.[34]

The Eucharist's character as memorial and as anticipation are intertwined. The same action memorializes and prefigures. Indeed, as I shall demonstrate, the reality it memorializes is the same as that which it prefigures.[35] In other words, just as Christ's sacrifice lies at the heart of the church's historical existence, it is also the destiny to which the church is ultimately called.

Wood has demonstrated that the structure of memorial, presence, and anticipation bears a formal similarity to the spiritual senses of Scripture in their doctrinal form.[36] Hence, the same basic hermeneutic of the two testaments that preoccupied de Lubac in *Medieval Exegesis* from

1959 to 1964 was already operative and in place, articulated using different terminology, as early as 1939, when *Corpus Mysticum* was first completed (though the original French edition was not published until 1944). Christ's sacrifice on the cross, of which the Eucharist is the memorial, is the fulfillment of the Old Testament sacrifices.[37] Hence, as in *Medieval Exegesis*, the cross occupies the position of allegory vis-à-vis the letter: the Christological fulfillment of the Old Testament. The Eucharist also stands in this position because of (1) its identity with Calvary[38] and (2) its identity with the New Covenant (see Luke 22:20; 1 Cor. 11:25).[39] Indeed, it is because of this relationship that the terminology of *truth* was applied to the Eucharist. Though eventually the language of truth came to be applied to a theology of real presence: the true body and blood of Christ, it was initially expressive of a theology of sacrifice. The sacrifice of the altar was the truth/fulfillment prefigured by the Old Testament's sacrifices.[40] As we have seen, though, the Eucharist is also itself a figure of a greater consummation still to come. It is so in a way analogous to how Christ is a figure of the eschatological *totus Christus*. In fact, the sacramental body of Christ is itself also a figure of the *totus Christus*.

Because the Eucharist belongs to the economy of the New Testament, it stands in the position of "fulfillment," but, like other aspects of this economy, it also stands in a position of anticipating the eschaton.[41] De Lubac expresses this with the triad of shadow, image, and truth, where the shadow is found in the law and the truth in the eschaton, while in between, "in the gospel," one finds the image.[42] Hence, depending upon one's reference point, the gospel or the New Testament can be seen as the fulfillment, or as the pledge of the final fulfillment.[43] Even Christ, who is the fulfillment of the Old Testament, and of history itself, is considered a sacrament.[44] De Lubac first expressed this notion of Christ as a sacrament in his first book, *Catholicisme* (1938), in which Christ was identified as the sacrament of God.[45] In *Corpus mysticum*, and later in *Medieval Exegesis*, he described Christ as the sacrament of his own fullness, the *totus Christus*. Both the Old and New Testaments are sacramental economies involving symbolic mediations.[46] The crucial difference is that the New Testament is also an unsurpassable fulfillment, and so its sacraments also share in the realities they signify.[47]

More specifically, Christ's sacrifice on the cross (the content of the allegorical sense) is a figure of a greater final sacrifice of the *totus Christus*,

Corpus mysticum verumque   101

which is, nevertheless, the same sacrifice.[48] Christ's redemptive work is what de Lubac refers to as "a vast liturgy, the earthly and temporal image of the eternal Liturgy . . . *Shadow in the law, image in the gospel, truth in the heaven.* Thus it is with the sacrifice of the Church, compared on the one hand with figurative sacrifices and on the other hand with what can be called the heavenly sacrifice."[49]

Susan Wood appeals to the scholastic category of *res et sacramentum* to explain the dynamic in question.[50] In the sacrament of the Eucharist, the eucharistic species are the *sacramentum tantum*, or sign only. The real presence of Christ is the *res et sacramentum*, or reality and sign. In other words, Christ's body is the reality signified by the sacramental species but also a sign of a greater reality: the *res tantum*, which is the whole Christ. The real presence of Jesus's body and blood in the Eucharist signifies this ultimate and eschatological union of Christ and the church. This terminology corresponds analogously to the spiritual senses. As Wood explains:

> The *res tantum* [read *sacramentum tantum*], considered as the eucharistic rite, corresponds to the idea of memorial and its association with the literal sense of Scripture. The *res et sacramentum*, considered as the actualization of the New Covenant which makes present both Christ and the Church, corresponds to the allegorical sense of Scripture. The *res tantum*, the ecclesial unity effected by the Eucharist, corresponds to the notion of anticipation and the anagogical sense of Scripture.[51]

As Wood notes, the "correlations . . . are only analogous," because the scholastic terminology is focused upon the real presence rather than the historical dynamic of Old Testament, New Testament, and eschaton.[52] Nevertheless, the formal parallels are striking.

In this connection, it is significant to note that the ecclesial body in view is an eschatological reality rather than the immanent and historical gathered community. As Laurence Paul Hemming notes, this eschatological understanding of de Lubac's thought stands in considerable contrast to the reading proposed within Radical Orthodoxy (to give but one example), which focuses upon ontology rather than eschatology, and so emphasizes the gathered community rather than the eschatologically complete body of Christ.[53] As we shall see in the next section, there is an intrinsic identity between them. However, the historical dynamism must not be missed; otherwise the picture de Lubac sketches will be distorted and denatured.

The unity of content between memorial and anticipation, image and truth (and allegory and anagogy) becomes clearer when de Lubac, immediately after describing the future fulfillment as unity and charity, also defines it as sacrifice. Just as the sacrament of the altar memorializes Christ's sacrifice on Calvary, it also prefigures "the 'true' sacrifice, of that interior and spiritual sacrifice by which the holy society of all those who belong to God is brought into being."[54] In discussing the commingling of water and wine in the chalice in connection with the water and blood that flowed from Christ's side on the cross, de Lubac writes:

> The sacrifice of the church—of each one of us—[is] inseparable . . . from the sacrifice of Christ. Thus the consideration of the water in its double relationship to the Eucharistic mystery—the mystery of the Passion and the mystery of the Church, the mystery of the body torn apart and the mystery of the unified body—opened one more route by which it was possible to see rejoined the idea of *power* [*virtus*] and the idea of *matter* [*res*], the idea of the most intimate union to the Saviour and the idea of the social building up of the Church, the idea of the union of the Church with Christ and the idea of the union of the members of Christ among themselves.[55]

The terms *power* and *matter* here build upon a previous discussion of the *virtus sacramenti* and the *res sacramenti*, respectively.[56] Broadly speaking, the *res sacramenti* was considered to be the unity of Christ's body, while the *virtus* was the spiritual life of the body. The former tended to be associated with the term *corpus*/body and the latter with *caro*/flesh, which more naturally connoted food. It was the genius of Augustine to synthesize these two. In the Tractates on the Gospel of John he identifies the body of Christ with the church's unity, the sacramental Eucharist, and the state of sharing eternal life.[57] Crucially, though, as the lengthy quote above indicates, it is precisely in connection with Calvary that these two senses can be synthesized. This coheres with de Lubac's statement, noted earlier, that the patristic focus was not so much on real presence as it was on the action of offering the eucharistic sacrifice, a sentiment that is reiterated throughout *Corpus Mysticum*.[58]

De Lubac credits Christ's sacrifice with bringing about the church, and doing so in a twofold sense. On the one hand, Christ's offering on the cross gathers into one and is the source of the church's life. On the other hand, it is through the church's union with Christ's sacrifice, a union effectively realized at the Mass, that it lives in charity and so in unity. In this connection, de Lubac once more draws upon Augustine, who identified charity with both the principle of the church's unity and the reality that lay at the heart of true sacrifice.[59] In fact, in *Catholicisme* de Lubac speaks of the eucharistic sacrifice as being offered for the sake of the church's unity. This final, perfect unity of the church is "the sacrifice for which the sacrifice of the altar is a preparation."[60] This places the sacrifice of the Mass in the position of *res et sacramentum* and the final unity of the church in the position of *res tantum*. For this reason, I propose that de Lubac's famous statement "Literally speaking, the Eucharist *makes* the church" should be read through a sacrificial lens.[61] After all, (1) it is Christ's sacrifice that brings about the church in the first place, (2) the Eucharist shares an identity with this sacrifice, and (3) the unity of the church as Christ's body, which is effected by the Eucharist, is itself a sacrifice, and, indeed, Christ's sacrifice.

The Church's Sacrificial Destiny

The idea that sacrifice is a particularly interior and spiritual reality allows us to see how the eschatological fulfillment is at once the unity in peace and charity of the church and a great sacrifice: the great sacrifice *is* the charity that binds the church together. Here the notion of the threefold body of Christ provides coherence to de Lubac's conception. The historical sacrifice of Christ on the cross was for the sake of this great final sacrifice of the whole Christ in eternity. For this reason, even Jesus of Nazareth may be said to prefigure a greater reality: the *totus Christus*.[62] The sacramental body of Christ memorializes the historical sacrifice and anticipates the eschatological one. That these three forms of Christ's body are not three bodies, but one, establishes that these sacrifices are not three, but one. The formal coherence of this formulation with de Lubac's theology of spiritual exegesis is unmistakable.

Turning to de Lubac's more explicitly ecclesiological writings, we see the same basic dynamic in play. To discern this, we must reprise some concerns discussed in chapter 5. Throughout *The Splendor of the Church*, de Lubac belabors the fact that the church in its historical existence is provisional. Like all sacramental realities, it will pass away at the coming of the eschaton, absorbed into its inmost reality: the *totus Christus*.[63] At the same time, though, as he stressed throughout his career, the earthly church and the heavenly church are by no means separate, but rather form one church that is identical across its successive states.[64] In this connection, it is crucial to recognize that de Lubac's account of the church's identity is pervaded with a historical dynamism. The heavenly church is not simply a static reality with which the earthly church (or the purgatorial church) is vertically and synchronously related. It is an eschatological reality, with a diachronic relation to the pilgrim church. This refusal to separate the church in its pilgrimage from its eschatological fulfillment also lies at the heart of de Lubac's persistent opposition to Joachim of Fiora, who expected the institutional church to be surpassed by a pneumatological freedom. Chapter 7 will return to the question of Joachim's theology of history. As de Lubac notes, the church is a mysterious reality shot through with paradoxes. It is of God (*de Trinitate*) and of humanity (*ex hominibus*), visible and invisible, earthly-temporal and heavenly-eschatological.[65] It is entirely provisional and must be entirely passed through, and yet is identical with its own eschatological completion and can never be surpassed.[66]

Once more, the historical framework provided by the spiritual senses correlated with sacramental terminology helps to elucidate de Lubac's thought. The church belongs to the economy of the New Testament and is therefore an aspect of the allegorical sense. At the same time, the church awaits, prefigures, and anticipates a greater fulfillment (anagogy). This essentially places it in the position of the *res et sacramentum*. It belongs to the economy of fulfillment (*res*), but also signifies (*et sacramentum*) a greater fulfillment (the *res tantum*), even as it participates in that reality. Hence, de Lubac's ecclesiological paradoxes are not contradictions. In affirming both the identity and the discontinuity of the historical church with the *totus Christus*, de Lubac is not inconsistent. Rather, the two are identical, but not coextensive. Only eschatologically will the union of the redeemed with Christ be fully consummated.

Corpus mysticum verumque   105

Nevertheless, that consummation is not other than the renewal and transfiguration of the church that concretely exists here and now.

In his consideration of ecclesiology, just as in his considerations of spiritual exegesis and the Eucharist, de Lubac envisions both the church's peregrination and its final dénouement in sacrificial terms. In a discussion of the general and ministerial priesthoods, de Lubac notes: "Every Christian participates in the unique priesthood of Jesus Christ."[67] Their participation in Christ's sacrifice is not, strictly speaking, liturgical. Instead, he suggests that "this priesthood of the Christian people is not concerned with the liturgical life of the Church, and it has no direct connection with the production of the Eucharist."[68] This statement may seem to be in some tension with *Lumen gentium*, no. 10, which speaks of the faithful joining in the offering of the Eucharist. However, it should be read in light of this statement of de Lubac: "At Mass the celebrant speaks in the name of the whole Christian community" and that, by the congregation's agreement with the priest's words and actions, they share in the offering.[69] While "at the essential moment, he [the celebrant] acts by the power of Christ,"[70] and not simply as a function of the gathered community—a statement that agrees with *Lumen gentium*'s insistence that the ministerial priesthood is qualitatively different than the general priesthood—it is still the case that the sacrifice of the Mass is the act of the whole church.[71]

The general priesthood offers spiritual sacrifices (i.e., the Christian life), while the ministerial priesthood, "the 'hierarchic' Church . . . produces the Eucharist."[72] De Lubac's statements about the ministerial priesthood are focused upon the question of consecrating the Eucharist, and not on the offering of the sacrifice of the Mass. Because of the unity of the episcopate, and the derivation of presbyteral order from episcopal order, and because all priesthood is really a sharing in the one priesthood of Christ, it follows that the whole church is present in the eucharistic offering.[73] At the same time, the hierarchy is ordered to serving the laity. First, because it is precisely by this sacrifice that the church is effected as Christ's body.[74] Second, because the ministerial priesthood's cultic sacrifice "would be of no value if it did not arouse in each assistant the interior sacrifice . . . our unity is the fruit of Calvary. It results from the application to us of the merits of the Passion, which is made at the Mass, in view of the final liberation."[75]

106   *Salvation Realized*

This distinction between the ministerial priesthood's cultic function and the general priesthood's noncultic vocation for sacrifice provides an important insight into de Lubac's thought at this point. Without it, one might think of the sacrificial aspects of the church's life as relegated to the cultic sphere. Of course, the cultic dimension is important, essential even: it brings about the congregation's own interior sacrifice. But this interior sacrifice, which is the mode in which "every Christian participates in the unique priesthood of Christ,"[76] extends beyond the liturgical cult, meaning that the sacrifice of Christ is a far more pervasive component of ecclesial existence. It is the principle of the church's life.

All Christians participate in Christ's sacrifice. This occurs both liturgically and extra-liturgically. And Christ offered this sacrifice, de Lubac writes, "so that we would be but one in that unity of the divine Persons."[77] Indeed: "We are not fully personal except as interior to the Person of the Son, by whom and in whom we partake in the exchanges of the trinitarian life."[78] Once more the theme of sharing in the trinitarian life through Christ's sacrifice reasserts itself. And, once more, this final integration into the life of God is itself seen as a sacrifice.[79] In the eschaton, when all sacramental mediation will have passed over into a "regime of perfect interiority," the redeemed city will be a great temple,

> and there will be no other Temple save the Lord, himself, no other light to shine except the Lamb. The altar will be that of incense, no longer that of holocausts, and the Church, whole and entire, will be no more than a single host of praise in Jesus Christ. At the Day of the Lord, when the "*catholica societas*" will be realized in its perfection, all will be found in God himself, at once unified, interiorized, and eternalized, because "God will be all in all."[80]

The theology of the threefold body, particularly of the spiritual senses, allows us to bind this together into a coherent statement: the fulfillment of history is the sacrifice of Christ (historical body), a sacrifice in which he includes his people and by which he invites them into the life of the Trinity.[81] Humanity shares in the triune life specifically as members of Christ's body (ecclesial body). This membership in Christ is signified and effected in the Eucharist and lived out in the life of the church, which the eucharistic sacrifice brings about (sacramental body). The life of the church's members is itself a spiritual sacrifice through which they

Corpus mysticum verumque   107

participate in Christ's own unique sacrifice. It is as the *totus Christus* that both Christ and his people dwell in the eschatological bliss of the one God, humanity enfolded by the eternal Son who has always shared this life with his Father and the Holy Spirit.[82]

Conclusion: Charity as the Tie that Binds

Attention to the sacrificial center of de Lubac's ecclesiology further underscores his theological vision of the church as the community of salvation, and does so in such a way as to reprise and reinforce themes that have emerged earlier in this study. Salvation is a social reality and is constituted by the supernatural virtue of charity, by which we are introduced into and come to share in the divine life, because God is love. Charity is, moreover, the formal content of Christ's sacrifice, a sacrifice that is also offered in the Eucharist. It is precisely because the Eucharist is Christ's sacrifice that the Eucharist makes the church, for it is by his saving act that Christ gathers and binds together humanity. The charity that constitutes Christ's sacrifice also constitutes the church's unity. In this way, the discussion of sacrifice reprises the notion of salvation as an authentic humanism.

De Lubac's sacrificial vision of the Eucharist and the church also dovetails with his theology of spiritual exegesis, and does so both formally and materially. The same structure that characterizes his understanding of the relation between the Testaments and between the New Testament and the eschaton occurs in his understanding of the Eucharist/Church relationship within the economy of salvation. The same sacrifice that inaugurates humanity's participation in God's life constitutes humanity's eternal destiny within the trinitarian joy. This is the *res tantum*, which forms the inmost reality of Christ's earthly life and sacrifice, of the Eucharist, and of the church. Christ, the church, and the Eucharist all belong to the fulfillment of all things (allegory) but are not yet the consummation. Hence, they are analogous to the *res et sacramentum*: reality, but still the sign of an ultimate reality. Nevertheless, there is an identity of content between them and the *res ultima*, which they all figure, for there is but one body of Christ and one sacrifice of that body, just as anagogy introduces no new content to allegory but is rather its full fruition.

Finally, the theme of incorporation into the life of the Trinity returns here with force. Through Christ's sacrifice we come to share in the divine life, because Christ's sacrifice is not so much his death as the charity that led him to suffer death on our behalf and because God himself is charity. De Lubac consistently understands our participation in the Trinity in sacrificial terms. By union with the Son we enter God's life interior to the Son, and do so as a great sacrifice of praise. This is what it means to be saved, and is, moreover, what it means to be the church, for it is within this community that salvation is realized.

PART FOUR

Salvation Consummated
Eschatology and the Theology of History

CHAPTER SEVEN

Salvation as the Meaning of History

In chapter 4 we noted that de Lubac's theology of spiritual exegesis, more than advocating a method for biblical interpretation, pointed toward a particular disposition according to which Scripture was approached as testifying to and centered upon Jesus Christ and his saving act and as disclosing a theology of history centered upon the same. As Kevin Hughes has noted, the outlook of spiritual exegesis exercises a "capillary influence" throughout de Lubac's œuvre.[1] We further noted both there and in chapter 6 that Henri de Lubac's theologies of spiritual exegesis and of the church and its sacraments unfold within a historically differentiated terrain. An ingredient of each is the relationship of the two testaments to each other and to eschatology. In both the theology of spiritual exegesis and ecclesiology, the turning point is the saving act of Christ. Theologically, the church is the realization of the salvation achieved by Christ, to which the Scriptures bear witness and into which we are thrust by grasping their spiritual meaning, which is precisely that salvation.

In those contexts, our focus remained fixed upon the form and content of spiritual exegesis as such, leaving to the side wider questions of the theology of history. In moving beyond those narrower considerations to de Lubac's more general theology of history, we most certainly do not move beyond Christ or his saving mystery or the church, which is its realization. Indeed, as we shall see, de Lubac's theology of history is focused upon insisting that such a moving beyond of Christ or the church is incompatible with the Christian faith. In the eschaton, salvation will be consummated, but what will be consummated is none other than what

112   *Salvation Consummated*

has been instilled as the deepest longing of the human heart, achieved by Christ, realized in the church, and disclosed in the Scriptures.

Hence, in what follows we shall be reprising themes that have been discussed earlier in this study, but now for a different purpose. In chapter 2 we saw that de Lubac characterized atheistic humanism as presenting a parodic and parasitic account of salvation that must be countered with the authentic humanism of Christian salvation. Now, in his theology of history, he returns to many of these figures, resolute in his conviction that Christ and his salvation represent the unsurpassable meaning of history. In chapter 5 we considered de Lubac's insistence on the ongoing place of doctrinal authority and ecclesial structure. Here we shall see that he viewed moving beyond them as implying that we could move beyond the achievement of Christ. Here the theology of spiritual exegesis will return in force, for it both provides the basic structure of de Lubac's theology of history and is also the basis of his disagreements with Joachim of Fiore's. In this way, we shall see the unity of de Lubac's pre- and post-conciliar concerns as we trace two career-long themes: resistance to Joachim of Fiore and his influence upon the subsequent intellectual history, and the diachronic unity of the church across the eschatological caesura.

De Lubac's Writings on Joachim and his Spiritual Posterity

Throughout his career, de Lubac expressed his fascination with, admiration of, and opposition to the exegetical and historical thought and influence of Joachim of Fiore (1135–1202), an abbot who lived in Calabrais and wrote several exegetical works while longing for a spiritual purification and reform of the church.[2] In this somewhat obscure figure de Lubac discerned the seeds both of atheist humanism and of the paracouncil, and gradually we see his interest in Joachim turn from matters of exegesis to ecclesiological, trinitarian, and historical and eschatological concerns.[3]

De Lubac's first substantive discussion of Joachim is found in *History and Spirit*, where he discusses the notion of an "eternal gospel."[4] Both Origen and Joachim utilized this phrase, and the conventional wisdom suggested that Origen was the origin for the Calabrian abbot's dream of an eternal gospel and a spiritual church. However, de Lubac insists that any similarity between the thought of the two is merely verbal. They are both using the same phrase, one that comes from Scripture (Revelation 14:6), but they intend by it entirely different things. For Origen, the "eternal Gospel is the antithesis and anticipated antidote of that of the Calabrian monk."[5] Whereas Joachim's vision turned upon prognostications for a coming world and ecclesial order, Origen's understanding of the eternal gospel was at once "completely eschatological" and yet in deep continuity with the gospel of the church's proclamation.[6] In other words, as the church advances toward its ultimate goal, it never progresses beyond its most fundamental message: the saving gospel of Christ.

Writing eleven years later, in the third volume of *Medieval Exegesis*, de Lubac engaged with Joachim in greater detail.[7] In the monk's intricately detailed exegetical system, history bears a trinitarian cast, consisting of three ages, each of which discloses one of the divine persons: the Father under the law, the Son in the time of grace, and the Holy Spirit in an anticipated age of fuller grace and freedom.[8] The relation between letter and spirit is not that of the Old Testament to the New but rather of both testaments to a (soon?) coming third age of the Spirit.[9] In this lies the principle error of Joachim, for it at once compromises the Christian novelty—Christ has not, in fact, brought all newness in bringing himself; there is evidently more to come—and detaches the work of Christ and the Holy Spirit, such that the latter operates independently of the former.[10]

This consideration paves the way for a bifurcation between two streams of successors to Joachim's thought. On the one hand, there are those of his exegetical posterity, who follow him in seeking concords between the testaments, especially a spiritual meaning in the New Testament, thereby, in de Lubac's view, reducing it to another letter. On the other hand, there are those de Lubac identifies as spiritual posterity and with whom the two volumes of *La postérité spirituelle de Joachim de Flore* are concerned.[11] The spiritual posterity were those who, in various forms, looked for a coming third age of the Spirit. Joachim's exegetical posterity was by no means unproblematic (De Lubac understatedly observes that Joachim's "fantastic" exegesis "would not be all that bad, provided that all these 'phantasmagoria' did not flow from principles that ruin the whole economy of Christian revelation").[12] But at least it operated within a theological framework, such that Christ gave way to another divine hypostasis. The spiritual posterity, though, eventually come to see Christ

114   *Salvation Consummated*

and Christianity as simply surpassable, ultimately giving way to purely human endeavors.[13] De Lubac traces the steps by which this notion of a third age becomes denatured and secularized.

We need not detain ourselves here with all of the contours of this genealogy nor with the extent to which all of the ills laid at Joachim's feet rightly belong there, both of which matters are contested territory.[14] It is especially worth noting that Marjorie Reeves and Bernard McGinn have both challenged the notion that Joachim saw the third status (as Reeves notes, he spoke in terms of a *status*, not an *age* in this connection)[15] as surpassing Christ, or the spiritual church as supplanting the institutional church.[16] Joachim insisted, for instance, on the permanent validity of the papacy. His vision of the successive statuses had all three divine persons inseparably operative throughout the whole of history, and his threefold division was complemented by a twofold one. The threefold schema, based upon the capital Alpha (A), reflected the way that two (the Son and Holy Spirit) proceed from and are sent by one (the Father), while his twofold schema, patterned on the lowercase omega (ω), reflects the procession and mission of one (the Holy Spirit) from two (the Father and the Son).[17] Joachim, then, found a spiritual sense in the New Testament because the Spirit proceeds from the Son, to whom the New Testament testifies.[18] And so McGinn is insistent that Joachim had not lost sight of Christ's constitutive role in history and salvation.[19]

However, as important as it surely is to (1) interpret Joachim accurately as a thinker in his own right[20] and to (2) avoid going further than the textual evidence allows in our tracing of intellectual genealogies, in a work focused on de Lubac's theological vision our concern must be with the lessons that de Lubac wishes to impart through his survey of Joachim and his spiritual posterity. In this connection, though, Patrick Gardner has pointed out that de Lubac's approach is not especially focused on laying responsibility for his posterity at Joachim's feet but rather on seeing in Joachim a certain destabilizing and disruptive figure in the history of thought, a man whose ideas were often developed in problematic ways in excess of—and, at times, contrary to—the intention of their progenitor.[21] Indeed, as we shall see momentarily, this assessment is reflected in de Lubac's engagement with what he dubs "semi-joachimism." Hence, whether or not Joachim ever actually held the dangerous theological views against which de Lubac warns, and whether or not they can be directly traced back to him, these views will be our focus.

Salvation as the Meaning of History   115

De Lubac's concerns can be distilled into three primary areas that, in the end, are reducible to one. He opposes Joachim's reduction of the New Testament to another letter, his vision of an age of the Spirit that surpasses Christ, and his vision of a spiritual church that surpasses the visible and institutional church along with its sacraments as they exist in history. In the end, the problem with all three of these Joachimite commitments is that they compromise the novelty of Christ and amount to a surpassing of the salvation he has achieved. The consequences of this view, then, are "dangerous," even "fatal."[22]

These three Joachimite positions are closely related to one another because they all turn upon whether or not Christ's salvation is definitive and eternally valid. To view the New Testament as another letter awaiting its spiritual fulfillment is to "compromise . . . the full sufficiency of Jesus Christ."[23] The traditional understanding of the spirit's relation to the letter presumed that "every revelation has been given by Christ and every work of salvation has been accomplished in him."[24] There did indeed lay ahead the eschatological consummation of this salvation, but within the frame of history, the last days have been inaugurated by the events of the cross, the resurrection, and Pentecost.[25] The content of the spiritual sense is Christ and his mystery, and the event of the Holy Spirit's bestowal is closely tied to, indeed integral to, this mystery rather than separate from it.

Alek Zwitter summarizes the concern well. For de Lubac and Origen, what allows for the spiritual understanding of Scripture is the paschal mystery, and so Joachim's emphasis on the third age

> radically changes traditional exegesis. If for traditional exegesis the challenge was the deepening of the mystery, the driving idea of Joachim is a secret to find or an enigma (regarding the unfolding of the history of the world) to decipher. From this "literal concord" results a new spiritual intelligence. The principal mystery "revealed" to Joachim through the concord of the two testaments is the mystery of the third age.[26]

By locating the spiritual meaning of Scripture found not in Christ or the paschal mystery but rather in the third age, Joachim articulates a deficient Christology whereby "the novelty of Christ does not have an absolute relation to history, it is solely transitory."[27] Here lies the crucial difference between the Origenian and the Joachimite understandings of the eternal gospel. For Origen it was exclusively eschatological, while Joachim anticipated it within history. For Origen "the eternal Gospel remained bound to the mystery of Christ," while for Joachim it "presents itself as the surpassing of this mystery."[28] In the end, Joachim's eschatology is "non-Christic, because it doesn't reserve the central place to the paschal mystery."[29]

De Lubac saw distinct parallels between the Joachimite aspiration for a spiritual church free from hierarchical structure and doctrinal constraint and the post- and para-conciliar milieu that so disturbed him. Gardner notes distinct parallels, especially the tendency toward a "pneumaticism" that accompanied a "separation of the council's 'spirit' from its letter" in the service of transforming the church's institutional structure.[30] In this connection, the exegetical foundations of de Lubac's disagreement with Joachim's thought are especially pertinent. The separation of letter and spirit, whether with reference to the council or the Scriptures, is unthinkable. The spirit is transformative of, but nevertheless valorizes and upholds, the letter.[31] This parallel between the para-council and Joachimism remains more or less inchoate throughout most of de Lubac's survey of the spiritual posterity,[32] leading Michael Sutton to note, "This . . . preoccupation . . . in the long history of ideas recounted at length in the eighteen chapters of *La Postérité spirituelle*, surfaces only rarely. In contrast, it dominates the Conclusion of the work."[33] And de Lubac leaves no ambiguity about his position when, in *At the Service of the Church*, he explicitly states that Joachimite views are "a still-present and even pressing danger. I recognize it in the process of secularization which, betraying the Gospel, transforms the search for the kingdom of God into social utopias. I see it at work in what was so justly called the 'self-destruction of the Church.'"[34]

The concluding paragraphs of *La postérité spirituelle* give de Lubac's diagnosis of and prescription for the matter, showing two tendencies the church must avoid in order to be true to itself and avoid this self-destruction:

> It is impossible to take in, in faith and hope, the coming of God in our history without retaining, in an inseparable memory, that the *inexhaustible* infinite has been *given* to us. . . . Sometimes we re-

member that God has given himself at the time of his coming, but we think that the gift, the message, and the life of Christ are exhausted. Thus, there will be no further future or innovation, or life in a frozen, sclerotic Church reduced to the dead past of an epoch that it pleases our sentiments to remember. Other times, in an inverse sense, we forget that God has given himself absolutely in person, and so believe that everything is to be invented, that the Church has no heritage.

Church of the past, Church of the Father without inventive spiritual life; dead, frozen Church of the "integrists" of the past. Church of the future, without gathering the gift of God, in defiance of the institution; stale Church in an unreal spiritual future, Church of the "progressives." One and the other lack the present of the Church; one and the other have forgotten the inexhaustible gift of the infinity of God. And each of these abstractions that crucify the Church risks occupying turn by turn each Christian in order to ruin the sense and the living reality of fidelity. The necessarily incessant conversion to the God of the Gospel is without doubt the will always set up to find without pause in the Church the indivisible truth of the gift of God.[35]

We see here, then, the need to avoid both stagnation—as though the church of today must be locked in the past, with no room for growth or development—and dissipation—as though the church had not already received all of its identity and solidity in Christ. In this connection, we would be remiss were we to ignore de Lubac's observation that there is also a sort of "semi-Joachimism" that he regards as "perhaps less unfaithful to the aim of Joachim himself" and that might be considered "the tentative search for what was to be the normal development of Catholic tradition ... the discovery by the Church herself, all along her pilgrimage, of the perpetual fruitfulness of the Gospel, from which she draws in each new situation ... *nova et vetera*."[36]

De Lubac identifies Philippe Buchez, who believed that in holding fast to the initial principles of the faith one found limitless fecundity and possibilities for deepened engagement and development, all while "envisaging nothing beyond Catholic Christianity, and ceding no dissolving or deforming 'interpretation' of the mystery," as semi-Joachimite and

118   *Salvation Consummated*

suggests that the same impulse is found in the thought of Vladimir So-loviev.[37] Adam Mickiewicz probably also belongs under this umbrella.[38] Patrick Gardner and Alek Zwitter both suggest that de Lubac might be fruitfully understood as himself a semi-Joachimite.[39]

Without denying that there is some analogy or overlap, I believe that this assessment is anachronistic, exceeds the bounds of the available data, and is, ultimately, unnecessary. De Lubac does not use the phrase *semi-Joachimite* at all until 1981, and then just thrice, in a span of two pages. Eight years later, he will use it once more, and in a rather tentative fashion: "Still, I would not be far from admitting that a kind of semi-Joachimism (perhaps less unfaithful to the aim of Joachim himself), of which I spoke with regard to Buchez, was, on the contrary, the tentative search for what was to be the normal development of Catholic tradition."[40] Though he clearly sees something worthwhile in semi-Joachimism, and though he registers no opposition to it, neither does he at any point give a full-throated endorsement of it, much less apply the label to his own thought or positions. Finally, the wellspring of de Lubac's position was neither Joachim nor any of his posterity but rather Origen, who already in the third century had provided an articulation of the perpetual novelty and fruitfulness of the Christian mystery while also refuting Joachimism *avant la lettre*. To the extent that the semi-Joachimite label could adhere to de Lubac, it is because he was always already schooled in the "whole interpretation of Christianity, of which Origen . . . was less the author than the witness."[41]

In Christ all has been given, and in bringing himself, he has brought all newness. This is, then, an inexhaustible source of life. One can never advance beyond it, not because all discovery is at an end but because it is ever new and perpetually valid. The way forward for the church, then, is not a pretended advance beyond its past but a continual return to its inmost and founding reality.

The Sacramentality of Christ, the Church, and History

The first volume of *La postérité spirituelle* appeared when de Lubac was 83 years old. His energy was fading, and his friend, Hans Urs von Balthasar, had to goad him into completing Volume 2.[42] De Lubac reports

Salvation as the Meaning of History   119

that in 1980 "the time for stopping had come," and so he never completed a proper doctrinal conclusion to the work, ending it, instead, with a brief reflection on "*Néojoachimismes contemporains*."[43] Though the preceding eight hundred pages were not without evaluation of the movements they surveyed, we are, nevertheless, left without a clear word from de Lubac on precisely what to make of the intellectual history with which he has presented us. He notes that, apart from this missing conclusion, the book does not always rise above the level of "inquisitiveness [*curiosité*]."[44] We are not thereby left entirely without bearings, however. In a footnote he observes that "the outline of this missing conclusion was traced in 1952 in my *Méditation sur l'Église*, 175–80."[45]

Following upon this observation, Marie-Gabrielle Lemaire and Patrick Gardner have each attempted to sketch the outline of this conclusion that never was. Lemaire concentrates on the selection from *Méditation sur l'église* along with the various notes that de Lubac had assembled for but never transmogrified into the conclusion.[46] Gardner notes that de Lubac's writings are indeed refutations of Joachim *avant la lettre*, for both before and after the Council he had been engaged with the extrinsicist thought currents that characterized Joachim's spiritual posterity, whether in the form of neo-scholasticism and integralism, atheist humanism, or secularized immanentism.[47]

Turning to the passage de Lubac indicates sketched his conclusion to *La postérité spirituelle*, we see that it is focused upon the sacramentality of the church. The church is the sacrament of Christ, who is, in turn, the sacrament of God.[48] This notion of Christ and the church as sacramental reprises themes first taken up in *Catholicisme*, which bear their fruit in *Lumen gentium*'s identification of the church as the universal sacrament of salvation.[49] De Lubac's appeal to sacramentality here is for a specific purpose. He is concerned to speak about the church as at once provisional and unsurpassable.

Because a sacrament "is the sign of something else, it must be passed through [*traversée*], and this not in part, but wholly."[50] By definition, a sign is meant to lead us on to whatever it signifies. At the same time, though:

> This sacramental reality is not just any sign, provisional or changeable on a whim. It is found in an essential relation to our present

condition. . . . Its second character, indissociable from the first, will be then that it can never be dismissed as having ceased to be useful. This diaphanous milieu, which one must always traverse and traverse totally, one has never however finished traversing it. It is always in its traversal that one attains that of which it is the sign. It can never be outdated, nor its boundaries crossed.[51]

This provisionality and unsurpassability characterize, variously, both Christ and the church, albeit in different ways: Christ is the sacrament of God, and the church is the sacrament of Christ. We can come to the Father only through Christ, and it is through the church that we encounter Christ and his grace.[52] Neither is dispensable in the slightest, and yet both must be passed through entirely. It would seem that we are on the horns of a dilemma.

Because we are concerned here with the relation between Christ, the church, and the sacramental order of the eschaton, it would be helpful to have recourse to the Lubacian trope of the threefold body of Christ, which encompasses all three of the realities in question, and does so cognizant of both their unity and their differentiation. The three forms of Christ's body—the historical body, born of the Virgin, nailed to the cross, risen from the dead, and now seated at the right hand of the Father; the sacramental body, present on the altar; and the ecclesial body, the union of the faithful together with Christ, their head—are not three bodies, but one, for Christ is one.[53] Moreover, each is the reality signified by some sign and also the sign of some other reality. Here the scholastic distinction between *res* and *sacramentum* provides us with a clarifying framework for understanding this sacramental dialectic of signification and fulfillment, for it allows us to consider, in any sacramental reality, precisely what is provisional (because it is a sign of some other reality) and what is permanent (because it is the reality signified).[54] We shall consider each mode of Christ's body in turn.

The Historical Body

Most fundamentally, we must understand the historical body of Christ to occupy the position of *res*. He is the fullness of revelation; to him all the signs of the Old Testament pointed, and on him they all converge.[55] It is axiomatic for de Lubac that Christ is unsurpassable, and, as we have

Salvation as the Meaning of History   121

seen, this accounts for his opposition to Joachimism. At the same time, though, we have seen that de Lubac also identifies Christ with the *sacramentum*. He is, above all, the sacrament of God. Through him we pass to the Father who sent him, which is a theme of the Johannine farewell discourse (e.g., John 14:7–14).[56] Beyond this, though, Christ is also, in a manner of speaking, a figure of the church, which is to say that he signifies the mystical body in union with its head.[57] Crucially, although Christ does indeed await a greater fulfillment in the *totus Christus*, this does not amount to surpassing him, for in signifying the church "Christ signifies himself."[58] The historical Jesus is a sign of a greater fulfillment, the *totus Christus*.[59]

And so, analogously to how the real presence of Christ's body and blood is the *res et sacramentum* of the Eucharist—signified by the species of bread and wine (*sacramentum tantum*) and signifying the union of the whole Christ (*res tantum*)—the historical body occupies a position of *res et sacramentum*. He is the reality signified by the entirety of the Old Testament and of history itself, yet he also signifies the great eschatological consummation. However, while the historical body of Christ is the sign of a greater fulfillment, it remains permanently valid and never, in any sense, passes away. The mystical body that he signifies is united with its head, which is the historical Jesus Christ. The head assimilates the members to himself, not the other way around.[60] Turning to the framework of the spiritual senses: Christ accomplishes and constitutes the allegorical sense. His is the mystery contained in Scripture. The further senses of tropology, by which his mystery is reproduced in the lives of the faithful and of the church and of anagogy, where it is eschatologically consummated, does not move beyond or add to the allegorical sense, which is permanently valid.

The Sacramental Body

To an extent the inverse holds when we consider the sacramental body of Christ. Like the historical body, it should be seen as occupying the place of *res et sacramentum*. Indeed, it perhaps superlatively belongs in this position, as the sacramental analogy and scholastic framework we are utilizing are drawn from its domain. As discussed above, the Eucharist, the sacramental body of Christ, precisely is the *res et sacramentum*. Within the historical and eschatological framework we are interrogating, the same holds, though de Lubac expressed it using a different framework, that of shadow—image—truth. As we saw in chapter 6, de Lubac's treatment of the Eucharist in *Corpus Mysticum* turns, in part, upon its relation to the animal sacrifices of the Old Testament. It is the reality they signified: the image to their shadow. However, it holds this position in an entirely derivative way. It fulfills the Old Testament sacrifices because it is the sacrament of Christ's sacrifice on Calvary, with which it shares a mysterious union: they are the same sacrifice (sacrament of memory). Additionally, though, it also holds a middle position between the shadows of the law and the truth of the eschatological fulfillment. It signifies and anticipates the eschatological sacrifice of the *totus Christus* (sacrament of hope).[61] In this way, while it is the *res* of the Old Testament's figures (and of the sacramental species), the Eucharist is also the *sacramentum* of the church, both understood in its character as the body of Christ and insofar as it will be eschatologically offered as the sacrifice of Christ's body.

However, in contrast to the historical body, the sacramental body will not endure eschatologically. On this point, de Lubac is clear. Sacramental realities are necessary to us in our present condition, between the definitive fulfillment of the New Testament and the eschatological consummation in which faith will give way to sight and *spes* will give way to *res*. There will be no more need for sacraments because the reality they signify will be our possession.[62] Within history, the Eucharist is indispensable. In eternity, the Eucharist will be no more.

The Ecclesial Body

Like the historical and sacramental body, the ecclesial body of Christ has a twofold sacramentality. As we have already noted, it is the sacrament of Christ, as Christ is the sacrament of God. Through the church we pass into Christ, and so into God. And yet, in a sense, the ecclesial body is also the sacrament of itself because it is also an anticipation of its own eschatological fulfillment as the *totus Christus*; in this regard it remains the sacrament of Christ, of course, for the whole Christ is indeed the whole *Christ*. It is the *sacramentum*, then, of these *res*, and they are, in the end, not plural, but a singular reality. It is also, though, as we have seen, the *res* of which the Eucharist is the *sacramentum*, which it was the major burden of *Corpus Mysticum* to recover.

Like the historical body, but unlike the sacramental body, the ecclesial body will endure eternally. And here de Lubac is clear and consistent in saying that the eschatologically complete mystical body is not a different body than the ecclesial body as it exists in history. They are one and the same.[63] However, unlike the historical body, the church will undergo a radical transfiguration in its passage into the eschaton.[64] Insofar as this transfiguration is analogous to the resurrection of the dead, we might note that the historical body of Christ does indeed undergo this transfiguration, but that it has occurred in the midst of history—as history's very pivot—rather than beyond history's end. Nevertheless, as de Lubac has told us, the church "must be passed through, and this not in part, but wholly."[65] All of the church's visible and institutional apparatus will pass away with the eschaton.[66] Only the church's inner substance will remain, namely, the communion of all the faithful together with Christ. What will remain is love. What will remain is salvation, which is the theological meaning of the church.

And this is precisely why de Lubac insists, against Joachim, that the church cannot be superseded, for to do so would be a supersession of Christ and his salvation. Though the church is transformed, it nevertheless retains its most basic identity as the body of Christ and the community of salvation. We can affirm this because there is an identity of meaning between allegory and anagogy. Hence, whereas Joachim understands the relationship to be something like *institutional church* : *spiritual church* :: *Letter* : *Spirit*, for de Lubac the relation is *historical church* : *eschatological church* :: *allegory* : *anagogy*. For Joachim, both the institutional church and the spiritual church will occur within history in advance of the eschaton. For de Lubac, the institutional church will indeed give way to the wholly spiritual church, but only across the eschatological transom. In bringing himself, Christ has brought all newness, and so the same reality that gave rise to the church: salvation in Christ characterizes it during its pilgrimage and will be consummated in it at the end of history.

Conclusion: Christ, the Pivot of History

For de Lubac, Christ, the church, and history are all sacramental. It is important to note that this sacramentality is not static or Platonic but is shot through with a historical dynamism. History both discloses and is driven toward its eschatological completion. The paschal mystery has introduced the last times, which are at once the time of Christ, the Holy Spirit, and the church.[67] This is the acceptable time, the day of salvation (2 Cor. 6:2).

This leads Marie-Gabrielle Lemaire to suggest that the Lubacian theology of history is essentially the reverse of the Joachimite legacy. Whereas "modernity made of Christianity one historical event among others, or even a step to surpass," de Lubac insists that history's dignity and meaning arise from its coming to be salvation history with the gift of Christ.[68] The gift of Christ reveals that there is a history at all, and this gift, having been given in full, admits of no surpassing. To do so would be decadence rather than progress.[69] Dogma can develop, our experience of the saving mystery can be deepened, but none of this changes the constitutive meaning that has been bestowed in Christ.[70]

This is a rather crucial point. Joachimite thought saw the whole of history as revealing the Trinity. With this de Lubac would agree. Yet, as Gardner notes, the Trinity is already fully revealed in the paschal mystery and the mystery of redemption.[71] There is no more to reveal. Hence, rather than a linear progression, with Christ's mystery occupying either the *terminus a quo* or a midpoint along the way to some future state or time, history is entirely centered upon this mystery, which has been given in its fullness.[72] Because it has been fully given, and because the church is part of this mystery's intelligibility as the realization of salvation and as the fullness of Christ, it also follows that the time of the church cannot be surpassed either.[73]

In these various ways de Lubac insists that history bears no other meaning than Christ and his salvation: a salvation that is accomplished in the paschal mystery of Christ's death, resurrection, and gift of the Holy Spirit and realized in the church. These elements cannot be separated, for their meaning is one: the one God and our coming to share in his life through the saving act of the one Christ.[74] History turns upon this event, which is inexhaustibly rich and whose depths will never be fully plumbed nor its meaning fully expressed.

CHAPTER EIGHT

Salvation as Eschatological Sacrifice

In the previous chapter we considered de Lubac's theology of history, especially as articulated in response to Joachim of Fiore and his spiritual posterity. In opposition to Joachimism, de Lubac was resolute that Christ and his salvation constitute the unsurpassable meaning of history. Now, though, we shall range more broadly still and consider history in its widest sweep. De Lubac's writings on Pierre Teilhard de Chardin help to establish this wider context.

Teilhard is well known for his attempts to articulate the Christian faith within the context of the shifts in understanding brought about by the recognition of time's immensity—the universe's staggeringly ancient character—and evolutionary accounts of life's emergence and development.[1] De Lubac's engagement with Teilhard allows us to look at history, particularly salvation history, in its cosmic scope and significance, from its beginnings to its final consummation and convergence in the kingdom where God is all in all—what Teilhard terms "Omega." The meaning of history is Jesus Christ and the salvation he accomplished upon the cross. De Lubac's engagement with Teilhard allows him to articulate this as the act toward which everything in the cosmos tends and into which it all will be gathered.

The Character of De Lubac's Writings on Teilhard

It is difficult to assess precisely how de Lubac's own thought relates to Teilhard's. He wrote five books about him: as many as about spiritual

125

126 *Salvation Consummated*

exegesis and more than about the supernatural,[2] and he was preoccupied with rehabilitating him during the Second Vatican Council.[3] As Éric de Moulins-Beaufort notes, de Lubac's pro-Teilhardian campaign at Vatican II unfolded in three primary stages. Initially he worked to defend his late confrère from possible condemnation at the Council, an outcome that some expected. Subsequently, though, he began to position himself as an interpreter of Teilhard, highlighting especially the apologetic thrust of Teilhardian thought. Finally, toward the end of the Council, de Lubac saw in Teilhard a resource for the Council's work and for the future fruitful implementation of conciliar teaching.[4] This final stage is on display in *Athéisme et sens de l'homme*, where de Lubac sees in Teilhard anticipations of the solutions proposed by *Gaudium et spes*.[5]

And yet, for all the vigor of de Lubac's defense and advocacy, in his candid moments he noted dissatisfaction with the task and the distance between his thought and Teilhard's. Consider his words to Gaston Fessard: "[Writing] about Teilhard and again about Teilhard, it tires and bores me, all the more so as I feel very well that there is little Teilhardian in me."[6] This disparity, then, means that we must tread lightly in de Lubac's writings on Teilhard, for it is not always apparent when de Lubac is simply reporting and interpreting the views of his friend and when his own commitments are on display.

Because this is a study of de Lubac's theology and not a purely constructive enterprise, we must differentiate between de Lubac's actual views and his reportage of Teilhard's. Here a few principles can guide us. First and most obviously, we can note those junctures at which de Lubac explicitly distances himself from Teilhard. He was quite willing to note where Teilhard's writings led to problematic conclusions, either because of what they actually affirmed or due to Teilhard's own lack of precision.[7] At times, though, one wishes he had been more pointed in his denunciations. For instance, under de Lubac's pen, Teilhard's eugenicism gets off entirely too easily in my view, with de Lubac simply noting that Teilhard recognized that human capacities had developed to the point at which we had more direct control over which traits were passed on than we did through mere natural selection and that we ought to proceed in this arena carefully and informed by religious and moral concerns.[8] So far as that goes, it is probably accurate. We *are* capable of this greater control, and our response to it *should* be religiously and morally informed. Yet

Salvation as Eschatological Sacrifice   127

Teilhard's thoughts on the matter seem to have extended beyond this fairly minimalist position to advocate for actions that, frankly, ought to chill us.[9] De Lubac records Teilhard's recognition that human progress was not without ambivalence, along with his awareness that we were capable of becoming a "*Nouveau Moloch*,"[10] and I would propose that it is precisely in this light that we should read Teilhard's eugenicism. The religiously and morally responsible approach to the recognition that we can do more than what merely natural selection permits is to refuse any such tampering. That said, those areas in which de Lubac differentiates himself from Teilhard obviously indicate aspects of Teilhardianism that ought not inform our understanding of de Lubac other than by way of contrast.

I further assume that, in those areas in which we can discern a formal or material overlap between de Lubac's presentation of Teilhard's thought and what we discern elsewhere in his œuvre, we can take his statements as indicative of his own views as well. Beyond such direct parallels, we must be more tentative. And so in what follows I will be confining myself to de Lubac's own views rather than Teilhard's per se. In this context it matters little if Teilhard was correct on any given issue or if de Lubac is correct in his interpretation of Teilhard. While I will provide some references to Teilhard himself, mainly to *The Human Phenomenon* or *The Divine Milieu*, I will primarily be citing de Lubac's writings. At the same time, to avoid clumsy verbiage, I will refer to Teilhard directly in attributing notions and ideas rather than using such constructions as "According to de Lubac's understanding of Teilhard, . . ." However, it is not my intention to present any of this as Teilhard scholarship, and such references to him should be understood in this qualified sense.

De Lubac's initial motivation for engaging the thought of Teilhard seems to have been a compulsion toward justice. After Teilhard's death in 1955 on Easter Sunday, a pall of suspicion overhung him and his views, and he was no longer capable of speaking for himself. De Lubac, himself still forbidden from publishing on or teaching theology, sought to come to his departed friend and confrère's defense. At that time the Society of Jesus was unwilling to allow its members to publish on Teilhard, but de Lubac spoke on his behalf and produced a short work on him that was not intended for circulation but began to circulate in samizdat form without his knowledge. However, in 1961 de Lubac received not only permission but *instruction* to produce work on Teilhard's behalf and to begin immediately, allowing no other obligations to encroach upon his availability for this work.[11] He followed this directive with gusto, as we have seen.

De Lubac knew well what it meant to be unfairly suspected and marginalized.[12] He could not countenance the same happening to his friend, a man he knew to be an earnest, sincere, and pious Christian.[13] Indeed, whatever one's misgivings about Teilhard's project (and I myself have several), it is difficult to read de Lubac's works on him without being drawn into a greater admiration for him as a man and as a Christian. Yet these impulses of justice and friendship do not fully account for de Lubac's array of writings on Teilhard. Instead, as Jean-Pierre Wagner notes, there are more substantive theological commitments that account for the hospitality toward Teilhard evident in de Lubac's thought.[14] In general, it is upon these theological commitments that I shall focus. Beyond them, though, there was something about Teilhard's comportment that attracted de Lubac and drew forth his admiration. In de Lubac's own estimation, Teilhard was a mystic,[15] a characteristic especially on display in Teilhard's *La messe sur le monde* (1923). And Éric de Moulins-Beaufort has argued persuasively that de Lubac saw in Teilhard an exemplary case of the *vir ecclesiasticus* about whom he wrote in *Méditation sur l'église* and saw in Teilhard's creativity, harnessed to an unflagging desire to remain in communion with the church, the solution to the crises facing the church.[16]

Moulins-Beaufort suggests that these dispositions were primary in de Lubac's assessment of Teilhard, and this does seem plausible, especially given de Lubac's own distancing from Teilhard and his demurral from identifying too fully either with Teilhard's project or his own works on Teilhard. While de Lubac did indeed see value in Teilhard's ideas, it was Teilhard's personal integrity and convictions that really drove him. In David Grumett's significant study of Teilhard he notes that Teilhard represents a synthesis of Blondel's emphasis on the will (in his account of humanity's "passivities") and Rousselot's intellectualism (in his account of human action).[17] Blondel and Rousselot were, of course, major influences upon de Lubac's own intellectual formation, so it should be unsurprising that he would find sympathy with a figure in whom their distinct emphases were synthesized.

Most significantly of all, there are considerable structural similarities between Teilhard's account of the spiritualization of matter and the culmination of all things in Christ-Omega and de Lubac's notion of the Christian newness, especially as expressed in his theology of the supernatural and of spiritual exegesis. Both of their visions, in the end, turn upon the incarnate Christ and the saving act of the cross.

Christocentrism and Cruciformity

As we have seen, de Lubac was clear that he did not consider himself to be a Teilhardian. Still, he found much to commend in Teilhard's writings, and all the more so if one remembered to keep the main thing the main thing. *The Religion of Teilhard de Chardin* opens with an observation that when it comes to Teilhard, readers are missing the point:

> It is only too easy to dismiss, in a writer's thought, anything that makes no special appeal to us, to minimize or even completely overlook its importance. This may lead us, in all good faith, to distort the whole meaning of his work, even if any analysis we include is itself accurate.... [An example of this is] the biblical exegesis of the Fathers of the Church. This rests in its entirety on a keen perception of a relation, unique of its kind, the relation of the two "Covenants" or the two "Testaments." There we have the key without which it cannot be properly understood.[18]

Similar distortions occur when readers separate out *The Divine Milieu* from *The Human Phenomenon*. The former is the key to a proper understanding not only of the latter but of Teilhard's overall perspective, because it helps us to see that Teilhard is far more concerned with cultivating a particular disposition than with advancing any particular positions, and that this central disposition is a devotion to Jesus Christ.[19] Hence, it is especially appropriate that de Lubac marshaled the example of spiritual exegesis to illustrate the tendency to miss Teilhard's point, for it, too, is entirely focused upon the event of Christ. And indeed, as we shall see, there are distinct similarities between de Lubac's account of spiritual exegesis and his account of Teilhard's thought, as both hinged upon the event of Christ within a context of historical development.[20]

130 *Salvation Consummated*

De Lubac wants us to see how, all of his neologisms and idiosyncrasies aside, Teilhard is, at heart, a rather traditional sort of Christian. If we would listen to his self-explanation in *The Divine Milieu*, we would recognize this for ourselves.

> The purpose of this Essay—on life or on inward vision—is to prove by a sort of tangible demonstration that this fear [that Christianity is incompatible with the new, emerging understanding of the world] is unfounded, since the most traditional Christianity, expressed in Baptism, the Cross and the Eucharist, can be translated so as to embrace all that is best in the aspirations peculiar to our times.[21]

This passage could almost function as a quod erat demonstrandum for de Lubac's main thesis regarding Teilhard: whatever else his Jesuit elder might have said and done, it was all meant to be in the service of articulating a traditional Christianity. Teilhard's was a religion of the incarnation and redemptive passion and of special devotion to the Eucharist, to the sacred heart of Jesus, and to the immaculate conception of his blessed mother.[22]

Evolution's Culmination and Convergence in Christ

As is well known, Teilhard sought to give expression to Christianity within the recently widely accepted evolutionary account of the universe and of life's emergence and development. While there had certainly been precursors to this outlook, Darwin's account of natural selection provided a coherence, plausibility, and explanatory power that had hitherto been lacking in accounts of emergence. Teilhard, trained as an archaeologist, was attuned to thinking in terms of time's immensity, so it seemed only natural to him to situate his Christian faith within the context of an evolving cosmos.[23] Yet his approach to doing so was not a simple matter of combining the two. In fact, his methodology sought to keep his work in these two areas distinct. When he wrote about evolution, he did so as a scientist, without recourse to theological categories. Hence his primary work on evolution, *The Human Phenomenon*, turns to what he calls "the Christian Phenomenon" only in an epilogue, a point to which I will return below.[24] And the text de Lubac identifies as the key to Teilhard's entire thought, *The Divine Milieu*, devotes scant attention to evolutionary science because its aim was not to give a scientific account of the life's origins and development but rather to articulate a version of Christianity informed by such an account.[25]

As Teilhard saw it, the universe is expanding and complexifying, which means that the emergence of increasingly complex life, including the emergence of consciousness, is not a mere accident but rather part of the larger cosmic trend. This grants a priority to life within the universe and, beyond mere life, to personality. The evolutionary process is also the process of greater personalization: from pre-life to life to thought to what he calls "superlife," or the social nature of humanity, which is now no longer merely personal but inter-personal. Eventually, all things will converge in their point Omega, which turns out to have been functioning as a sort of final cause of the whole process.[26] Having articulated this march toward and culmination in Omega, Teilhard pivots to identify the Omega point as God, specifically the union of all things with God in and through Christ, echoing the Pauline "God will be all in all" (1 Cor. 15:28).[27]

Christian Newness: Continuity and Discontinuity

Teilhard's account of emergence, evolution, and culmination in Omega, at least as understood by de Lubac, generates a vision of history wherein genuine change and novelty occur, but do so in such a way as to preserve continuity with what has come before. This preservation and transfiguration are discernible in the purely scientific arena as life emerges from mere matter, leading Teilhard to understand it not just as matter but as pre-life. Yet biogenesis does not do away with matter but rather transforms it into new configurations. Similarly, life gives rise to spirit, to personality, to thought. There is rupture and change, yet for all its difference, the life of spirit is still life. As de Lubac notes, for Teilhard the emergence of consciousness is not the end of a process but rather the beginning of the preparations.[28] Society and cooperation transfigure the mode of life for individuals, yet those individuals are not obliterated by their cooperation.[29] The evolutionary drama is at once genetic, bestowing continuity upon the whole, and dynamic, granting novelty.[30] For all the rupture of evolutionary change, new forms can emerge only from predecessors. "While the new reality is not completely new, the old reality is none the less given an entirely new form."[31] This continuity and transformation characterizes not only evolution but also the supernatural: "And just as animal realities—hunger, love, the feeling for conflict, the hunting instinct—are still with us . . . so supernatural charity, for example, is nourished by our natural capacities for love while at the same time it transforms them." Our supernatural fulfillment transcends and reorders but is still rooted in our nature.[32]

De Lubac summarizes this dialectic of continuity and novelty well while also gesturing toward important connections with other areas of his thought:

> Created nature remains itself, it is not absorbed or annihilated, and nevertheless it is transposed into a completely different state; it is re-cast . . . —and not simply made greater, prolonged, or completed in its own order—that is what calls for the effective reality of the divine principle to which classic theology has given the name of supernatural. We may add that Christian tradition, as we know, has readily accepted the changing of water into wine at the marriage feast of Cana as a symbol both of the transition from the Old Testament to the New and of the divinization of our nature by Christ.[33]

The reference to the changing of water into wine is followed by a footnote wherein de Lubac cites his own treatment of this theme in *Medieval Exegesis*, along with a reference to "the words in the Ordinary of the Mass, before the offering of the chalice."[34] This connection between divinization and the sacrifice of Christ, particularly as represented in the Mass, will be important in our subsequent reflection.

As noted before, *The Human Phenomenon* presents itself primarily as a scientific, not a theological or metaphysical, work. Yet it concludes with a consideration of the "Christian Phenomenon," which Teilhard presents in an epilogue.[35] De Lubac discerns great significance in its status as an epilogue.[36] Had it been an appendix, this would have indicated too extrinsic a relation between the Christian and supernatural character of the universe's fulfillment and its natural development throughout history. An additional chapter, or even a conclusion, would have given insufficient regard to the novelty and discontinuity of that

Salvation as Eschatological Sacrifice   133

fulfillment. In the literary form of the epilogue, de Lubac apparently discerns a complement to his own views on the supernatural and its relation to the natural order.

The Jesus of History and the Cosmic Christ

A frequently recurring theme in de Lubac's writings on Teilhard is that of optimism. One might expect that this grand vision of spirit's victory over matter, leading to an ultimate culmination in point Omega, would view time and history as a sort of inevitable, unambiguous march of progress. And while Teilhard does indeed see history's outcome in Omega as certain, de Lubac wants us to see that this is not a trite optimism grounded in human capacities but rather the outcome of a movement from above, the movement of grace, a supernatural reality. As he puts it, "Final progress does not come automatically: but neither is there a final end that is obtained by the unaided action of man's will. The final end is divine, and however necessary and fine man's effort may be (whether individual or collective) it cannot by itself [obtain] that end. It is 'of another order.' The result of man's effort can never by itself have any positively supernatural value."[37] For this reason, though he was not consistent on the point, Teilhard distinguished between omicron and Omega, the former being the term of merely human effort and the latter being the term of radical transfiguration and transposition of the realm of human activity.[38] In the end, for Teilhard, all turns upon love, for personalization and amorization turn out to be the same movement.[39] And yet, "No one is naturally 'charitable,'" for charity is a supernatural virtue.[40]

Hence, to reach the ultimate destination, human action will need to be transfigured, purified, and transformed.[41] At the same time, we should recognize that according to de Lubac, Teilhard's was not an activist project at all. *The Divine Milieu* presents a vision whereby in all aspects of life we are summoned to union with Christ and, through this union, to deification. Human activity can be carried out and perfected in communion with Christ.[42] More tellingly, our passivities and diminishments are capable of deifying union.[43] Teilhard placed a greater emphasis upon humanity's passivity, of which he considered death to be the great sign— and not just any death, but death as transfigured by Christ.[44]

Within an evolving cosmos, this attention to death is of particular importance. Recognizing the long history of the universe and the rise and fall of species through natural selection and periodic mass extinctions, all before we get to the emergence of humanity and, with it, the possibility of sin and a fall, brings death to the forefront of our considerations in a new way. Traditionally, theology has seen death as a result of human fallenness. Now we recognize that it antedates humanity by millennia and is, in many ways, the matrix of life's development. Neither Teilhard nor de Lubac presents us with a fully coherent synthesis regarding the theological understanding of death within an evolutionary view of the world. However, by (1) recognizing the mystery of Christ as the pinnacle and axis of history, which gathers up and recapitulates all that has come before, and (2) recognizing death as a locus of encounter with him, they certainly gesture in a direction in which such a synthesis could develop. More germane to our purposes, they gesture toward a framework within which we might discern the centrality of Christ's sacrifice upon the cross for the whole of cosmic history, a point to which we shall turn as we conclude.

For Teilhard, the process of evolution leads to and culminates in Christ. Cosmogenesis is ordered to biogenesis, which is ordered to noogenesis, which makes possible Christogenesis, which ultimately makes possible the universal convergence in the Omega Point, which is the union of all things in Christ, the cosmic Christ.[45] Littered with neologisms as this system is, in its basic affirmations it is the same as the vision articulated within de Lubac's theologies of nature and grace and of spiritual exegesis. As de Lubac demonstrates, Teilhard's cosmic Christ is essentially the mystical body, or *totus Christus*, the contours of which we traced in chapters 4 through 6.[46] Teilhard's articulation of this theme adds three key factors to our consideration: it widens the scope to encompass the entirety of creation, it provides an account of eschatological differentiation, and, crucially, it centers the entire vision upon the redemptive action of the cross.

The Jesus of History

Though its distinctive idiom may give the impression that Teilhard's vision of the cosmic Christ is somewhat outré or untethered from traditional conceptions of Christology, this is not the case. Teilhard is resolute that only the historical Jesus, who was born of the Virgin Mary, lived and ministered in Judea, was crucified under Pontius Pilate, and rose again on the third day before ascending to his Father's right hand, is of any value. There is no difference between the historically incarnate Jesus and the Omega's cosmic Christ.[47] This presents us with an important formal parallel with the theology of spiritual exegesis and a crucial ingredient to de Lubac's theology of history. Recall that most basically there are two senses of Scripture: the letter and the spirit, or history and allegory, with the advent of Christ transforming the former into the latter.

This rupture and transfiguration itself represents the discontinuity that is the Christian newness. Apart from Christ's coming, the Hebrew Bible would and could never have referred to him, but by his act it now does and we realize has, in fact, always done so. Apart from the actual gift of grace, humanity would never attain to our supernatural end (our orientation to which is itself gratuitous), but by the coming of Christ, we can and do. Similarly, the drawing on of history towards its culmination in Omega is the result of a definitive movement from above and could never be arrived at by the efforts of immanent forces, no matter how highly evolved, and yet the pleroma is the fullness and completion of the long history of the cosmos and of humanity.

Moreover, though, the allegorical sense of Scripture expands into the further senses of tropology, by which the mystery of Christ is interiorized and reproduced within the Christian, and anagogy, by which it culminates in the eschatological dénouement. Yet, crucially, neither tropology nor anagogy introduces any additional content to the spiritual sense: all is already given in Christ. It is precisely his mystery that is reproduced in us and consummated at the end of all things. And Teilhard's pleromatic Omega is none other than the incarnate Christ of history and our union with him. The import of this parallel extends further, though. Teilhard sees a twofold development: the emergence of humanity represents a "victory of Spirit over matter," which leads to "a second victory, involved in and conditional upon the first . . . the victory of the risen Christ, whose Pleroma will one day be accomplished."[48] Throughout, the principles of the Christian newness and of the identity of allegory and anagogy characterize the exposition. None of the preparations for Christ—whether in evolutionary history or the history of Israel— brought about the incarnation, and similarly, none of our preparations or development will bring about the Parousia.[49]

136   *Salvation Consummated*

This brings us to the crucial point: all things find their term in Christ. The ultimate universal convergence of the Omega, which is none other than the recapitulation and union of all things in Christ, is the end toward which history is tending; it is the purpose and the meaning of history and the universe itself. And this meaning is introduced in the middle of history with Christ's incarnation, death, and resurrection.[50] The time between Christ's advents is the outworking of that meaning on the way to its consummation, but the meaning of all is that act whereby the meaning of history has been introduced. As we saw in previous chapters, de Lubac places a special emphasis upon the cross in this connection. If anything, Teilhard makes this connection even more forcefully, which in turn will allow us to gather together some of the threads that we have observed throughout this study of de Lubac in the coda, but first we must introduce one further bridge concept.

A Eucharistic Bridge

Christ's sacrifice transfigures humanity, our experience of death, and, through us, the cosmos as a whole. Christ's cross is the axis of the universe's ultimate convergence. It is precisely in his sacrificial act, expressed and represented in the Eucharist, that Christ gathers all things to himself, taking on the cosmic dimensions of the pleroma.

De Lubac identifies the Eucharist as central to Teilhard's devotion to Jesus, providing an integrative principle to the elder Jesuit's spiritual life as a whole and giving expression to the continuity Teilhard saw between the historical Jesus, the evolutive Christ, and the cosmic point Omega.[51] Teilhard's extensions of the Eucharist are well known and perhaps most famously expressed in his *La messe sur le monde*, which grew out of a period in which he had been unable to celebrate the Mass and had been compensated by a modification of a spiritual communion. In an act of spiritual communion, one who is incapable of receiving the Eucharist sacramentally, through an act of interior devotion, expresses a desire for communion with Christ and, in so doing, experiences a real communion with the Lord in spirit. In the Mass upon the world, Teilhard, lacking an altar or the proper elements, makes the world his altar and offers to God, in an expanding movement, the whole of human history with its travails and suffering and, ultimately, the entirety of the cosmos, praying that they should be transformed into Christ's body and blood just as really as are the eucharistic species.[52] As de Lubac explains, "In the Eucharist, which is the central mystery, Père Teilhard contemplates both the extension of the Incarnation of the Word and the promise of the world's transfiguration."[53]

Crucially, though, Teilhard's notion of eucharistic extension is not simply a matter of "transubstantiating" the universe. Teilhard recognizes that the reality of transubstantiation does not apply to the world as transfigured by Christ in the same way that it does to the sacramental species.[54] Yes, the world is transfigured by and incorporated into Christ, but the eucharistic consecration results in what had formerly been bread or wine now being bread and wine no longer, but rather Christ's body and blood. This does not occur with the extensions of the Eucharist. More importantly, though, the Mass upon the world unfolds in a distinctly sacrificial modality.

It is sacrificial, first of all, in a nearly tautologous—and, yet, foundational—sense: the Mass is a true sacrifice, offered for the living and the dead.[55] And indeed, Teilhard's language in *La messe sur le monde* is distinctly that of offering and calling upon the fires of heaven to descend upon the offering. Teilhard consistently refers to the Host, and while in much contemporary parlance *Host* tends to be merely a synonym for *wafer*, one gets the sense that Teilhard really means it: the Host is the sacrificial victim. Indeed, the very form leads us to a sacrificial understanding: Teilhard does not offer ruminations on a spiritual communion—though there is a moment of communion in the dénouement—but rather on a spiritual *Mass*, that is to say, the sacrificial act itself. This proves to be rather decisive, for it is precisely by the cross that Christ has effected the transformation of the world about which Teilhard speaks.[56] This becomes all the more striking when we consider that Teilhard's vision also turned upon the axes of personalization and love, the latter of which has long been identified as the substance of Christ's redemptive act. The same charity that burned in Christ's heart upon the cross is kindled in our own hearts so that, through Christ, we might become partakers of God's life.

This, then, is an account of sacrifice that can encompass the reality of violence and death but does not require, underwrite, or further them.

What is essential to sacrifice is charity, even if in its actualization, in the actual world order, it has turned out to be, in the words of the *Petite catéchèse*, "A darksome drama . . . a bloody drama, the climax of which is Calvary."[57] Christ's sacrifice did indeed involve his passion, but it was not the suffering that made it a sacrifice but rather his love. In a world so often torn by bloodshed, war, and the like, in a world in which life has emerged from death in the eons-long process of natural selection, we can recognize this as Christ coming to embrace the human condition not in order to endorse it, but to redeem it. But that last moment, redemption, is crucial, for the darksome drama has a "luminous conclusion,"[58] our deification. It is a matter of elevating transformation rather than destruction.

Teilhard is unmistakably sacrificial in his understanding of how deification will occur. Writing to Auguste Valensin about areas of agreement and disagreement with Maurice Blondel, he writes:

> I agree first of all, without difficulty, that the universal Effort of the World can be understood as *the preparation of a holocaust*. By its spiritual acquisitions (in which are summed up all the others), the World develops essentially a capacity, a power of adoration, that is, of renunciation. The final use of individual and collective consciences that it elaborates—the supreme act in view of which it nourishes them, refines them, and frees them, is their voluntary return to God, and the sacrifice of their apparent (or immediate) autonomy. . . . All our work, finally, results in forming the host upon which the divine fire must descend.[59]

Beyond this, though, the question becomes whether the divine fire that descends upon the sacrifice is a "fire that devours" or a "fire that transfigures," a bifurcation that Blondel had used to contrast his and Teilhard's positions. Teilhard suggests, though, that at base, the two "amount to the same thing."[60] In the case of a devouring fire, whatever destruction it might entail, it does not utterly annihilate us but leaves at least something of us intact, which means:

> In my act of deciding to give myself over to God, all of me passes into the supernatural. . . . If . . . it is fire that is to recast me, then it is also quite true to say that this fire will consume me and spell my

Salvation as Eschatological Sacrifice   139

death. In speaking of its flames, one must say that they devour in order to emphasize the unimaginable grandeur of their work of recasting. But one should also add that they preserve us too, to make this point—as our natures undergo sublimation we retain all the elements our human liberty has amassed, the large and the small alike. For Grace, consuming and transfiguring are one and the same process.[61]

Lengthy though they may be, and their provenance from a pen other than de Lubac's notwithstanding, these quotes are well worth our attention, for they open to us a vista from which we can survey de Lubac's work as a whole and discern their motive force. After all, it was de Lubac who curated and compiled *these* particular exchanges from his mentors and friends. Moreover, the vision articulated here is deeply consonant with the emphases we have witnessed in de Lubac's own works. Indeed, as I noted above, this image of a cosmic and eschatological sacrifice provides us with a means by which we are able to draw together a number of themes that have emerged over the course of this study and present them in a more synthetic fashion, which is the task of the following coda.

Coda

Mysterium Crucis

The previous chapter ended with the notion, drawn from Teilhard de Chardin, that the outcome of history will be a cosmic oblation, and that history itself comprises a preparation of the sacrificial host. This is a viewpoint that de Lubac also discerned in Origen's work, writing in *History and Spirit*, "Now the divine Logos, uncreated Image of the Father, 'assumes' miserable flesh in order to purify it and to ignite the universe in the fire of his spiritual holocaust."[1] When set within the context of de Lubac's understanding of Christian mysticism, this trope allows us to synthesize the scattered references to sacrifice that we have noted throughout the Lubacian corpus. Mysticism, as we have seen, reproduces in the believer the Christian mystery, which is a saving mystery concentrated in the mystery of the cross, through which Christ takes our humanity into himself through death and into eternal life in God the Trinity. Recognizing this allows us to account for the several references to a sacrificial substance of or outcome to the Christian life, as well as the way in which salvation stands as the pivotal content of the diverse areas of de Lubac's work.

Recently Bertrand Dumas has demonstrated the way in which de Lubac's account of mysticism informs the whole of his work. As we saw in chapter 3, through a diachronic investigation Dumas demonstrates a developing position on the relation between mysticism (*mystique*) and theology (*théologie*) for de Lubac. They go from being more or less interchangeable to a relationship wherein theology is subordinated to mysticism until, in de Lubac's mature position, theology is included within mysticism without any subordination or opposition between the two.[2] The proper end of and mode for theology, then, is mysticism, meaning that proper theological reflection will aim for and support a properly Christian mysticism.

Coda   141

With this thesis, Dumas does little more than verify what de Lubac himself said when he wrote, "I truly believe that for a rather long time the idea for my book on Mysticism has been my inspiration in everything; I form my judgments on the basis of it, it provides me with the means to classify my ideas in proportion to it." While de Lubac never wrote his book on mysticism, judging it to be "in all ways beyond my physical, intellectual, spiritual strength," and finding himself unable to move beyond what he judged to be merely "preliminary, banalities, peripheral discussions, or scholarly details," it is fair to see in his notion of mysticism a guiding principle for interpreting his work, because he himself did the same.[3]

Since the book on mysticism was never written, our best insight into the mystical vision animating de Lubac's work comes from his 1965 article "Mystique et Mystère."[4] In this article de Lubac delineates what he considers to be the features of Christian mysticism, which he contrasts to the various natural mysticisms that also exist. Mysticism aspires to—and, in some measure, also attains—a true union with God. Hence, "for the Christian, it can only mean the union with the tripersonal God of Christian revelation, a union realized in Jesus Christ and through his grace."[5] While other religions have their own mysticisms and spirituality, not all religions are mystical, nor are all mysticisms religious.[6] And while people besides Catholic Christians have mystical experiences, de Lubac insists: "If mystical life at its summit consists of an actual union with the Divinity, such a union could be possible only through a supernatural grace whose normal setting is the Church and whose normal conditions are the life of faith and the sacraments."[7] A properly Catholic mysticism is one that interiorizes the life of Jesus, and thus springs from the same fount as Christianity itself.[8] It springs, then, from Christ and his redemptive act. In contrast with other types of mysticism, then, a truly Christian mysticism will be marked by a certain passivity; it receives more than it strives, dependent always upon a grace freely given, and its reality lies not in itself, but in the objectively given mystery of God and his saving act in Christ.[9]

Mysticism interiorizes this mystery and exists in a certain reciprocity with the mystery. On the one hand, the mystery must be received and interiorized; else it remains external to us and bears no fruit. An extrinsicist account of the mystery misses the entire point of the incarnation and redemption, for Christ came to unite us to himself and in so doing to actually accomplish redemption. Unless his saving act comes to its term in us, it might be a nice story, and it might even be true enough, but it will not have been a saving act. On the other hand, apart from this mystery and its reception, mysticism lacks all substance and reality.[10]

Thus far, in the notion that mysticism consists in interiorizing the Christian mystery we have the pith of de Lubac's thought on the matter. Before proceeding, though, it is helpful to take note of several characteristics that de Lubac understands to mark Christian mysticism, which we have noted in passing throughout this study. The first such characteristic is that "it is a mysticism of 'likeness,'" referring to the typical distinction in theological anthropology between image and likeness. Humanity is created in the image of God, and summoned to be conformed to God's likeness. It is this focus upon likeness that ensures that Christian mysticism depends upon "the gracious intervention of God in giving the mystery."[11] This, then, reproduces the basic structure of de Lubac's position on the supernatural: oriented toward a union with God by virtue of our supernatural vocation, yet utterly dependent upon God's gracious gift to realize it.[12] Moreover, it introduces a telos into the Christian life, a telos that will never be completed in this life, so "it contains an element of eschatological hope."[13]

Second, because the mystery interiorized by the mystic is revealed in Scripture, it follows that "Christian mysticism is essentially an understanding of the holy Books. The mystery is their meaning; mysticism is getting to know that meaning."[14] Dumas notes that, as de Lubac's thought developed, he placed an increasing emphasis upon Scripture and the "intelligence spirituelle" as the concrete form of mysticism, with spiritual exegesis as the locus in which this spiritual understanding occurred.[15] This thesis has been extended by Alek Zwitter, who moves its considerations into a more eschatological register.[16] Hence, for an adequate understanding of mysticism and its centrality, we shall need to return to a consideration of spiritual exegesis. Dumas's thesis represents, then, both a verification and a refinement of Susan Wood's contention that the unity of de Lubac's thought is found in his "immersion in the patristic and medieval practice of spiritual exegesis."[17] The unity of de Lubac's thought is found in spiritual exegesis because spiritual exegesis is the privileged locus for articulating the meaning of mysticism, which was the driving force undergirding his work and within which theology is properly situated.

Following from its scriptural character, Christian mysticism will be ecclesial, because it is in the church that the fruit of the mystery is realized.[18] Finally, because the redemptive incarnation is the act, revelation, and gift of the Holy Trinity, Christian mysticism will be trinitarian.[19] De Lubac notes that these characteristics actually "define all Christian reality," leading him to conclude that "what the Catholic Church calls mysticism is only the conscious actualization of the gift of God."[20] In this way de Lubac outlines the basic contours of his corpus and indicates that the same reality, the mystery of Christ, especially its fruition in the lives of the faithful, pervades the whole. We are now in a position to consider how it all fits together.

God is love, not a generic affection or positive regard. The Holy Trinity, the source of all things, is an infinitely generous exchange of self-gift. Having created us in his image, God also ordains us to be assimilated to his likeness. This, our supernatural vocation, culminates in love—once more not a generic affectivity, but love as union with God, a specifically trinitarian and gift-oriented union. De Lubac characterizes this as our coming to share in the Son's filiation, as sharing through him in the trinitarian exchanges, and as giving an unreserved gift in the sacrifice of praise.[21] These three designations name the same reality. Our sharing in Christ is a sharing in his sacrifice and a participation in the trinitarian life, particularly construed as gift exchange. This is hardly novel; de Lubac here is simply attentive to the theological tradition, especially, though not exclusively, in its Augustinian stream, which identified true sacrifice with charity.[22] Christ's saving sacrifice consists in the love that informed the act. Our own participation in that sacrifice likewise consists in love. Rather similar statements can be found in Thomas Aquinas, who received and refined the Augustinian position.[23]

Salvation is necessarily social, for humanity is social, and Christ came not to save isolated individuals, but rather to gather into one body the scattered children of God. In *Catholicisme* de Lubac casts this relationship as a *concorporatio*, by which humans come to really share in Christ's body, in which they are borne through Christ's on Calvary to his resurrection on Easter.[24] Marc Pelchat and Étienne Guibert in particular have developed the paschal and trinitarian dimensions of this concorporation into Christ's body. Our entry into Christ's body is indeed an entry into the exchanges of the Trinity's life,[25] and we pass into it through the pasch of Christ's death and resurrection, the *mysterium crucis*.[26]

The church is the sacrament of this salvation, displaying and playing an instrumental role in God's mission of reuniting the members of the human family with one another and with himself. In a manner of speaking, the church also *is* this salvation, for it shares an identity with the mystical body of Christ in which salvation consists.[27] The mystical body is bound together by charity, in which consists the supernatural order; and charity is the created echo of the uncreated life of God.[28] It is no coincidence, then, that at the heart of the church is the Eucharist. In the sacrament of the body of Christ, the church is formed as the body of Christ, further assimilated to its head. The Eucharist occurs on a historically differentiated terrain. It memorializes Christ's one sacrifice, making it present here and now in the life of the church while also anticipating the eschatological completion of that same sacrifice. The sacrificial dimension is essential to de Lubac's understanding, for it is by the sacrifice of Calvary that Christ gathers humanity into one body. It is by coming to share in the charity in which that sacrifice consists that the church is bound together as one body. And the sacrifice of the Mass turns out to be a preparation for the primary work of sacrifice to which the church is called, a calling that unfolds both proximately within history and ultimately in the eschaton. The church attains its ultimate destiny when, united as Christ's mystical body, it is offered as a great sacrifice of praise. Within the church and by the Eucharist, Christians internalize and are assimilated to Christ's saving act.[29]

De Lubac's understanding of an authentic Christian humanism is a corollary of this ecclesial vision. A true humanism respects the supernatural vocation of humanity, recognizing that we attain our noblest aspirations only in union with one another and with God, and so will be grounded in charity. Salvation, because it is social, realizes itself in such an authentic humanism.[30] Here the sacramentality of the church is on display. The meaning of the church is to be the charitable union of humanity with one another and with God in one body. This union is realized in the church, but it is not limited to or enclosed by the church. The same love that gathered and binds together the church is at work in the world, for Christ assumed not ecclesiality but humanity, and the church is the sign of what God intends for the whole of humanity. That toward which authentic humanism tends is an anticipation of the gift that is fully realized within the church.

Such assimilation into Christ and his mystery is also disclosed by and realized through the contemplation of Scripture, and is so in a way intrinsically connected to its realization in the church and the Eucharist. In his study of Origen, de Lubac identified three "incorporations of the Logos:" in Scripture, in the church, and in the Eucharist. Scripture, as the Word of God, testifies to and reveals the Word who was with God in the beginning and is himself God.[31] In fulfilling the letter by the Spirit, Christ at once clothes himself with the Scriptures and fills them with himself so that, in contemplating Scripture, we contemplate and are drawn into Christ himself. This being drawn into Christ is the meaning of the spiritual interpretation of Scripture and is also the meaning of mysticism. Moreover, it is Christ's saving sacrifice in particular that bestows upon the Scriptures their spiritual meaning, and in which this meaning consists. That which we contemplate and into which we are drawn is the saving mystery, the *mysterium crucis*.[32]

Our being drawn into the mystery is necessarily ecclesial, both for the reasons we elucidated above and also because the spiritual meaning of Scripture is the mystery of Christ and his church.[33] Redemption occurred in order for us to be united to Christ as his body. The church is, then, part of the intelligibility of the spiritual sense. Surveying this logic in Origen, de Lubac notes:

> Scripture, Church, Eucharist: if he did not always succeed in elucidating perfectly the relation of these three terms, Origen at least saw that they were related. Situating himself at the center of the faith, he made an effort to understand them by means of each other. It would be, not to criticize him, but to betray him to separate his assertions in their regard. . . . Origenian doctrine wishes to establish an organic relation between these three "bodies" of Christ that can be called his individual body [Eucharist], his social body [church], and his intelligible body [Scripture]. In this doctrine, Scripture plays a privileged role, because it is itself Logos. . . . However, let us notice that it is only in the Church, through the effect of the Church's preaching, that this Scripture ceases to be a simple mass of letters in order to become a living language. As to this spiritual manducation of the Word, the effect of meditation on Scripture and of the sacrament received in the Church, it is itself, in the end, in its reality, only

still symbolic in relation to what it will become in the other life, or rather, what the other life will be.[34]

What we have here is an articulation of the *nexus mysteriorum* that goes beyond merely considering the interconnection of the mysteries to provide an account of how and why it is that the nexus between them exists. They are all informed by the same content, the mystery of redemption by the triune God through the incarnate Christ. The Christological concentration of the mysteries leads to a coherent account of their relation to one another. As Dumas clarifies, de Lubac "distinguishes Mystery and myster(ies)—without great rigor in his use of capitalization—to signify the Mystery of God or to designate one of the mysteries of the faith. The Mystery is always Mystery-for-us. Strictly speaking, it is Christ, in the Holy Spirit; in a derivative way, mystery is all that is intimately related to the divine plan."[35] In other words, the mysteries are interconnected because they are all linked with the one great mystery: the mystery of redemption in Christ and his cross.

The passage from the Old Testament to the New is accomplished through the new Passover of the paschal mystery, to which Scripture testifies and that is enacted in the eucharistic sacrament, which lies at the heart of the church's existence, distilling the theological meaning of the church's identity as the body of Christ.[36] It is this that is attested to in Scripture's spiritual meaning and into which one is drawn through spiritual exegesis. As we saw, de Lubac's theological epistemology turned not upon factual data about God—not that this was entirely absent—but rather upon contemplation of the mystery, by which one was drawn into the very life of God. This is, at once, the meaning of mysticism and of spiritual exegesis.[37]

Crucial to de Lubac's account of Christian mysticism is the relationship between mysticism and mystery. This relationship is expressed in the relationship between allegory and the other spiritual senses of Scripture. Recall that, most fundamentally, the mystery of Christ is disclosed in the allegorical sense and, further, that the transition from letter to spirit represented a leap of sorts across the caesura of Christian novelty. The mystery of Christ is not more of the same, nor is the spiritual sense simply an extension of the literal sense. Yet it is the definitive content and meaning of Sacred Scripture. The tropological sense, we might say, *is* more of the same, insofar as it does not add any further content or meaning to Scripture. Its content is Christ and his paschal mystery. In bringing himself, Christ has brought all newness, and so, while the Christian novelty also characterizes tropology, this novelty is not in addition to allegory but rather unfolds within it.[38]

This unfolding within allegory is precisely an unfolding of the mystery, especially its unfolding in the lives of the faithful. While there is a certain analogy between history's relation to allegory and allegory's relation to tropology and anagogy, since in both cases the former is the foundation of the latter, de Lubac insists on an abyssal difference between them. Allegory is "no longer simply the letter of a text, this fact is not a simple history, it is indeed a sign, but an efficacious sign. It is no longer solely mystery: it is, in its principle, the entire mystery. Tropology will describe only the fruit, anagogy will evoke only the consummation . . . in reality what the investigation of these two brings adds nothing to the mystery of Christ; it does not bring us outside or beyond it: it only manifests its fecundity."[39] Note once more de Lubac's use of the sacramental category of an effective sign to describe the relation between the spiritual senses of Scripture, displaying once more the connection between the various incorporations of the Logos and the sacramental character of de Lubac's theology of history.

The fecundity of the Christian mystery is not simply efficacious, but also assimilative. The mystery of Christ does not simply bring about the life of the church, or of the individual Christian, or of the eschatological kingdom. Rather, "these are entirely constituted by the assumption of humanity into the interior of the mystery of Christ,"[40] precisely the meaning of Christian mysticism. Crucially, this interiority to the Christian mystery is possible "in virtue of the cross of Christ,"[41] and can be ultimately "reduced to a single word: charity."[42] Hence, our interiority to the mystery and its interiority to us shares an identity with the mystery itself. Precisely the same content is unfolded within our own lives as unfolded at Calvary and as eternally unfolds within the Trinity: love. Recall also that for Augustine, whom de Lubac follows, the interior reality of true sacrifice is love.

History moves toward its consummation, a consummation we have seen that de Lubac, following both Origen and Teilhard, construes in sacrificial terms. A consideration of how his eschatology relates to both history and mysticism clarifies precisely why it is that the end is sacrificial. Once more, it is within the framework of the spiritual senses of Scripture that de Lubac's logic is most clearly ascertained. Turning to the anagogical or eschatological sense of Scripture, de Lubac notes that there are really two anagogies that correspond to different ways of ordering the scriptural senses. One is doctrinal and fulfills the fourfold list of history, allegory, tropology, and anagogy. The other is mystical and fulfills the threefold list of history, tropology, and anagogy. Of these, "the one [doctrinal anagogy] is defined by its object, and the other [mystical anagogy] by the manner of apprehending it."[43] As Alek Zwitter explains, "The first is speculative, the second contemplative," and both are rooted in the Christian mystery.[44] If we follow Dumas in seeing *théologie* as included in *mystique*, the picture becomes even more coherent. As he writes, "One could say that we are finally in the presence of a double inclusion: of theology in mysticism, and finally of the two in the Mystery."[45]

In this way, de Lubac states: "Anagogy realizes the perfection both of allegory and of tropology, achieving their synthesis. It is neither 'objective,' like the first, nor 'subjective,' like the second. Above and beyond this division, it realizes their unity. It integrates the whole and final meaning. It sees, in eternity, the fusion of the mystery and the mystic."[46] Anagogy represents the culmination of both history and mysticism. As Zwitter explains, the mystical anagogy roughly corresponds to the category of realized eschatology, a term de Lubac did not utilize, and highlights the continuity between the present and the eschatological states, for it is the completion of the process of interiorization already begun in us here and now. On the other hand, doctrinal anagogy corresponds more to future eschatology and underlines the rupture between present and future, the great transfiguration that all things must undergo in order to reach their fulfillment in Christ.[47]

Yet whatever transformations it may involve, this fulfillment is not other than what has already been bestowed in the mystery of Christ (in the allegorical sense). We may see his mystery's perfection, but we never move beyond it, never find any additional meaning. True to the relation among the spiritual senses, the culmination of each shares an identity of meaning, for that which is culminated is, in both cases, the same reality: the mystery of Christ. Insofar as anagogy perfects mysticism, it is the fulfillment of what is begun here and now in the Christian life—

interiority to Christ's paschal mystery and, through it, interiority to the Trinity's life. Insofar as anagogy perfects history itself, it is as the fruition of that same mystery. Though there remains a greater fulfillment, there is no "third Testament." Instead, "the mystery of Christ, given one time, was given in its entirety. The anagogical sense can only be glimpsed, but the reality that it glimpses is already there."[48]

Hence, those instances in which de Lubac speaks of the end in sacrificial terms must be understood not generically, as if the eschatological oblation were unrelated or only extrinsically related to the central mystery, but specifically, as the fulfillment of Christ's sacrifice, for there is no other meaning they could bear that does not betray de Lubac's fundamental commitments. Even though he does not make this connection explicit, the entire momentum of his thought leads ineluctably to this synthesis, for the meaning of all has been definitively given in Christ. In bringing himself, he has brought all newness, and no other sacrifice could possibly suffice.

This is the mystery that lies at the heart of the world's history and gives meaning to it. This is the mystery that lies at the heart of the church's existence and gives meaning to it, that lies at the heart of the church's Eucharist and is continually represented in it. This is the mystery that lies at the heart of Christian Scripture, the contemplation of which draws us into the mystery itself. This is the mystery that lies at the heart of the Christian life, which turns out to be an ongoing conversion to and interiorization of the mystery itself. This is the mystery that informs an authentic humanism, which is attainable only through charity, the same reality that informed the redemptive sacrifice and informs our participation in the supernatural order, which is itself the life of God. We are made fully personal by sharing in the Son and, through him, in the infinitely generous exchange that is God the Trinity.[49] This is the mystery the contemplation of which is the goal of our theological investigations, for to know God is to be drawn into his life, and it is in the mystery of Christ and his redemption that God has been fully revealed. And this is the mystery into which all things shall finally be drawn as they reach their consummation, for having given himself in the Son, God has given all that could possibly be given, and history's fulfillment cannot advance beyond or be other than what has been given in Christ.

Conclusion

From the previous eight chapters and their coda, a fairly consistent profile of the Lubacian corpus has emerged. For all of his various concerns and interlocutors, Henri de Lubac's vision was dominated by a vision of Christ and his gathering of all things to himself. The act by which he gathers us is the Christian mystery—his incarnation, death, resurrection, and gift of the Holy Spirit—which act constitutes the meaning of history and the content of Scripture, the substance of salvation, the destiny of humanity, and the essence of the church and its sacraments. Our coming to share in that mystery is the essential meaning of mysticism, which consists in a passing into that mystery. Theology was properly located *within* mysticism for de Lubac. Hence, his entire theological vision was in service of articulating the way in which we come to share in the mystery of salvation.

We can construe this in more or less accurate ways. It would be a distortion of de Lubac's intent to suggest that, in any given context, what he was *really* concerned about was salvation and not, say, spiritual exegesis, ecclesiology, or what have you, and so lose the distinctive contours of his œuvre. Just as grace does not abolish but rather preserves nature, just as the spiritual meaning does not abrogate the literal sense, just as an eschatological perspective does not render the institutional church or its sacraments obsolete (at least within history), recognizing de Lubac's soteriological impetus does not flatten out his corpus into an undifferentiated mass. Rather, by locating theology within mysticism we preserve its integrity and that of its constituent elements, even as we recognize that they are ordered to and in service of assimilation into the Christian mystery.

This recognition allows us to account for the ways in which the disparate areas of de Lubac's thought interpenetrate and influence one another. They all intend to give expression to the same mystery, and they

150

Conclusion   151

all play out in the arena of a vision of humanity's incorporation into that mystery. At various junctures this mystery is identified as the mystery of Christ, of the church (or Christ and the church, for they are together "one great mystery"), of the paschal mystery, the mystery of the supernatural, and the mystery of the Trinity. De Lubac does not elide these realities such that they lose all distinctiveness, but neither does he separate them. I propose, then, that the framework that best allows us to articulate this relationship is the notion of the nexus of the mysteries with one another and with humanity's final end. Throughout his career, de Lubac drew upon this principle, so it is not an imposition to see it operative here, though I am proposing a refinement, a refinement that cuts both ways.

Speaking in terms of the nexus of mysteries allows us to better recognize the pluriformity of the Christian economy and to better distinguish between *theologia* and *oeconomia*, as well as between nature and grace. This is fairly essential when among the elements of the mystery are God the Trinity—who exists necessarily and would be the same God even were there no creation, and realities pertaining to us and our salvation, which are both contingent and gratuitous. De Lubac labored to keep these distinct, even as he resisted any extrinsicist account of their relation. However, if our vocabulary speaks *only* of the mystery, singular, then this distinction can be rather difficult to maintain. Recovery of the framework of Vatican I's *Dei Filius* allows us to do so.

At the same time, de Lubac's emphasis on the unity of the mystery ensures that the nexus is rather tight indeed, neither haphazard, ad hoc, nor merely notional. Each of the "mysteries" is actually a facet of a single reality whose expression defies and exceeds our capacities, categories, and frameworks. We never gain mastery, and our knowledge remains always provisional, till faith gives way to vision and we finally achieve that for which we've longed from our being's inmost depths, and toward which all of our theological efforts—indeed, all of history—have been directed: assimilation into the life of God the Trinity.

This consistent concern and impetus, then, bestows a structural consistency upon de Lubac's thought. This structure, as we have seen, following the trail pioneered by Susan Wood, is most readily grasped in the categories of spiritual exegesis, which, following Bertrand Dumas, Lubac saw as the concrete expression of the mysticism that pervaded his writings. The Christian novelty, an outcome of the act of Christ, at once preserves, transcends, and transforms that which had come before. Whether we consider the spirit's transformation of the letter, the supernatural's transformation of nature, the passage of the image of God into the likeness of God, the transformation of history into salvation history, the redirection of intellect toward contemplation by spirit, or the Teilhardian Christogenesis, the structure remains the same. The Christian novelty does not mean the end of all progress—dogma develops, history continues, the exegete continually returns to the sacred text—however, all subsequent development occurs within and never moves beyond the mystery of Christ, who, in bringing himself, has brought all newness. Tropology and anagogy unfold within allegory; the age of the Spirit is coincident with the age of Christ; the church, as Christ's body, remains itself within history and beyond; and the same charity that characterizes the life of the redeemed here and now will characterize our lives eschatologically, because God is love.

This structural feature of de Lubac's thought also provides insight into the nature of his *ressourcement* and his relation to the two Vatican Councils. De Lubac is typically, and rightly, associated with Vatican II, which is, often enough, framed in contrast with Vatican I. It is also no secret that de Lubac remained troubled by what he called the "paracouncil," which, in some quarters, is identified with the spirit of Vatican II. Para-conciliar developments took a variety of forms, but a consistent theme was the eschewal of doctrinal authority and a downgrading of the Christian novelty, which either flattened the mystery of Christ into a mere continuation of what had always been the case or sought a further "newness" beyond it. Our Lubacian structure, though, allows us to thread the needle differently. Developments never move beyond the past in such a way as to render them utterly obsolete: the letter is always preserved by the spirit. At the same time, the full meaning has already been given in the Christian mystery.

This, then, presents an argument for the hermeneutics of continuity (as opposed to the hermeneutics of rupture) while yet recognizing that Vatican II represents and was a decisive event at which real change occurred. This recognition remains, though, located within a prior commitment to the vision that *the* decisive event has already occurred in the paschal mystery of the incarnate Word. This, I would suggest, is a pos-

Conclusion   153

ture and commitment that contemporary Catholic thought—grappling, as it does, for a renewed footing and a way forward in a constantly and rapidly changing world—would do well to appropriate. Later developments neither entirely supersede their precursors nor fail to be genuine developments. The measure of and criterion for all development remains, though, the mystery that has definitively and for all time been given in Christ. The infinite riches of this mystery mean that development is not only possible, but necessary. Yet development will occur by a continual retortion to the original event. In this recursive movement of development lies the meaning of *ressourcement*.

Ressourcement, then, is neither a method nor even a sensibility, but rather the outgrowth of a conviction: that in the mystery of Christ—incarnate, crucified, and risen—a definitive and unsurpassable gift has been given, one that constitutes the meaning of the world and its history, one whose riches can never be exhausted. Scrutinizing the signs of the times and interpreting them in the gospel's light involves a continual return to that definitive and founding event with new questions, new conceptual tools, new insights, so that once more we can bring forth treasures old and new. The Scriptures, the liturgy, and the theological tradition are privileged loci for this return because they, in their varying ways, bear witness to and express this mystery and its unfolding in the life of the church. *Ressourcement* represents the conviction that the past is never simply past, never a dead letter, to be locked away and forgotten. Instead, with varying degrees of faithfulness and adequacy, it is informed and pervaded by the mystery of Christ, the font, form, and telos of all Christian life. We return to the past not to repristinate it, nor out of a misguided nostalgia, nor even from a naïve conviction that our forebears were more faithful than we, but because the past bears witness to the unique mystery, which, like refracted light, can be fruitfully approached from multiple angles. Insight into the problems we face might be found by investigating the way this mystery was expressed by those who operated according to a different framework.

This further and finally allows us to recast the place of speculative theology within de Lubac's thought. On the one hand, speculative theology is typically associated with scholasticism, of which de Lubac was certainly not an exemplar, though I contend it would be inaccurate to understand him as *anti*-scholastic. On the other hand, an undeniable speculative vision has emerged over the course of this study, one that follows from the location of *théologie* within *mystique* and turns upon the incorporation of humanity into the life of the Trinity by the paschal mystery, interior to the incarnate Son. This incorporation is first given as a gift, and it takes the form in us of our assimilation into that same gift as we come to share in the life of the God who is himself pure gift: a living sacrifice that flows from and shares an identity with the one sacrifice of Jesus Christ upon the cross, upon the altar, in the hearts of the faithful, as the substance of the church, and as the ultimate destiny in which history will be consummated.

This speculative vision is never given systematic articulation, and de Lubac would probably be resistant to such systematization. To do so would be to misconstrue the nature of theology, failing to recognize its interiority to mysticism. It would be to prioritize the intellect, when instead it should be the more fundamental élan of the spirit that is kept in view. The speculative vision operative in de Lubac's theology is not principally in the service of gaining a more adequate understanding, though, again, it is not opposed to this. Rather, it is in the service of fostering interiorization of and assimilation to the mystery. We might, then, call it a contemplative-speculative theology, recognizing that it consists in and aims for the contemplation of God, beholding the mystery and refusing to reduce it to our proportions, not even for the sake of resolving logical aporiae.

In this way, though, it becomes apparent that de Lubac's theology is animated by the spirit of Vatican I.[1] It recognizes and respects the limitations of the human intellect in the face of the infinite mystery of God. A fruitful understanding of the mysteries is indeed possible, but this understanding will never be equivalent to the knowledge of objects that fall within the purview capacities of the natural intellect. De Lubac's contemplative-speculative theology invites us to consider of what the fruitfulness of our understanding of the mysteries would consist: of neither the satisfaction of intellectual curiosity nor full logical consistency,[2] but of our coming to share in the mystery whose meaning we interrogate and contemplate. Moreover, the form of this speculation takes the form of a consideration of the nexus of mysteries also commended by *Dei Filius*: the doctrines of the Trinity, of Christ, of humanity, of the church, and of the sacraments are all bound together in a synthetic vision that considers their relation to one another and to humanity's final end.

While the spirit of Vatican I undeniably animates de Lubac's theology, it is also clear that the *form* of his thought more closely resembles its sequel, though, of course, most of his major works antedate it. In line with Vatican I's theological affirmations as he was, de Lubac's writing breaks free from its propositionally focused and schematic character and so anticipates and comes to inform the narratival and essayistic documents of the Second Vatican Council, themselves replete with references to Scripture, the liturgy, and the church fathers.

De Lubac's speculative-contemplative theology at once affirms the renewal of Vatican II and insists that all true renewal will occur through continual recourse to the mystery of faith, delivered once and for all in Jesus Christ. That it is *speculative* insists that it remain tethered to and reason from its first principle: the mystery of Christ. The need for a speculative theology, beyond just positive theology, flows from the inexhaustible fecundity of the mystery of faith. It is not enough to articulate it, nor to uncover its historical origins or the ways it has been expressed in the past. One must continually advance in one's understanding of the mystery. That it is *contemplative* insists that it aims toward our deeper incorporation and assimilation into that mystery. Vital as intellectual understanding or social praxis and action may be, the goal is our coming to share in the reality itself.

Salvation is achieved by humanity's passage through Christ into the life of the Trinity. We share in the triune life by sharing in Christ's identity as members of his body. We come to share in the divine life through charity, which is God's very nature and, within God, takes the form of an infinitely generous gift. We are brought into salvation by Christ's sacrifice on the cross, which has charity as its inmost content. This charity informs the life of Christ's body, the church, and the life of his individual members. His saving sacrifice is the fulcrum and the meaning of history, and history's fulfillment will likewise be this same sacrifice, as the body of Christ is offered, in union with its head, to the Father as a supreme act of loving worship. This is the same sacrifice by which we were saved, and it is ultimately as this sacrifice that we are saved, entering into the loving beatitude of the Holy Trinity.

This speculative vision accounts for the organic unity of de Lubac's theology, and does so while following the commendations of Vatican I (respecting the mysteries' transcendence, pursuing their nexus) and moving into the idiom and sensibility of Vatican II, for which de Lubac paved the way and to which he helped give shape. This integrative vision presents not only a unified account of the Christian faith but also gestures toward and calls for a renewed speculative theology in the spirit of both Vatican Councils.

NOTES

Introduction

1. de Lubac, *Religion of Teilhard*, 11. "Qu'il est facile de laisser tomber, de la pensée d'un auteur, ce qui n'intéresse pas! de n'attribuer à cette part jugée inintéressante qu'une importance minime, ou même de ne pas l'apercevoir! On fausse ainsi de bonne foi la signification de toute une œuvre en en faussant les proportions, même si l'on n'en présente que des analyses exactes" (*Pensée religieuse du père Pierre Teilhard*, 11).

2. Irenaeus, *Against Heresies*, 4.34.1. See especially Hercsik, *Jesus Christus als Mitte der Theologie*; Zwitter, *Histoire en présence de l'Éternel*.

3. Balthasar, *Theology of Henri de Lubac*, 23.

4. de Lubac, *At the Service of the Church*, 143. "On cherchait en vain dans l'ensemble de publications si diverses les éléments d'une synthèse philosophique ou théologique—ou, comme certains l'ont dit, 'gnoséologique'—vraiment personnelle, que ce soit pour la critique ou pour l'adopter" (*Mémoire sur l'occasion de mes écrits*, 146–47).

5. Chantraine, *Henri de Lubac, tome I*, 53.

6. Balthasar, *Theology of Henri de Lubac*, 127.

7. The "Œuvres Complètes du Cardinal Henri de Lubac," to be published by Cerf, will encompass fifty volumes. I am including only monographs as "major works," excluding articles, edited collections, memoirs, and the like.

8. So also Hemming, "Henri de Lubac: Reading *Corpus Mysticum*," 520–21.

9. *Dei Filius*, chapter 4, "On Faith and Reason" (Tanner, 2:808). All conciliar documents are cited from the edition edited by Norman Tanner.

10. Ibid.

11. de Lubac, "Apologetics and Theology," 95. "Et le Concile du Vatican ne nous invite-t-il pas à rechercher ces liens, lorsqu'il enseigne que la méthode de la théologie consiste à étudier le rapport, non seulement des divers dogmes entre eux, mais de l'ensemble du dogme avec la fin dernière?" ("Apologétique et théologie," 101).

12. de Lubac, *Un-Marxian Socialist*, 242–43, 258–60; *Discovery of God*, 106–14, 119–40; *Christian Faith*, 261–89; "Problem of the Development of Dogma," 264–66.

13. de Lubac, "Theological Foundation of the Missions," 382; *Church: Paradox and Mystery*, 33; *At the Service of the Church*, 329; *Révélation divine*, 75; *Athéisme et sens de l'homme*, 107. De Lubac's notebooks from Vatican II mention the nexus of mysteries in connection with a series of addresses given by Gustave Martelet, which de Lubac attended and seems to have greatly appreciated. *Vatican Council Notebooks*, 1:240, 263–64, 280, 478.

14. de Lubac, "Problem of the Development of Dogma," 278. "Ce texte m'est très cher. J'avais l'occasion de le citer moi-même, dès ma première publication (*N.R.th.*, 1930, p. 366). Je m'en suis souvent inspiré depuis lors" ("Problème du développement du dogme," 69).

15. Henri de Lubac, *Splendor of the Church*, 23. "N'est pas un luxe mais une nécessité" (*Méditation sur l'église*, 16).

16. de Lubac, *Christian Faith*, 227–59. See also *Discovery of God*, 211; "Light of Christ," 216–17; "Problem of the Development of Dogma," 274–75.

17. de Lubac, *Christian Faith*, 237. "Elle [l'Église] est mesurée par l'unique Parole" (*Foi chrétienne*, 274). As we shall see in chapter 4, the unity of the Word is a major theme of de Lubac's theology of spiritual exegesis.

18. de Lubac, *Christian Faith*, 243.

19. Ibid., 243–45 (243). "On peut légitimement dénombrer des dogmes, on peut aussi dénombrer des mystères. . . . Mais si 'le Dogme' fait leur unité, comme on l'a dit par l'origine, 'le Mystère' fait leur unité intérieurement, par la substance" (*Foi chrétienne*, 282–83). See further *Révélation divine*, 71–77. On the relationship between dogma and mystery in de Lubac, see Dumas, *Mystique et théologie*, 79–85.

20. Dumas, *Mystique et théologie*, 83; de Lubac, "Apologétique et théologie," 101. "Rapport, non seulement des divers dogmes entre eux, mais de l'ensemble du dogme avec la fin dernière?"

21. See, e.g., Jean Daniélou's famous statement that "the Christian faith has only a single object, which is the mystery of Christ dead and risen. But this unique mystery subsists under different modes." "Symbolisme des rites baptismaux," 17. My translation: "La foi chrétienne n'a qu'un objet qui est le mystère du Christ mort et ressucité. Mais ce mystère unique subsiste sous des modes différents." Karl Rahner similarly argues that all of the various mysteries (plural) find their unity as expressions of the holy mystery (singular) that is God in his self-communication. "Concept of Mystery," 36–73. De Lubac approvingly quotes Rahner's essay in *Christian Faith*, 245. One might also discern it in the mystery theology of Odo Casel. E.g., *Mystery of Christian Worship*. See the discussion of the function of "mystery" in de Lubac and his contemporaries and its

Christological concentration in Wagner, *Théologie fondamentale*, 78–82, 202–14; Dumas, *Mystique et théologie*, 79–96, 235–77. As we shall see in chapter 4, de Lubac's account of spiritual exegesis is likewise preoccupied with the mystery of Christ.

22. On the transition, see Joseph Ratzinger, "Dogmatic Constitution on Divine Revelation," 170–71; de Lubac, *Révélation divine*, 163–65, 190–93, 196–97; Sauer, "The Doctrinal and the Pastoral," 198–99, 210–15; Demers, "'Nouvelles' notions de Révélation et de Foi," 19–35; Lenehan, "Unfolding in Friendship," 175–91.

23. *Dei Verbum*, nos. 2–4 (Tanner, 2:972–73). See further de Lubac, *Révélation divine*, 49–51, 59–62, 71–138; Ratzinger, "Dogmatic Constitution on Divine Revelation," 171–75. De Lubac was involved in the preparatory work for the schema on revelation, but not the final drafting of *Dei Verbum*. See Chantraine, *Henri de Lubac, tome II*, 243–81.

24. Boeve, "Revelation, Scripture and Tradition," 416–33; Gaillardetz and Clifford, *Keys to the Council*, 31–38; Lenehan, "Unfolding in Friendship," 175–91. Because of these differences, Jean-Pierre Wagner identifies *Dei Filius* with the outmoded apologetics de Lubac opposed in his inaugural lecture. *Théologie fondamentale*, 80–83. Yet, such an understanding fails to reckon with the deliberate appeal de Lubac makes to *Dei Filius* not just throughout his œuvre, but also in the very essay in which he opposes apologetics to fundamental theology.

25. On this, see Ratzinger, "Dogmatic Constitution on Divine Revelation," 164–65, 168–69, 177–80; Boeve, "Revelation, Scripture and Tradition," 420–22. See also *Dei Verbum*'s repeated citations of *Dei Filius*, which are traced in Meszaros, "Revelation in George Tyrrell, Neo-Scholasticism, and Dei Verbum," 535–68.

26. de Lubac, *Catholicism*, 20. "Au reste, ce sont là seulement, groupés en un ordre peu rigoureux, quelques matériaux, doublés de quelques réflexions" (*Catholicisme*, xiv).

27. E.g., Balthasar, *Theology of Henri de Lubac*, 35–43; O'Sullivan, *Christ and Creation*, 85–89; Hillebert, "Introducing Henri de Lubac," 11–13.

28. de Lubac, *At the Service of the Church*, 113. "C'est, je crois bien, depuis assez longtemps, l'idée de mon livre sur la Mystique qui m'inspire en tout; c'est de là que je tire mes jugements, c'est lui qui me fournit de quoi classer à mesure mes idées. Mais ce livre, je ne l'écrirai pas. Il est de toute manière au-dessus de mes forces, physiques, intellectuelles, spirituelles" (*Mémoire sur l'occasion de mes écrits*, 113).

29. Probably the most substantive English-language discussions of mysticism in de Lubac are Hollon, "Mysticism and Mystical Theology," 307–25; Hillebert, *Henri de Lubac and the Drama of Human Existence*, 169–99. In an important essay, Aidan Nichols suggests that we may indeed find the unity of

de Lubac's thought in a consideration of mysticism. "Henri de Lubac: Panorama and Proposal," 3–33. Joseph Flipper notes the importance of the theme for de Lubac and writes that this presents a genuine interpretive challenge, given the dearth of material written directly on the theme. *Between Apocalypse and Eschaton*, 305–9.

30. Cholvy, *Surnaturel incarné dans la création*; Moulins-Beaufort, *Anthropologie et mystique*; Zwitter, *Histoire en présence de l'Éternel*.

31. Dumas, *Mystique et théologie*, 235–77.

32. Milbank, *Suspended Middle*; *Theology and Social Theory*, 206–57; Boersma, *Nouvelle Théologie and Sacramental Ontology*. Similarly ontological, but not Platonic, is Hollon, *Everything Is Sacred*. A different iteration of this interpretation is Mulcahy, *Aquinas's Notion of Pure Nature*, which takes the Radical Orthodox reading of de Lubac as accurate while criticizing it.

33. Wood, *Spiritual Exegesis and the Church*. Wood's work is extended in that of her students, who have brought a greater concern for the eschatological dimension of this theology of history into their considerations. Flipper, *Between Apocalypse and Eschaton*; Schlesinger, "Threefold Body." Flipper also recognizes in the work of Brian Daley ("Nouvelle Theologie and the Patristic Revival" and "Knowing God in History and in the Church") a more historically oriented approach. *Between Apocalypse and Eschaton*, 12.

34. de Lubac, *Catholicism*, 107–32. Flipper's work has fairly decisively, I hope, put to rest the thesis that de Lubac represents a Christianized Platonism. *Between Apocalypse and Eschaton*, 100–115.

Chapter One. Saving Grace

1. This theme tends to be underdeveloped in English-language scholarship on de Lubac, with my own "Integrative Role of Sacrifice" a somewhat lonely exception. It is, though, a major theme of Guibert, *Mystère du Christ*. Guibert's emphasis on this trinitarian incorporation has influenced subsequent francophone scholarship. E.g., Cholvy, *Surnaturel incarné dans la création*; Geneste, *Humanisme et lumière du Christ*; Zwitter, *Histoire en présence de l'Éternel*.

2. On the axial significance of *Surnaturel*, see, e.g., Kerr, *Twentieth-Century Catholic Theologians*, 70–75; Milbank, *Suspended Middle*, 16–37; O'Sullivan, *Christ and Creation*, 217–47; Bonino, ed., *Surnaturel: A Controversy*; Rober, *Recognizing the Gift*, 14–22. See the rather important discussion of the historical setting of de Lubac's writings on nature and grace, including post-revolutionary France's secularism and the experience of the world wars, in Swafford, *Nature and Grace*, 28–36; Rober, *Recognizing the Gift*, 2–14.

Notes to Pages 4–5   161

3. See the succinct distillations of de Lubac's basic position on nature and grace in the form of several theses in Healy, "Christian Mystery of Nature and Grace," 181–203; Flipper, *Between Apocalypse and Eschaton*, 265–70.

4. See de Lubac's reminiscences of the entire affair, including the various thaws and relaxations that occurred before his complete reinstatement, in *At the Service of the Church*, 67–92. See also Komonchak, "Theology and Culture at Mid-Century," 579–602.

5. de Lubac, *Aspects du Bouddhisme I*, 13–164; *Amida*, 167–524.

6. de Lubac, *At the Service of the Church*, 31–32. See also Grumett, *De Lubac: A Guide*, 145; Hillebert, "Introducing Henri de Lubac," 22.

7. de Lubac, *At the Service of the Church*, 74–75.

8. Ibid., 88–89. See also Grumett, *De Lubac: A Guide*, 51.

9. Pius XII, *Humani generis*, no. 26.

10. E.g., Milbank, *Suspended Middle*, xiii (approvingly); Feingold, *Natural Desire* (disapprovingly). David Braine believes that de Lubac makes enough qualifications to avoid direct conflict with *Humani generis*. "The Debate," 574. Nicholas Healy sides with de Lubac. "Henri de Lubac on Nature and Grace," 551–52. Reinhard Hütter, while finding de Lubac's position theologically inadequate, judges him to be operating within the required doctrinal parameters. "*Desiderium naturale*," 81–183. Bernard Mulcahy recognizes some ambiguity regarding this question: the Holy See never formally disciplined de Lubac, but the encyclical's defense of scholasticism was such that any suggestion of a positive reading of it is "exaggerated." *Aquinas's Notion of Pure Nature*, 165–68 [167] (cf. de Lubac's contention in the next note). Cholvy notes de Lubac's concerted efforts to operate within the parameters set by the Church's magisterium. *Surnaturel incarné dans la création*, 371–88. See especially Jacob Wood's treatment of this question against the backdrop of de Lubac's appropriation of the little-known Aegidian tradition. According to Wood, the answer to whether or not *Humani generis* condemns de Lubac depends upon precisely which figures and their respective positions de Lubac intended to endorse in *Surnaturel*. "Henri de Lubac, Humani Generis, and the Natural Desire," 1209–41; *To Stir a Restless Heart*, 357–415.

11. de Lubac, *At the Service of the Church*, 71.

12. Ibid., 78. "Dans toute l'affaire . . . affaire qui dura tant d'années, je ne fus jamais interrogé, je n'eus jamais un seul entretien sur le fond des choses avec aucune autorité romaine de l'Église ou de la Compagnie. On ne me communiqua jamais aucun chef précis d'accusation" (*Mémoire sur l'occasion de mes écrits*, 79–80).

13. On this see especially Jacob Wood's painstaking analysis of the development of Thomas's own thought on the question (*To Stir a Restless Heart*,

162 Notes to Pages 5–6

136–356) and his summary of the question of de Lubac's exegesis of Aquinas (424–28). See also the various evaluations of Feingold, *Natural Desire*; Long, *Natura Pura*; Hütter, "*Desiderium naturale*" and "Aquinas on the Natural Desire," 523–91; Healy, "Henri de Lubac on Nature and Grace" and "Christian Mystery of Nature and Grace"; Grumett, "De Lubac, Grace, and the Pure Nature Debate," 123–46; Moloney, "De Lubac and Lonergan," 509–27; Larsen, "Politics of Desire," 279–310; S. Wood, "Nature-Grace Problematic," 389–403.

14. For de Lubac's account of "the twins," see *At the Service of the Church*, 123–31.

15. On the relationship between the original *Surnaturel* and de Lubac's *Augustinianism and Modern Theology*, see Michel Sales's preface to *Surnaturel*, especially the "Genetic Schema" of de Lubac's publications on the supernatural. *Surnaturel*, i–xvi. O'Sullivan also helpfully traces the developments between these works, especially in the area of Christology. *Christ and Creation*, 251–63.

16. See, e.g., de Lubac, *At the Service of the Church*, 123, where he claims that his *Mystery of the Supernatural* does not change "the least point of doctrine" from the 1949 article of the same name ("sans y changer le moindre point de doctrine" [*Mémoire sur l'occasion de mes écrits*, 124]) . This is in direct contrast to Milbank, who suggests a sort of career-long subterfuge on de Lubac's part (*Suspended Middle*, xiii), and to Feingold, who also senses equivocation and revisionist history in de Lubac's later works (*Natural Desire*, 306–7, 384–85). See, instead, the judgment of Swafford, *Nature and Grace*, 56–59. Jacob Wood notes three distinct stages in the development of de Lubac's thought, during which he was more dependent upon different figures from the Aegidian tradition. *To Stir a Restless Heart*, 416–20.

17. This is ably traced by O'Sullivan, *Christ and Creation*, 251–55, and "An Emerging Christology," 327–48. It is also developed at some length by Cholvy, *Surnaturel incarné dans la création*, 149–71; Geneste, *Humanisme et lumière du Christ*, 178–85.

18. de Lubac, *At the Service of the Church*, 198–99. "Enfin, la transformation, ou plutôt le retournement du désir de Dieu sous l'action de la grâce, sa métamorphose (partielle) en charité, était à peine indiquée en quelques mots dans la conclusion, mais cela eût été l'objet d'un autre ouvrage" (*Mémoire sur l'occasion de mes écrits*, 202).

19. de Lubac, *Mystery of the Supernatural*, xxxiv. "N'a-t-il considéré ni le rôle médiateur du Verbe incarné, ni l'entrée de la créature adoptée dans les relations trinitaires" (*Mystère du Surnaturel*, 14).

20. It is worth noting that this sort of bracketing of other issues to deal with one particular matter is a thoroughly scholastic approach to things, which undercuts any suggestion that de Lubac was *anti*-scholastic. In chapter 3 we shall assess de Lubac's relationship to scholasticism.

21. de Lubac, *Mystery of the Supernatural*, xxxv. "Tout ce qui vient du Christ, tout ce qui doit conduire à Lui, est si bien relégué dans l'ombre, qu'il risque d'y disparaître à jamais" (*Mystère du Surnaturel*, 15).

22. So also Guibert, *Mystère du Christ*, 124–27.

23. In this regard, de Lubac carries forward trajectories evident in Maurice Blondel (*Action*, 330–57, 422–24, 445–46) and Pierre Rousselot (*Intelligence*, 12, 30–39, 141–52). See, though, the contention of Jonathan Heaps that Blondel's methodological self-restriction to philosophy, rather than theology, means that his account of the supernatural will remain far more notional and unspecified than de Lubac's. "Ambiguity of Being," 147–53.

24. de Lubac, *Surnaturel*, 9–13; *Augustinianism and Modern Theology*, xvii–xxi. See further, e.g., O'Sullivan, *Christ and Creation*, 256–63; Grumett, "De Lubac, Grace, and the Pure Nature Debate," 125–31; Cholvy, *Surnaturel incarné dans la création*, 210–15; Swafford, *Nature and Grace*, 41–49. On Jansenism more broadly (irrespective of de Lubac's engagement with it) see, e.g., Radner, "Early Modern Jansenism," 436–50; Feingold, *Natural Desire*, 277–93.

25. Once more, I reiterate that my task here is not evaluative. In dealing with these controversial early modern theological movements, particularly with Jansenism, the picture is rather complex. It is not a foregone conclusion that Cornelius Jansen held all of the positions attributed to him, and later Jansenists tried to position themselves as within the required norms of fidelity to Catholic teaching. Additionally, this study does not presume that de Lubac was always historically accurate or fair in his analysis of Jansenism. Rather, the goal is to take note of the soteriological thrust of his engagement with it.

26. de Lubac, *Augustinianism and Modern Theology*, 1–5; *Surnaturel*, 15–16.

27. de Lubac, *Surnaturel*, 16. My translation: "Baius ne conçoit pas la charité divine qui est au principe de la vocation surnaturelle de l'homme et qui, pour ainsi dire, enveloppe toute l'économie du salut."

28. de Lubac, *Augustinianism and Modern Theology*, 37–43, 48–49. For a very helpful sifting of the controversy surrounding these two terms, see De-Meuse, "World Is Content with Words," 245–76. Feingold, *Natural Desire*, 277–83. See also Feingold's contention that Jansen sought to avoid the very scholastic distinctions that would have prevented him from lapsing into error.

29. de Lubac, *Augustinianism and Modern Theology*, 87–104.

30. Ibid., 67–69, 78–80.

31. Ibid., 80–83, 89. This problem also attends Baianism. As Swafford notes, these two "Augustinianisms" go astray precisely by failing to recognize the different "states" in which human nature can exist, has existed, and does exist. *Nature and Grace*, 44–47. In their correspondence, de Lubac suggests that Blondel had paved the way philosophically for de Lubac's theological undertaking. The

incommensurability of created beings and God fully guarantees the gratuity of grace, which could only possibly come as a gift. *At the Service of the Church*, 187.

32. On this, see Heaps, "Ambiguity of Being," 1–46.

33. On this development, see Lonergan, *Grace and Freedom*.

34. de Lubac, *At the Service of the Church*, 154.

35. Cholvy, *Surnaturel incarné dans la création*, 388–99.

36. de Lubac, *Augustinianism and Modern Theology*, 32–33, 50.

37. Ibid., 14–15; *Surnaturel*, 25. This novelty is a major theme of Hercsik, *Jesus Christus*, and Zwitter, *Histoire en présence de l'Éternel*, and will be especially pertinent in our treatments of spiritual exegesis and the theology of history.

38. de Lubac, *Augustinianism and Modern Theology*, 23. "Saint Augustin montrait l'achèvement de la nature dans sa surnaturalisation. Baius, lui, naturalise le surnaturel. Il transforme une doctrine spirituelle en thèse d'ontologie" (*Augustinisme et théologie moderne*, 40). Also *Surnaturel*, 32. See further O'Sullivan, *Christ and Creation*, 258–59; Swafford, *Nature and Grace*, 46–47.

39. John Milbank, *Suspended Middle*, xii.

40. See especially Milbank, *Theology and Social Theory*, but also *Suspended Middle*, 53–61.

41. de Lubac, *Surnaturel*, 24. My translation: "Comment une participation à la filiation du Verb n'engenderait-elle qu'une activité au mérite tout humain? Comment l'acte d'obéissance que toute créature doit à son auteur aurait-il pour effet, par sa propre vertu, d'introduire la créature au sein de la vie divine?" See also *Augustinianism and Modern Theology*, 13.

42. de Lubac, *Surnaturel*, 366 (citing Cyril of Alexandria, *In Joannem*, 1. 2., c. 9).

43. de Lubac, *Surnaturel*, 368. My translation: "Le surnaturel ne serait donc pas seulement au-dessus de la nature, de ses exigences et de ses forces . . . il serait au-dessus de sa perfection même."

44. Ibid., 421. My translation: "Il est destiné à l'union divine, à la participation de la Vie trinitaire dans la 'vision béatifique.' Le surnaturel, c'est donc essentiellement la vision de Dieu. . . . Mais par extension, tout ce qui a rapport à cette fin."

45. Ibid., 101–27; *Augustinianism and Modern Theology*, 105–83.

46. de Lubac, *Surnaturel*, 145. Emphasis original.

47. Ibid., 153. See further S. Wood, "Nature-Grace Problematic," 389–90, on de Lubac's desire to avoid the twin dangers of an immanentism that elided grace and nature and secularism, which separated them.

48. de Lubac, *Surnaturel*, 155.

49. Ibid., 424: "Le surnaturel est donc ainsi nommé à la fois parce qu'il est divin et parce qu'il est gratuit, et ces deux raisons n'en font qu'une en fin de compte, l'absolument gratuit coïncidant nécessairement avec le divin."

50. The most thorough treatment of this theme is Moulins-Beaufort, *Anthropologie et mystique*.

51. de Lubac, "Tripartite Anthropology," 117–200.

52. de Lubac, *Surnaturel*, 483. My translation: "Paradoxe de l'esprit humain: créé, fini, il n'est pas seulement double d'une nature; il est lui-même nature. Avant d'être esprit pensant, il est nature spirituelle. Dualité irrésoluble, autant qu'union indissoluble. Image de Dieu, mais tire du néant. Avant donc d'aimer Dieu, et pour pouvoir l'aimer, il desire. Fait pour Dieu, l'esprit est attire par lui. . . . L'esprit est donc désir de Dieu."

53. de Lubac, *Mystère du Surnaturel*, 135–41, 248, 253, 260–67. The English translation is inconsistent in its translation of *esprit*, rendering it sometimes as "spirit," other times as "mind" (*Mystery of the Supernatural*, 101–6, 200, 204, 209–16). Given the distinctions drawn in "Tripartite Anthropology," this is especially unfortunate.

54. de Lubac, *Surnaturel*, 101–55; *Augustinianism and Modern Theology*, 147–234.

55. E.g., de Lubac, *Surnaturel*, 197–98, 475–80; *Catholicism*, 117, 248. The fullest English-language treatment of this theme is O'Sullivan, *Christ and Creation*, 174–201. See also Cooper, *Naturally Human, Supernaturally God*, 194–202; Moulins-Beaufort, *Anthropologie et mystique*, 37–67; Guibert, *Mystère du Christ*, 211–18.

56. de Lubac, *Surnaturel*, 483–85.

57. Ibid., 483.

58. Ibid., 492, 494: "L'ordre surnaturel, qui est l'ordre de la charité pure . . . parce que Dieu, étant lui-même charité."

59. Cholvy, *Le surnaturel incarné dans la création*, 434–38: "une métaphysique de l'amour."

60. de Lubac, *Surnaturel*, 487–89 [487]: "Dieu, en couronnant nos mérites, couronne ses propres dons."

61. Ibid., 490.

62. Ibid., 492–94: "Identiquement, la béatitude est le service, la vision est adoration, la liberté est dépendance, la possession est extase. Lorsqu'on définit notre fin surnaturelle par la possession, la liberté, la vision, la béatitude, ou n'en définit qu'un aspect. On ne l'envisage que du point de vue *anthropocentrique*, ce qui est d'ailleurs assez naturel, puisqu'on s'occupe de la fin de l'homme. En soi, ce point de vue n'est pourtant pas le principal, s'il est vrai que Dieu, qui a créé le monde par pure générosité, l'a néanmoins créé pour lui-même et pur sa gloire. . . . Le monde tout entier parvient à sa fin grâce à l'être spirituel, que le reçoit en lui pour le rapporter à son Créateur. L'esprit donne à Dieu le monde en se donnant lui-même, dans un acte de remise totale. Or cet acte n'atteint sa perfection, c'est-à-dire qu'il ne s'achève en toute sa pureté, que dans l'ordre surnaturel, qui est

l'ordre de la charité pure. Rien ne manque alors à la plénitude du 'sacrifice de louange.' Tel est l'aspect essentiel, aspect *théocentrique*. . . . Il lui devrait toujours le service, l'adoration, l'amour tels qu'ils sont réalisés chez les bienheureux. Tout le *sacrificium laudis*. . . . Dieu, étant lui-même charité et désintéressement, n'envisage notre service que comme une participation bienheureuse à sa vie." While this final phrase actually occurs in a negative construction in the original text, the wider context shows that de Lubac would affirm its positive meaning.

63. Cholvy, *Surnaturel incarné dans la création*, 302–3, 408–9.

64. De Lubac calls for a renewed Augustinianism that, among other things, involves "a clearer distinction between [the] natural order in itself and the order that results from sin." *Mystery of the Supernatural*, 19. "Peut-être ce nouvel effort de pensée . . . devra-t-il consister, par rapport à l'augustinisme, surtout à mieux assurer la consistance réelle de l'ordre naturel à tous ses degrés, comme à mieux distinguer cet ordre naturel pris en lui-même de l'ordre qui résulte du péché" (*Mystère du Surnaturel*, 41). Susan Wood also notes this development in de Lubac's thought. "Nature-Grace Problematic," 398–401. Once more, the most comprehensive presentation of this distinction is Cholvy, *Surnaturel incarné dans la création*, especially 388–99.

65. de Lubac, *Mystery of the Supernatural*, 29. "Il lui faut consentir un sacrifice bien plus complet" (*Mystère du Surnaturel*, 52).

66. de Lubac, *Mystery of the Supernatural*, 35, 37–52.

67. Ibid., 48. See further Swafford, *Nature and Grace*, 49–51.

68. de Lubac, *Mystery of the Supernatural*, 48. Also discussed by Cholvy, *Surnaturel incarné dans la création*, 214–15.

69. de Lubac, *Mystery of the Supernatural*, 53–62. See further Cholvy, *Surnaturel incarné dans la création*, 220–27.

70. de Lubac, *Mystery of the Supernatural*, 73. Emphasis original. "La fin surnaturelle ne peut *en aucun cas* l'objet d'une exigence, même de la part d'un être qui, *hic et nunc*, n'en saurait avoir une autre" (*Mystère du Surnaturel*, 102–3).

71. de Lubac, *Mystery of the Supernatural*, 76–80; Cholvy, *Surnaturel incarné dans la création*, 371–88.

72. de Lubac, *Mystery of the Supernatural*, 84–88. Here de Lubac distinctly echoes Blondel, *Action*, 445–46, and Rousselot, *Intelligence*, 146–52, both of whom he cites throughout *Mystery of the Supernatural*, 25–30, 187–89.

73. de Lubac, *Mystery of the Supernatural*, 24, 39–40, 98, 224, 228, 235.

74. Ibid., 96. See also S. Wood, "Nature-Grace Problematic," 393–96.

75. The most comprehensive treatment of finality in de Lubac is Cholvy, *Surnaturel incarné dans la création*, 87–199.

76. See Guibert's discussion of creation through and for the divine Word. *Mystère du Christ*, 211–18.

Notes to Pages 13–15   167

77. de Lubac, *Mystery of the Supernatural*, 119–39.

78. Ibid., 140–84. In chapter 3 I shall attend to the precise role that the category of paradox plays in de Lubac's theological epistemology.

79. Ibid., 221. The relationship between supernatural revelation and the natural desire for God will be developed in our consideration of de Lubac's theological epistemology in chapter 3. See also the exposition in Guibert, *Mystère du Christ*, 35–57; Geneste, *Humanisme et lumière du Christ*, 79.

80. de Lubac, *Mystery of the Supernatural*, 228. "À l'ἐπιστροφή platonicienne a succédé—combien différente et combien plus radicale—la μετάνοια chrétienne. La 'vision béatifique' n'est plus la contemplation d'un spectacle, c'est une participation intime à la vue que le Fils a du Père au sein de la Trinité. En nous faisant connaître dans son Fils le Dieu d'amour, le Dieu personnel et trinitaire, le Dieu créateur et sauveur, le Dieu 'qui se fait homme pour nous faire dieux,' la Révélation change tout" (*Mystère du Surnaturel*, 280).

81. de Lubac, *Brief Catechesis*, 20–21. "N'est pas tant Dieu ou l'ordre des choses divines considéré en lui-même, dans sa pure transcendance, que, d'une façon générale et encore indéterminée, l'ordre du divine envisagé dans son rapport d'opposition et d'union à l'ordre humain. Refuser cette distinction . . . serait aussi bien refuser, tout idée de révélation, de mystère, d'incarnation divine, de rédemption, ou de salut" (*Petite catéchèse*, 206–7).

82. Hence, de Lubac insists on the adjectival "supernatural" rather than the nominal "supernature." *Brief Catechesis*, 33–41. See also S. Wood, "Nature-Grace Problematic," 397–98; Cholvy, *Le surnaturel incarné dans la création*, 367–71.

83. de Lubac, *Brief Catechesis*, 41.

84. Ibid., 43; "Le modèle parfait se trouve dans la circumincession des trois Personnes de la Trinité" (*Petite catéchèse*, 217). This trinitarian dimension of deification will help us to integrate the perspectives offered in *Surnaturel* with those found in *Catholicisme* and *Meditation sur l'église*.

85. de Lubac, *Brief Catechesis*, 48–49.

86. Ibid., 55–64. On the theme of humility, see Geneste, *Humanisme et lumière du Christ*, 79–82.

87. de Lubac, *Brief Catechesis*, 61. See Joseph Komonchak's excellent exposition of the relation between de Lubac's basic position on the supernatural and his writings on atheism. "Theology and Culture at Mid-Century." Chapter 2 will demonstrate the particularly soteriological impetus that lies behind the works on atheism.

88. de Lubac, *Brief Catechesis*, 61. "Dieu . . . qui souverainement libre en sa transcendance, se fait partiellement immanent à sa créature par cette 'kénose,' cette 'excentration,' ce 'mouvement de descente' qu'est l'incarnation du Verbe" (*Petite catéchèse*, 226).

168   Notes to Pages 15–16

89. de Lubac, *Brief Catechesis*, 61. "Comme les 'missions' des personnes divines reproduisent en quelque sorte librement au-dehors leurs 'processions' internes, on a même pu parler d'une humilité de Dieu plus radicale encore, congénitale à son Être éternel, consistant dans l'excentration (l'extase) de chaque personne se rapportant toute aux deux autres" (*Petite catéchèse*, 226). This offers a rather interesting point of contact with the trinitarian theology of de Lubac's friend Hans Urs von Balthasar, who, drawing from such figures as Sergius Bulgakov, proposed just such a kenosis within the life of the Trinity. E.g., *Mysterium Paschale*; *Theo-Drama, Volume 4*. This is also noted by Geneste, *Humanisme et lumière du Christ*, 81. Elsewhere I have developed my own speculative account of incorporation into the trinitarian processions through the trinitarian missions, especially in their concretion in the paschal mystery (*Sacrificing the Church*). Precisely for this reason, I am cautious about developing this tantalizing statement from de Lubac further. My aim is to give an accurate account of de Lubac's own thought, and while his statement is ripe for development along the lines of what I have suggested, he does not do so himself, and I wish to avoid imposing my own views upon his.

90. See Guibert's discussion of the terms *kénose* and *sacrifice* in de Lubac. *Mystère du Christ*, 235–39. See also Cholvy, *Surnaturel incarné dans la création*, 194.

91. de Lubac, *Brief Catechesis*, 117. O'Sullivan, *Christ and Creation*, 251–55; "An Emerging Christology," 328–31.

92. de Lubac, *Brief Catechesis*, 118. "La grâce est aussi pitié et pardon" (*Petite catéchèse*, 253).

93. de Lubac, *Brief Catechesis*, 119–21. See also Guibert, *Mystère du Christ*, 258–62.

94. de Lubac, *Brief Catechesis*, 121–22. "Si l'union de la nature et du surnaturel est consommée en principe par le mystère de l'Incarnation, l'union de la nature et de la grâce ne peut être consommée que par le mystère de la Rédemption" (*Petite catéchèse*, 254).

95. de Lubac, *Brief Catechesis*, 135. "Sombre drame. . . . Drame sanglant, dont le sommet est au Calvaire. Et ce sommet est lui-même sanglant. . . . Mais au regard de la foi, dénouement lumineux, joie de la réconciliation, du retour à la Vie. Car le Sacrifice du Christ, abolissant de façon définitive les inventions impuissantes de l'homme depuis toujours en quête d'expiation et de pardon, est capable d'apporter à tous le salut" (*Petite catéchèse*, 261). See also S. Wood, "Nature-Grace Problematic," 398–401; Zwitter, *Histoire en présence de l'Éternel*, 222–23; Cholvy, *Surnaturel incarné dans la création*, 192–99, 440; Geneste, *Humanisme et lumière du Christ*, 248–53.

96. de Lubac, *Brief Catechesis*, 155.

Notes to Pages 16–17   169

97. Ibid., 157–66.

98. I have defended this outlook, with particular reference to the theologies of Jon Sobrino and Ignacio Ellacuría in *Missa Est*, 35–45, 81–83; "Eucharistic Poverty of the Church," 627–51. See Flipper, *Between Apocalypse and Eschaton*, 246–54.

99. de Lubac, *Brief Catechesis*, 168–69; Cholvy, *Le surnaturel incarné dans la création*, 192–99, 440.

100. de Lubac, *Vatican Council Notebooks*, 1:165, 255, 327, 356, 418, 521; 2:45, 55.

101. Ibid., 2:195. Nearly all remaining references to Schillebeeckx in the notebooks express some measure of concern (2:198, 221, 225, 234, 277, 294, 310, 319, 322, 347, 409, 411).

102. Ibid., 2:195 (October 16, 1964). He mentions Edward Schillebeeckx's "Église et le monde," and "Église et l'humanité," 57–78, and relates that it was after hearing Schillebeeckx address an assembly that he drafted his resignation letter to Rahner (*Vatican Council Notebooks*, 2:409 [November 10, 1965]).

103. De Lubac wrote to Rahner about the article on October 17, 1964 (*Vatican Council Notebooks*, 2:197–98) and also spoke to him at a party for the journal on October 23, 1964, after which de Lubac relates being "only half reassured" (221).

104. Recorded in an entry dated April 28–30, 1965 (ibid., 2:354–55). The official letter of resignation is dated November 10, 1965 (2:409).

105. Schillebeeckx, *Approches théologiques*, 3:145–49. See also S. Wood, *Spiritual Exegesis and the Church*, 112–15.

106. de Lubac, *Brief Catechesis*, 195–96, 193. Susan Wood has shown that one of the citation errors noted by de Lubac, the omission of the phrase *cum Deo*, is a peculiarity of the French edition. The phrase appears in the original Dutch edition. The other citation problem, that the council never used the term "sacrament of the world," is indeed accurate. *Spiritual Exegesis and the Church*, 110.

107. de Lubac, *Brief Catechesis*, 194.

108. Ibid., 195–212. See also S. Wood, *Spiritual Exegesis and the Church*, 109–12, 115–17; Portier, "What Kind of a World of Grace?," 142–45.

109. Schillebeeckx, *Approches théologiques*, 3:146. For de Lubac's criticism of Schillebeeckx on these points, see *Brief Catechesis*, 194–96, 219–20.

110. Schillebeeckx, *Approches théologiques*, 3:152–56, 162–67.

111. Ibid., 3:155.

112. Ibid., 3:210. In chapter 4 we shall see how central the distinction between the Old and New Testaments was for de Lubac's conception of the Christian novelty.

113. Note de Lubac's criticism. *Brief Catechesis*, 195.

170 Notes to Pages 18–22

114. Chantraine and Lemaire, *Henri de Lubac, tome IV*, 307–10, 573–77.

115. de Lubac, *Mystery of the Supernatural*, 14, 32.

Chapter Two. Authentic Humanism as Salvation

1. See de Lubac, *At the Service of the Church*, 35, 59.

2. de Lubac, *Drama of Atheist Humanism*, 20–23. This understanding would also inform Vatican II's *Gaudium et spes*, nos. 12–21 (Tanner, 2:1075–83). De Lubac had a significant role in shaping this section of the Constitution. See, e.g., Chantraine and Lemaire, *Henri de Lubac, tome IV*, 310–31; Rowland, "Neo-Schlolasticism of the Strict Observance," 41–42; Riches, "Henri de Lubac and the Second Vatican Council," 121–56; Routhier, "Finishing the Work Begun, 5:124–26; Hünermann, "Final Weeks of the Council," 5:394, 398. See de Lubac's own reflections on the relation between the Constitution, atheism, and humanism in *Athéisme et sens de l'homme*, 13–33, 42–46.

3. de Lubac, *Drama of Atheist Humanism*, 24–25. This earlier work was focused more on the positivist strain of atheism common in the late nineteenth and early twentieth centuries. In *Athéisme et sens de l'homme*, following *Gaudium et Spes*, de Lubac acknowledges that not all atheism is so committed to the absolute rejection of transcendence. On this transition, see Nguyen Tien Dung, *Foi au Dieu*, 153–204. Hence, it would be inaccurate to conclude that de Lubac considers atheists necessarily immoral or atrocity-prone. As we shall see in chapter 3, de Lubac's theological epistemology recognizes a primordial affirmation of God at the base of all operations of affirmation (or rejection), because humanity's identity as created spirit cannot be effaced.

4. de Lubac, *Drama of Atheist Humanism*, 11–12, 58–72. The most wide-ranging discussion of de Lubac's humanism is Geneste, *Humanisme et lumière du Christ*, which itself builds upon Wagner, *Théologie fondamentale*, 149–71.

5. Gardner, "Inhuman Humanism," 229; Murphy, "Influence of Maurice Blondel," 68.

6. de Lubac, *Catholicism*, 342.

7. de Lubac, "Nietzche as Mystic," 469–509. See also Wagner, *Théologie fondamentale*, 98–112.

8. de Lubac, *Drama of Atheist Humanism*, 114–19.

9. Ibid., 128–29.

10. Ibid., 82–95. On Bergson, see Grogin, *Bergsonian Controversy*. On these dynamics more generally, see Schloesser, *Jazz Age Catholicism*.

11. de Lubac, *Drama of Atheist Humanism*, 91. "Mythe et mystère, l'un et l'autre engendrent, si l'on veut, une mystique" (*Drame de l'humanisme athée*, 91).

Notes to Pages 22–23   171

12. See the excellent overview of the circumstances surrounding the publication of *Drama of Atheist Humanism* by Komonchak, "Theology and Culture at Mid-Century," 595–602. Note especially Komonchak's observation that de Lubac's "critique of Feuerbach and Nietzsche addresses the roots of Nazi neo-paganism, while the chapters against Comte surely have in mind the positivism that underlay the collaborationists of Action française" (599). See also Kirwan, *Avant-Garde Theological Generation*, 212–15; Dansette, "Contemporary French Catholicism," 230–74. For a comprehensive treatment of the rise of fascism in France, including its roots in Proudhon and Action Française, see Sternhell, *Neither Right nor Left*. Sternhell ably demonstrates how fascism was able to take hold so quickly and without a struggle because, even if full-fledged, self-identified fascists were a minority in French society, the intellectual atmosphere was replete with fascist-leaning ideals, meaning that the movement had great popular support. It arose in continuity with what had come before and was not imposed from the outside. See also Nolte, *Three Faces of Fascism*, 29–141. Nguyen Tien Dung enriches this perspective by looking beyond Europe to consider atheistic regimes in Eastern cultures. *Foi au Dieu*, 15–21.

13. de Lubac, *Drama of Atheist Humanism*, 215–37.

14. Ibid., 139–47. This meta-narrative has become fairly commonplace in Enlightenment and Post-Enlightenment contexts.

15. Ibid., 158–67.

16. Ibid., 180–86.

17. Ibid., 192–203.

18. This is Komonchak's appraisal. "Theology and Culture at Mid-Century," 599.

19. de Lubac, *Drama of Atheist Humanism*, 266. "La foi qui jadis fut adhésion vivante au Mystère du Christ, finit alors par n'être plus qu'un attachement à une formule d'ordre social, elle-même faussée et détournée de sa fin. Sans cris apparente, sous des dehors qui sont parfois l'inverse d'une apostasie, cette foi s'est lentement vidée de sa substance" (*Drame de l'humanisme athée*, 276–77).

20. Komonchak, "Theology and Culture at Mid-Century," 599.

21. In a different essay, de Lubac does make an explicit comparison of Comte and Action Française, specifically on the matter of anti-semitism. "New Religious 'Front,'" 478–79. See further the discussion in Prévotat, "Note sur Auguste Comte, Charles Maurras, et le christianisme," xxi–xxviii.

22. de Lubac, *At the Service of the Church*, 41. "*Le Drame*, spécialement dans la partie consacrée à Auguste Comte, ne plut guère aux maurassiens. Dependant j'ai su que, dans sa prison, Charles Maurras m'avait lu, la plume à la main, et qu'en plusiers endroits il avait noté qu je voyais juste" (*Mémoire sur l'occasion de mes écrits*, 39). These annotations are reproduced in *Drame de l'humanisme athée*, xxviii–xxxv.

172   Notes to Pages 23–25

23. Nolte, *Three Faces of Fascism*, 71.

24. See Bernardi's treatment of how Pedro Descoqs was able to recognize grievous errors in Maurras and yet completely bracket them for the sake of focusing on the natural order. *Maurice Blondel, Social Catholicism, and Action Française.* The reverse side of this is seen in a story related by de Lubac in which an Italian theologian took him to task for advancing a critique of Marxism from a specifically Christian, rather than a generically (natural) philosophical perspective. *At the Service of the Church*, 59.

25. de Lubac, *Drama of Atheist Humanism*, 440; Zwitter, *Histoire en présence de l'Éternel*, 189–94. In contrast and complementarity, see Sternhell's explanation of fascism as a revolution of "spirit" against Marxist and capitalist materialisms. *Neither Right nor Left*, 213–65.

26. de Lubac, "Search for a New Man," 451–55.

27. Ibid., 466–67.

28. Ibid., 467. "Au renouvellement du Mystère de Pâque" (*Affrontements Mystiques*, 305). See further Zwitter, *L'Histoire en présence de l'Éternel*, 222–23; Cholvy, *Le surnaturel incarné dans la création*, 192–97; Geneste, *Humanisme et lumière du Christ*, 249–51.

29. de Lubac, *Un-Marxian Socialist*, 156. "Le socialisme est la doctrine de la conciliation universelle" (*Proudhon et le Christianisme*, 167).

30. For Proudhon's understanding that religion should be surpassed, see *Un-Marxian Socialist*, 229–44. De Lubac also traces Proudhon's overlap with and distinction from the dialectics of Marx, Hegel, and Feuerbach (129–39, 151–65), noting that in some cases his similarity with their systems was only superficial, with Proudhon operating in an entirely different register (138–39, 152–53), but that he was able to learn from these other dialectics and use them to refine his own form of thought. Also note his difference from and dependence on their dialectics.

31. On this dynamic, see Gardner, "Inhuman Humanism," 239–40; M. Sutton, "Henri de Lubac," 81–82; Wagner, *Théologie fondamentale*, 112–19; Nguyen Tien Dung, *Foi au Dieu*, 63–70.

32. de Lubac, *Un-Marxian Socialist*, 271–73, 293–95.

33. Ibid., 180–81.

34. Ibid., 240–41, 296.

35. Ibid., 241–42.

36. Ibid., 169–226. See also "Homo Juridicus," 502–4.

37. de Lubac, *Un-Marxian Socialist*, 278–80.

38. Ibid., 242–43.

39. Ibid., 285–86.

40. Ibid., 295 (citing Proudhon's *Note-books*, 1847). "Il se demandera même . . . si . . . 'la fin de l'humanité' ne serait pas au contraire 'sa réconciliation

définitive avec Dieu, et son passage du temps à l'éternité'" (*Proudhon et le Christianisme*, 315).

41. de Lubac, *Un-Marxian Socialist*, 226, 295–96. See also Nguyen Tien Dung, *Foi au Dieu*, 47–69. In this way, de Lubac anticipates key affirmations from *Gaudium et spes*, no. 21 (Tanner, 2:1080–81). See also de Lubac, *Athéisme et sens de l'homme*, 16–19. For the relationship between de Lubac and *Gaudium et spes*, see note 2 above.

42. de Lubac, *Catholicisme*, 323. On the Christian humanism of *Catholicisme*, see Wagner, *Théologie fondamentale*, 153–54.

43. de Lubac, *Catholicism*, 20. "Le dogme n'y apparaît que sous quelques-uns de ses aspects" (*Catholicisme*, xiv).

44. de Lubac, *Catholicism*, 353. "Des aspirations les plus profondes" (*Catholicisme*, 309).

45. de Lubac, *Catholicism*, 358–59.

46. de Lubac, "Christian Explanation of Our Times," 441–43 (443). "Le sens profond de l'Église, qui est communauté fraternelle, se perdait. . . . L'homme se trouve isolé, déraciné, 'déboussolé.' Il est asphyxié" ("Explication chrétienne de notre temps," 234–35).

47. de Lubac, *Catholicism*, 353. "Ce rêve, le catholique ne saurait ni le faire sien tel quel, ni le repousser simplement comme une chimère néfaste" (*Catholicisme*, 309).

48. de Lubac, *Catholicism*, 353–55. See further Nguyen Tien Dung, *Foi au Dieu*, 173–88, as well as Kirwan's account of *Catholicisme*'s relationship to the exigences disclosed by atheistic humanism and its dependence upon Blondel's outlook. *Avant-Garde Theological Generation*, 167–71.

49. de Lubac, *Catholicism*, 25–47.

50. Ibid., 37–39. My bracketed substitution: "Car le Verbe n'a pas seulement pris un corps humain; son incarnation ne fut pas une simple *corporatio*, mais, comme dit saint Hilaire, une *concorporatio*. Il s'est incorporé à notre humanité, et il se l'est incorporée. . . . En assumant une nature humaine, c'est *la nature humaine* qu'il s'est unie, qu'il a incluse en lui, et celle-ci tout entière lui set en quelque sort de corps. . . . Tout entière il la portera donc au Calvaire, tout entière il la ressuscitera, tout entière il la sauvera" (*Catholicisme*, 14–16). See the important discussion in O'Sullivan, *Christ and Creation*, 317–18, 378–87; Guibert, *Mystère du Christ*, 139–58.

51. de Lubac, *Catholicism*, 48–55, 77–81. Chapter 5 will return in a more focused way to questions of ecclesiology.

52. Ibid., 82–111. The relation between sacraments and ecclesiology will also be more fully explored in chapters 5 and 6.

53. Ibid., 112–33.

54. Ibid., 130 (citing Aquinas, *Contra Gentiles*, lib. 4, c. 50). "La béatitude . . . ne peut consister que dans le règne de Dieu, lequel à son tour n'est rien autre que la société ordonnée" (*Catholicisme*, 101).

55. de Lubac, *Catholicism*, 116–19.

56. Ibid., 319–25. For accounts of the marked influence exerted by the Tübingen School, particularly Johann Adam Möhler, on de Lubac's socially inflected account of Catholicism, see Kirwan, *Avant-Garde Theological Generation*, 161–66; Boersma, *Nouvelle Théologie and Sacramental Ontology*, 41–52.

57. de Lubac, "Christian Explanation of Our Times," 450–52. "Le catholicisme ne réalise le type ni d'un indiviualisme cosmopolite, ni d'une sorte de socalisme [*sic*] unitaire . . . le biene de cette communauté, ou bien commun universel, coïncide en dernier ressort, d'un façon parfait, avec le bien personnel de chacun" ("Explication chrétienne de notre temps," 243–44). See also Cholvy, *Surnaturel incarné dans la création*, 151–62; Geneste, *Humanisme et lumière du Christ*, 245–54; Guibert, *Mystère du Christ*, 227–35.

58. de Lubac, *Catholicism*, 361–66; "Christian Explanation of Our Times," 454.

59. de Lubac, *Catholicism*, 355. "Humanisme social qui renouvelle aujourd'hui l'effort désespéré de l'homme pour se sauver seul . . . qui réfute en sauvant" (*Catholicisme*, 311).

60. de Lubac, *Catholicism*, 313. "Les courants naturalistes de la pensée moderne et . . . les confusions d'un augustinisme dévoyé" (*Catholicisme*, 270–71).

61. de Lubac, *Catholicism*, 313–14. "Cette chose si bien séparée, quelle inquiétude pouvait-elle inspirer désormais au naturalisme? . . . Les penseurs les plus résolument laïques trouvait en lui, malgré lui, un allié" (*Catholicisme*, 271).

62. de Lubac, *Catholicism*, 298. "N'est-il rien d'excellent que le catholicisme ne soit prêt à revendiquer pour sien" (*Catholicisme*, 255).

63. de Lubac, "Light of Christ," 205–206.

64. de Lubac, *Catholicism*, 298. "La seule religion vraie, la seule discipline efficace. . . . Il est la forme que doit revêtir l'humanité pour être enfin elle-même" (*Catholicisme*, 256).

65. de Lubac, *Catholicism*, 361–62.

66. Ibid., 362–64.

67. Ibid., 364–65. "Non qu'il puisse question . . . de transposer purement et simplement sur le plan naturel ce que la foi nous enseigne du monde surnaturel: ce serait transformere une réalité divine . . . en vaine idéologie . . . laïcisation téméraire, à propos de laquelle on pourrait bien parler une fois de plus de vérités chrétiennes devenues folles" (*Catholicisme*, 320).

68. de Lubac, *Catholicism*, 365–66.

69. de Lubac, "Internal Causes," 231. "ne sont pas seulement . . . nos collaborateurs ou nos instruments pour des taches purement humaines, mais des

êtres spirituels, faits comme nous pour Dieu seul et, si misérables, si fermés, si éteints qu'ils puissant nous paraître, tout au fond de chacun d'eux brille encore au moins une étincelle sacrée, et toutes ces étincelles sont destinées à se rejoinder pour un salut que Dieu veut fraternel" ("Causes internes," 21).

70. de Lubac, *Catholicism*, 344–45, 365, 368; "Light of Christ," 215; "Christian Explanation of Our Times," 252–53; "Spiritual Warfare," 501.

71. de Lubac, *Catholicism*, 342.

72. Blondel, *Action*, 373–88.

73. de Lubac, *Catholicism*, 332. "En l'Être qui se suffit, point d'égoïsme, mais l'échange d'un Don parfait" (*Catholicisme*, 288–89). Cf. *Surnaturel*, 494; "Christian Explanation of Our Times," 453–54. See also Guibert, *Mystère du Christ*, 214; Cholvy, *Surnaturel incarné dans la création*, 162–68, 302–3, 424–40; Geneste, *Humanisme et lumière du Christ*, 170–71, 238–54; Nguyen Tien Dung, *Foi au Dieu*, 253–65.

74. de Lubac, *Catholicism*, 332–35. See also Guibert, *Mystère du Christ*, 220–63.

75. de Lubac, *Catholicism*, 326, Latin translation mine. "La formule augustinienne où se condense, ainsi que nous l'avons vu, la doctrine exposée jusqu'ici: *unus Christus amans seipsum*" (*Catholicisme*, 283).

76. de Lubac, *Catholicisme*, 298, my translation. "Nous ne sommes pleinement personnels qu'à l'intérieur de la Personne du Fils, par laquelle et en laquelle nous avons part aux échanges de la Vie Trinitaire."

77. de Lubac, "Light of Christ," 209. "Un grande Geste . . . le Geste de la Charité" ("Lumière du Christ," 1:211). See discussion in Nguyen Tien Dung, *Foi au Dieu*, 246–65.

78. de Lubac, *Catholicism*, 368. "D'aucun amour naturel on ne passe de plain-pied à l'amour surnaturel. . . . L'humanité tout entière doit mourir à elle-même en chacun de ses membres pour vivre, transfigurée, en Dieu" (*Catholicisme*, 323).

79. de Lubac, *Catholicism*, 37–39. Bracketed French from *Catholicisme*, 16.

80. de Lubac, *Catholicisme*, 323, my translation. "Par le Christ mourant sur la croix, l'humanité qu'il portait toute en lui se renonce, et meurt."

81. On this, see, e.g., de Lubac, *At the Service of the Church*, 32; Hillebert, "Introducing Henri de Lubac," 22; Balthasar, *Theology of Henri de Lubac*, 38–43.

82. Chantraine, *Henri de Lubac, tome I*, 172–75.

83. de Lubac, *At the Service of the Church*, 32. "J'avais toujours eu un certain attrait pour l'étude du bouddhism, que je considère comme le plus grand fait humain, à la fois par son originalité, son expansion multiforme à travers l'espace et le temps, sa profondeur spirituelle" (*Mémoire sur l'occasion de mes écrits*, 30).

84. de Lubac, *Catholicism*, 224. "A juger en tout cas non des âmes individuelles" (*Catholicisme*, 185).

85. So Grumett, *Henri de Lubac and the Shaping of Modern Theology*, 55–56.

86. de Lubac, *Aspects of Buddhism*, 30–32. See also Grumett, *De Lubac: A Guide*, 137–41; Balthasar, *Theology of Henri de Lubac*, 54–59; Zwitter, *Histoire en présence de l'Éternel*, 52–59.

87. de Lubac, *Aspects of Buddhism*, 37.

88. Ibid., 32–34, 44.

89. Ibid., 34–37 (37).

90. Grumett, *De Lubac: A Guide*, 135–36.

91. de Lubac, *Aspects of Buddhism*, 37–42.

92. Ibid., 41.

93. Ibid. "Pour le chrétien, le commandement d'aimer Dieu est fondé sur l'amour de Dieu pour l'homme, et cet amour de Dieu pour l'homme exprime l'Être même de Dieu: Deus est caritas" (*Aspects du Bouddhisme I*, 48).

94. de Lubac, "Fondement théologique," 2:178–79, my translation. "Le chrétien ne sert pas de l'infidèle qu'il convertit en vue de se réaliser lui-même. . . . Sa vie est ce don même, parce que donner d'est participer à la Vie divine, qui est Don. . . . Le chrétien offre son individualité à la charité divine . . . comme le bois s'offre à la flamme our lui permettre de brûler." See also Wagner, *Théologie fondamentale*, 70–78.

95. de Lubac, *Aspects of Buddhism*, 46. "Étant provisoire et non définitive, demeurant moyen extrinsèque à la fin rechérchée, la charité bouddhique s'évanouit fatalement si l'on se place au point de la vérité absolue" (*Aspects du Bouddhisme I*, 54).

96. de Lubac, *Amida*, 221–44; "Notion of Good and Evil," 349–52.

97. de Lubac, *Amida*, 509–11. See "Notion of Good and Evil," 351–54, for a discussion of the similarities between Amidism and Catholic and Lutheran views of grace and merit.

98. Ibid., 434–36; "Notion of Good and Evil," 354. My use of quotation marks indicates that "orthodoxy" is not a concept native to Buddhism but rather a Christian projection on de Lubac's part.

99. de Lubac, *Amida*, 343; "Notion of Good and Evil," 336–37.

100. de Lubac, "Faith and Piety," 366–67; "Notion of Good and Evil," 347.

101. de Lubac, *Aspects of Buddhism*, 72–73.

102. Ibid., 73–74.

103. Ibid., 74. "Dans le christianisme, le Christ cosmique, ou plutôt hyper-cosmique—est encore le Christ personnel, Jésus de Nazareth, Homme et Dieu pour l'éternité, seul auteur du salut" (*Aspects du Bouddhisme I*, 96). See also *Amida*, 434–35; "Faith and Piety in Amidism," 365–66. See further Zwitter, *Histoire en présence de l'Éternel*, 50–51.

Notes to Pages 32–39   177

104. de Lubac, *Aspects of Buddhism*, 74. "Dans le christianisme, ce centre [du monde]—qui, à vrai dire, est moins un point dans l'espace qu'un événement dans le temps, moins le centre d'un univers matériel que le centre de l'histoire, moins une hauteur topographique qu'un sommet spirituel—c'est le Calvaire" (*Aspects du Bouddhisme I*, 96).

105. de Lubac, *Aspects of Buddhism*, 130. "Il s'agit d'être délivré d'un mal trop réel, de triompher d'une mort trop réele. Voilà pourquoi ce n'est pas dans un instant privilégié d'illumination—la bodhi—que réside le principe de notre salut: la rédemption du monde sera l'effet de l'Acte qui se consomme sur la Croix" (*Aspects du Bouddhisme I*, 164).

106. de Lubac, *Amida*, 457, my translation. "une illumination, non un salut."

107. de Lubac, "Faith and Piety," 368; "Buddhist Messianism?," 371–73.

Chapter Three.   Knowing the Mystery

1. de Lubac, *Mystery of the Supernatural*, 119–39.

2. Wagner, *Théologie fondamentale*, 201–27; Dumas, *Mystique et théologie*, 119–21; Swafford, *Nature and Grace*, 51–55.

3. de Lubac, "Mystique et Mystère," 42, my translation. "Une certaine union effective à la Divinité . . . au Dieu Tri-personnel de la révélation chrétienne, union réalisée en Jésus-Christ et par sa grâce."

4. de Lubac, "Mysticism and Mystery," 57, 51–52.

5. de Lubac, "Mystique et Mystère," 62, my translation. "Une mystique de la *seule* image serait une prise de conscience de soi, du fond de l'être, sans intervention gracieuse de Dieu par le don du mystère. . . . Mystique de la ressemblance, la mystique chrétienne est par le fait même orientée vers l'avant, vers un terme, vers Dieu qui nous appele et nous attire au bout du chemin." See also Dumas, *Mystique et théologie*, 154–65; Zwitter, *Histoire en présence de l'Éternel*, 78–79.

6. de Lubac, *Discovery of God*, 12. "Dieu se révèle incessamment à l'homme en imprimant incessament en lui son image. C'est cette opération divine qui constitue l'homme en son centre. C'est elle qui le fait esprit (*Sur les chemins de Dieu*, 15–16). For further overlap between image and spirit, see *Discovery of God*, 6–7, 12–13, 112–13.

7. de Lubac, "Anthropologie tripartite," 177.

8. These themes are ably explored by McCool, *Catholic Theology*; Livingston, *Modern Christian Thought*, 1:58–77, 342–53; Boersma, *Nouvelle Théologie and Sacramental Ontology*, 36–41.

178   Notes to Pages 39–42

9. McCool, *Catholic Theology*, 216–26; Kerr, "A Different World," 129–31.

10. *Dei Filius*, chap. 4, "On Faith and Reason" (Tanner, 2:808).

11. Ibid., chap. 2, "On Revelation" (Tanner, 2:806).

12. Ibid.

13. Ibid., chap. 4, "On Faith and Reason" (Tanner, 2:808).

14. McCool notes, importantly, that *Dei Filius*, while influenced by the neo-scholastic outlook and certainly capable of being interpreted in such a manner, held back from staking out any particular positions vis-à-vis scholastic theology. *Catholic Theology*, 218–21, 224–26; contra Boersma, *Nouvelle Théologie and Sacramental Ontology*, 40.

15. See further McCool, *Catholic Theology*, 226–32; *From Unity to Pluralism*, 5–14.

16. Modernism was condemned by Pope Pius X in his encyclical *Pascendi Dominici Gregis*. I call this an "unfortunate" sequel, not because the modernists were correct, but because of the culture of fear and suspicion that characterized this period of the church's life. The specter of modernism frequently overshadowed the "*nouvelle théologie*" movement with which de Lubac was associated and provided the answer to the titular question of Garrigou-Lagrange's "Nouvelle théologie où va-telle?," 126–45. For assessments of the relation between modernism and the *nouvelle théologie*, see, e.g., Loughlin, "*Nouvelle Théologie*," 36–50; Kirwan, *An Avant-Garde Theological Generation*, passim, but especially 44–134; Mettepenningen, *Nouvelle Théologie*.

17. McCool, *Catholic Theology*, 236–40; *From Unity to Pluralism*, 12–35; Kerr, *Twentieth-Century Catholic Theologians*, 1–16.

18. Kerr, "A Different World," 3–5; McCool, *From Unity to Pluralism*, 32–35; Livingston, *Modern Christian Thought*, 1:344–45.

19. See, e.g., McCool's account of Kleutgen's synthesis (*Catholic Theology*, 167–215) or Livingston's account of Mercier and Garrigou-Lagrange (*Modern Christian Thought*, 1:345–52).

20. See, e.g., Gilson, *Philosopher and Theology*, 45–47.

21. Grogin, *Bergsonian Controversy*, 1–8, 37–58; Schloesser, *Jazz Age Catholicism*, 3–17.

22. Grogin, *Bergsonian Controversy*, 9–16.

23. For an overview, see ibid., 69–98, 107–32; McCool, *Catholic Theology*, 244–45, 247–48; Gilson, *Philosopher and Theology*, 133–52. Cholvy understands de Lubac to occupy a position distinct from either rationalism or vitalism. *Surnaturel incarné dans la création*, 76–77.

24. Grogin, *Bergsonian Controversy*, 139–68; Gilson, *Philosopher and Theology*, 107–31.

25. See the important accounts in McCool, *Catholic Theology*, 241–67, and *From Unity to Pluralism*, passim.

Notes to Pages 42–44   179

26. English translation: Rousselot, *Intelligence*, 13–49, 52–58. See the important discussion in McCool, *From Unity to Pluralism*, 39–58.

27. McCool, *Catholic Theology*, 249–51; Gilson, *Philosopher and Theology*, 170–71; Kirwan, *Avant-Garde Theological Generation*, 84–86; McDermott, "De Lubac and Rousselot," 736–40. Contra Boersma, who rightly recognizes Rousselot's critique of rationalism and revalorization of the intellect, but wrongly interprets this as a move away from epistemological realism. *Nouvelle Théologie and Sacramental Ontology*, 67–83. Later, Bernard Lonergan would even more firmly distinguish between Thomas's intellectualism—which grounds its epistemology in the operation of the intellect, and so allows for a critical realism—from conceptualism, which is grounded in the objects grasped by the intellect, and so does not. *Verbum*; *Insight*. Lonergan understood his study to have been anticipated by Rousselot, an assessment that is borne out by Andrew Tallon's introduction to the latter's *Intelligence*, in which he observes Rousselot's attempt to move beyond faculty psychology to an analysis of mental operations (iii–xxxii).

28. Rousselot, *Intelligence*, 25–30, 35–41, 50–68.

29. Gilson, *Thomist Realism*; *Christian Philosophy of St. Thomas*; Maréchal, *Point de départ de la métaphysique*; Bouillard, *Conversion et grâce chez S. Thomas d'Aquin*; Chenu, *Aquinas and His Role in Theology*.

30. McCool attributes this realization especially to the work of Gilson, who, in addition to his studies of Aquinas, also undertook important research on Bonaventure (Gilson, *Philosophy of St. Bonaventure*), thereby establishing their irreducible differences. *From Unity to Pluralism*, 161–99.

31. This is the ably documented thesis of McCool, *From Unity to Pluralism*. Geneste notes a similar disruption of scholasticism by earlier humanistic movements like the Renaissance. *Humanisme et lumière du Christ*, 83–94.

32. Leo XIII, *Aeterni Patris*, no. 31. Leo goes on to speak of "those rivulets which, derived from the very fount, have thus far flowed, according to the established agreement of learned men, pure and clear," thus also endorsing the commentaries on Thomas (so McCool, *Catholic Theology*, 232–36). However, we should note that this is in a subsidiary place, with preference given to the study of Aquinas himself.

33. De Lubac's formation is thoroughly documented in Chantraine, *Henri de Lubac, tome II*.

34. de Lubac, *Discovery of God*, 205–7 (207). "qui nous a nourri, c'est dans son climat que notre pensée ne cesse de vivre" (*Sur les chemins de Dieu*, 241–44).

35. Chantraine and Lemaire, *Henri de Lubac, tome IV*, 688. "renverser l'encyclique *Aeterni Patris* en substituant à la philosophie thomiste une philosophie moderne." The article was written by Giuseppe Colombo.

36. Ibid. "Rien de plus faux" (citing Centre d'Archives et d'Études des Cardinal Henri de Lubac 73405–73408).

180   Notes to Pages 44–45

37. de Lubac, *At the Service of the Church*, 269. "chez les jeunes générations, à un déficit dans la précision de la pensée qui n'est pas sans danger pour la rectitude théologique" (*Mémoire sur l'occasion de mes écrits*, 271).

38. de Lubac, *At the Service of the Church*, 269. "Je ne crois pas que ce mal soit par ailleurs sans compensations, aussi ne suis-je pas pessimiste relativement à ces jeunes générations; je constate néanmoins avec regret un déficit" (*Mémoire sur l'occasion de mes écrits*, 271).

39. de Lubac, *At the Service of the Church*, 270. "un certain thomisme étroit et sectaire" (*Mémoire sur l'occasion de mes écrits*, 272).

40. Rousselot, *Intelligence*, 181–84. De Lubac explicitly denounces rationalism in "Apologetics and Theology," 93–94; *Discovery of God*, 37–38; "Problem of the Development of Dogma," 277; "Internal Causes," 233–35; *Révélation divine*, 190–93.

41. While the main elements of this commitment may be discerned throughout de Lubac, *Discovery of God*, it is most directly developed in "Conditions of Ontological Affirmation," 377–92. See especially the discussion in Moulins-Beaufort, *Anthropologie et mystique*, 505–44.

42. de Lubac, "Tripartite Anthropology," 179–80 (179). "une théorie essentiellement 'scientifique' (philosophique), ayant peu de rapport à la vie spirituelle" ("Anthropologie tripartite," 178).

43. de Lubac, "Tripartite Anthropology," 184.

44. Rousselot, *Intelligence*, 2.

45. de Lubac, *Sur les chemins de Dieu*, 89. "L'*intelligence* est *faculté* de l'être parce que l'*esprit* est *capacité* de Dieu." I am indebted to Jordan Hillebert for this insight. See also Moulins-Beaufort, *Anthropologie et mystique*, 542–43; Chantraine, *Henri de Lubac, tome II*, 748. Chantraine also surveys several of de Lubac's philosophical writings from his formation, which display reception, modification, and moving beyond figures such as Rousselot and Maréchal (363–490). On Rousselot's developing position on the will and the intellect, see especially McDermott, *Love and Understanding*. It is worth noting, though, that even this modification is not a radical departure from Rousselot, who endeavored to move beyond faculty psychology and into an analysis of the mind's operations, such that acts of discursive reason, of intelligence, and of volitional choice are all expressive of the same dynamic spirit that is ordered to the intellectual apprehension of God. So Tallon, "Foreword" in Rousselot, *Intelligence*, iii–xxxii. See also de Lubac, *Sur les chemins de Dieu*, 63; Cholvy, *Surnaturel incarné dans la création*, 262–64; Wagner, *Théologie fondamentale*, 182.

46. de Lubac, *Discovery of God*, 48, 70.

47. Ibid., 7–9.

48. Ibid., 9, 35–55 (9). "Notre opération la plus naturelle et la plus spontanée ne peut jamais être qu'une réponse" (*Sur les chemins de Dieu*, 14).

Notes to Pages 45–48   181

49. de Lubac, *Discovery of God*, 40–41.

50. Ibid., 112–13, 150–54,

51. Ibid., 35–37, 48, 105.

52. Ibid., 50–51. "Il faut ici distinguer . . . le temps qui précède chez le sujet l'accueil de la grâce ou son refus, et le temps qui vient après. Dans le temps qui précède, la certitude ontologique est ce qu'elle est, sans qu'il y ait lieu de la déclarer illégitime ou, pour mieux dire, illusoire. Après le refus, ces épithètes prennent un sens—mais qui doit être rigoureusement spécifié. Car si l'on peut dire alors illégitime ou illusoire la certitude ontologique, ce n'est pas pour la déclarer telle en elle-même—la nature de l'intelligence n'a point changé—c'est parce qu'elle se trouve désormais contredite vitalement. . . . S'il va délibérément au rebours de sa vocation d'esprit, il introduit de la sorte une contradiction, non dans sa seule intelligence—qui peut continuer de fonctionner comme par le passé—mais, dans son être même, entre son intelligence et sa vie" (*Sur les chemins de Dieu*, 64–65).

53. de Lubac, *Discovery of God*, 117. "Un infini d'intelligibilité, tel est Dieu" (*Sur les chemins de Dieu*, 140). See also Dumas, *Mystique et théologie*, 83.

54. de Lubac, *Discovery of God*, 121, 128–35; *Un-Marxian Socialist*, 260; *Christian Faith*, 261–89.

55. "Théologie et ses sources: Reponse," 396, my translation. "L'anti-intellectuel est contre l'intelligence: aucun de nous n'accepte de l'être, et, encore un fois, l'on serait bien empêché de montrer que nous le sommes." See also S. Wood, *Spiritual Exegesis and the Church*, 17.

56. "Théologie et ses sources: Reponse," 397, my translation. "Il peut y avoir, en théologie, un certain intellectualisme contre lequel nous n'hésiterons point à prendre position."

57. Ibid., 398.

58. de Lubac, *Discovery of God*, 214. "Il y a dans l'esprit humain quelque chose de plus fondamental: non pas en dehors, mais au cœur même de l'intelligence . . . l'intellectualisme légitime n'est point un narcissisme du concept. Il n'est pas amour de l'intelligence pour elle-même ou complaisance dans le produit de ses actes: il est libre et confiant usage de cette intelligence dans la recherche du vrai" (*Sur les chemins de Dieu*, 250–51).

59. See further Dumas, *Mystique et théologie*, 242–43.

60. The oath was imposed in Pius X's motu proprio *Sacrorum antistitum*.

61. So Gilson, *Philosopher and Theology*, 84; Kerr, "A Different World," 131–36; D. Long, "Knowing God," 271.

62. de Lubac, *Surnaturel*, 483–85; *Mystery of the Supernatural*, 185–221.

63. de Lubac, *Sur les chemins de Dieu*, 16.

64. de Lubac, *Discovery of God*, 12–13, 98–113.

65. *Dei Filius*, chap. 2, "On Revelation" (Tanner, 2:806).

66. de Lubac, *Discovery of God*, 109. "La vie de charité, nous faisant participer à la Vie même de Dieu" (*Sur les chemins de Dieu,* 130). This accounts for the difference between de Lubac and Blondel observed in chapter 1. While Blondel's method of immanence restricts his reflections to philosophy, and so keeps his account of the supernatural largely notional, de Lubac does not maintain this distinction and fills out his account of the supernatural with actual content drawn from revelation.

67. de Lubac, *Christian Faith*, 14.

68. Ibid. "Le mystère de la Trinité ne nous est pas révélé d'abord en lui-même, mais dans l'action de la Trinité 'au-dehors,' dans son action salutaire, il n'en est pas moins vrai que le terme de cette action salutaire est bien, dès maintenant, la Trinité entrevue par la foi dans son être même" (*Foi chrétienne,* 15). See further *Christian Faith*, 87–89; Guibert, *Mystère du Christ*, 65–102.

69. de Lubac, *Christian Faith*, 91–92, 107.

70. Ibid., 88. "Si tout l'acte révélateur est en fin de compte une révélation de la Trinité, toute la révélation de la Trinité est une révélation en acte, et tout cet acte a un rapport direct à l'homme" (*Foi chrétienne,* 102).

71. de Lubac, *Christian Faith*, 92.

72. de Lubac, "Problem of the Development of Dogma," 274. "L'état premier de la doctrine . . . c'est l'Action rédemptrice: c'est le don que Dieu nous fait de lui-même en son Fils . . . c'est donc déjà une première abstraction que de mettre complètement à part le don et la révélation du don, l'action rédemptrice et la connaissance de la rédemption, le mystère comme acte et le mystère comme proposé à la foi" ("Problème du développement du dogme," 2:64–65). In this connection, de Lubac also speaks of "la nouveauté chrétienne." See also Cholvy, *Surnaturel incarné dans la création*, 76–77; Wagner, *Théologie fondamentale*, 68–71; Dumas, *Mystique et théologie*, 84.

73. de Lubac, *Christian Faith*, 92, 101. See further Guibert, *Mystère du Christ*, 95–97.

74. This gestures toward the importance of the revelatory function of Christ (as opposed to a Christology focused solely upon redemption), an aspect of de Lubac's thought for which O'Sullivan argues extensively and persuasively in *Christ and Creation*, esp. 325–39; "An Emerging Christology," 327–48. See also D. Long, "Knowing God," 279. At the same time, the affirmation goes beyond this, for even if there were no revelation, God would still be the same God.

75. Dumas, *Mystique et théologie*, 120, my translation. "deux manières typiquement lubaciennes de recourir à une présentation théologique apte à nourrir l'élan mystique: le paradoxe et l'intelligence spirituelle des Écritures."

76. de Lubac, *Christian Faith*, 237. "Chacun est un aspect d'une vérité globale et unique" (*Foi chrétienne*), 274. See also *Révélation divine*, 75.

Notes to Pages 50–52   183

77. de Lubac, *Christian Faith*, 243–45. See further Wagner, *Théologie fondamentale*, 205–15; Dumas, *Mystique et théologie*, 184–277.

78. See also Wagner's discussion of paradox's place in de Lubac's theological method. *Théologie fondamentale*, 215–28.

79. See chapter 1.

80. de Lubac, *Corpus Mysticum*, 221–62; *Medieval Exegesis*, 1:55–74; 3:311–26; *Exégèse médiévale*, 2:84–106, 369–91. See the excellent treatment in Zwitter, *Histoire en présence de l'Éternel*, 294–311.

81. Swafford, *Nature and Grace*, 68. See also the rather thorough treatment of "Apologétique et théologie" in Wagner, *Théologie fondamentale*, 23–35.

82. de Lubac, "Apologetics and Theology," 91–92.

83. Ibid., 93–94 (93). "Par une sorte de rationalisme inavoué, qu'ont renforcé depuis un siècle l'envahissement des tendances positiviste" ("Apologétique et théologie," 100).

84. de Lubac, *Discovery of God*, 145; *Medieval Exegesis*, 1:67.

85. de Lubac, *Discovery of God*, 32. "La dialectique est une arme puissante, parce qu'elle correspond à l'un des processus essentiels de l'esprit" (*Sur les chemins de Dieu*, 41).

86. de Lubac, *Discovery of God*, 32–33. "Mais si elle veut non pas organiser mais proprement engendrer la pensée, son âme est une nécessité aveugle" (*Sur les chemins de Dieu*, 41).

87. de Lubac, *Discovery of God*, 37–38.

88. Ibid., 33. "L'idée du Dieu vivant y sera, comme toute autre, soumise à la dialectique" (*Sur les chemins de Dieu*, 42).

89. de Lubac, *Discovery of God*, 33, ellipses original. "Loin qu'elle corresponde à une phase de la dialectique humaine, c'est au contraire celle-ci qui joue le rôle d'intermédiaire, se déroulant comme l'entre-deux d'une réalité perçue à un mystère pressenti et ne cessant d'être soutenue en son mouvement par une présence . . ." (*Sur les chemins de Dieu*, 42).

90. de Lubac, *Sur les chemins de Dieu*, 134, my translation: "Même une fois que la logique nous a contraints d'affirmer qu'il existe, son mystère demeure inviolé. Notre raison ne pénètre pas en Lui. Dialectique et représentation ne peuvent dépasser le seuil. Mais, en deçà de toute dialectique et de toute représentation, notre esprit affirme déjà Celui qui, atteint par la médiation de la dialectique et de la représentation, est au delà de toute représentation et de toute dialectique."

91. de Lubac, *Paradoxes of Faith*, 9. "Le paradoxe est l'envers dont la synthèse serait l'endroit. Mais cet endroit nous fuit toujours. . . . Le paradoxe, c'est la recherche, ou c'est l'attente de la synthèse. Expression provisoire d'une vue toujours incomplète, mais qui s'oriente vers la plénitude" (*Nouveaux Paradoxes*, 71).

184   Notes to Pages 52–54

92. de Lubac, *Paradoxes of Faith*, 228. "Le Dogme est un vaste domaine que jamais la théologie n'exploitera tout entier. Il y a toujours infiniment plus dans le Dogme . . . que dans cette 'science humaine de la révélation,' dans ce produit de l'analyse et de l'élaboration rationnelle qu'est toujours la théologie" (*Nouveaux Paradoxes*, 183).

93. Wagner, *Théologie fondamentale*, 224.

94. Swafford, *Nature and Grace*, 51.

95. Dumas, *Mystique et théologie*, 120, my translation. "Générateur de tension féconde par cette énonciation simultanée des contraires, le paradoxe lubacien se trouve constituer un chemin à la fois théologique et spirituel par lequel le Mystère est respecté dans sa nature profonde de mystère et d'appel au dépassement."

96. See de Lubac's remarks on speculation in *Drama of Atheist Humanism*, 103–5.

97. Cf. the similar approach (without appeal to paradox) in de Lubac, *Splendor of the Church*, 9: "What I have done is meditate, in the light of faith, on certain aspects of the mystery of the Church, as an attempt to work myself into the very heart of that mystery." In French: "Nous avons seulement, dans la foi, médité sous quelques-uns de ses aspects le mystère de l'Église, en nous enforçant de nous établir le plus possible en son centre" (*Méditation sur l'église*, lxi).

98. de Lubac, *Corpus Mysticum*, 221–47. Also relevant, and going into more technical detail, are "Conditions of Ontological Affirmation," which contrasts the Blondelian position with the pure intellectualism of Rousselot, and the two-part essay, "'Seigneur, je cherche ton visage,'" which involves a close reading of Anselm. These essays shed further light on the consequences of the fundamental place given to spirit in de Lubac's theological anthropology, as the earlier sections of this chapter explored.

99. de Lubac, *Corpus Mysticum*, 238. "Ce rationalisme chrétien ne pouvait plus envisager l'intelligence des mystères eu dehors de leur démonstration" (*Corpus mysticum*, 267).

100. de Lubac, *Corpus Mysticum*, 221–30, 236–38. See discussion in Dumas, *Mystique et théologie*, 214–19.

101. de Lubac, *Corpus Mysticum*, 220. "L'apologie du dogme succède à l'intelligence de la foi" (*Corpus mysticum*, 247).

102. de Lubac, *Corpus Mysticum*, 230–35 (231). De Lubac's conception of the *intelligence de la foi* or *l'intelligence spirituelle* is a major theme of Dumas, *Mystique et théologie*, especially 222–32.

103. de Lubac, *Corpus Mysticum*, 231–33. "Or, si le mystère est essentiellement obscur à nos facultés charnelles, il est en lui-même tout rayonnant d'une secrète intelligibilité . . . nous devinons qu'il comporte un arrière-fond lu-

mineux . . . c'est-à-dire qu'il en cherche et qu'il en obtienne toujours plus l'intelligence" (*Corpus mysticum*, 259–61).

104. de Lubac, *Paradoxes of Faith*, 103–4.

105. Rousselot, *Intelligence*, 13–49.

106. de Lubac, *Corpus Mysticum*, 235–36. "L'image incréée du Père et la créature faite 'à son image' avaient une intime parenté, que l'activité de la raison avait pour fin de parfaire. À partire de la Nature, à partir de l'Histoire, ou de l'Écriture, ou de la Liturgie, à partir de toute chose, l'esprit tendait d'un même élan à l'intelligence spirituelle" (*Corpus mysticum*, 264); see also *Catholicism*, 332–33.

107. Rousselot, *Intelligence*, 25–30, 35–41, 50–68.

108. de Lubac, *Corpus mysticum*, 235. See also Moulins-Beaufort, *Anthropologie et mystique*, 545–600; Dumas, *Mystique et théologie*, 226, 353–61.

109. Dumas, *Mystique et théologie*, 223, my translation. "L'intelligence de la foi n'est pas la théologie, mais un mouvement de tout l'homme vers Dieu qui conjugue ainsi le désir (mystique) de voir Dieu et les ressources de la science rationnelle (théologique)."

110. Ibid., 235–77.

111. de Lubac, "Anthropologie tripartite," 177–86. See further Cholvy, *Surnaturel incarné dans la création*, 265–67; Dumas, *Mystique et théologie*, 68–71; Hollon, "Mysticism and Mystical Theology," 307–25.

112. de Lubac, *Christian Faith*, 133–45; *Splendor of the Church*, 28–38.

113. de Lubac, *Christian Faith*, 146. See the exposition in Guibert, *Mystère du Christ*, 263–70; Wagner, *Théologie fondamentale*, 224–25.

114. de Lubac, *Christian Faith*, 107 (quoting Erik Przywara, *Philosophie de la religion catholique*, 2e partie, *in fine*). "Car la Trinité ne nous est révélée que dans la mesure où elle permet notre élévation et notre rédemption dans l'œuvre du salut" (*Foi chrétienne*, 124). See also *Christian Faith*, 149–50.

115. de Lubac, "Development of Dogma," 275; *Révélation divine*, 56–60.

116. de Lubac, *Christian Faith*, 246–59. "développement du dogme, approfondissement du mystère" (*Foi chrétienne*, 286–306).

117. See discussion in Guibert, *Mystère du Christ*, 173–329; Dumas, *Mystique et théologie*, 285–322.

118. de Lubac, "Light of Christ," 215–17. This commitment on practice and charity distinctly echoes Blondel's philosophy of action. *Action*, 373–424.

119. de Lubac, *Christian Faith*, 292. "ce mouvement qui ratifie librement, à l'audition de la Parole, la destinée inscrite dans l'être même par le Créateur; autrement dit, la reprise et la transformation du mouvement secret qui est essentiel à la créature, par l'élan de la foi" (*Foi chrétienne*, 355).

186   Notes to Pages 57–58

120. E.g., Augustine, *Teaching Christianity* 1.11.11–14.14, 34.38 (pp. 110–12, 122–23); *Confessions* 7.18.24–19.25 (pp. 178–79); *Trinity* 4.10.13–18.24 (pp. 166–71); *City of God* 9.15 (pp. 293–95).

121. Augustine, *Teaching Christianity* 1.11.11 (p. 110). De Lubac explicitly draws from Augustine, *Christian Faith*, 297–302, and points to his importance for the pedagogical account of revelation in *Dei Verbum* in *Révélation divine*, 122–23.

122. de Lubac, *Christian Faith*, 292–302; *Sur les chemins de Dieu*, 130.

123. de Lubac, *Christian Faith*, 128. "Tout vient *du* Père, *par* le Fils, *dans* l'Esprit" (*Foi chrétienne*, 144).

124. de Lubac, *Discovery of God*, 220. "Le chrétien sait qu'il n'est, pour une rencontre réelle avec Dieu, qu'un seul Chemin: le Chemin Vivant qui a nom Jésus-Christ" (*Sur les chemins de Dieu*, 257). Here also de Lubac cites Augustine (*ciu.*11.2; *s.* 117; *in Io. eu* 10.26).

125. de Lubac, *Christian Faith*, 314. "est élan de foi, adoration, extase en Dieu. Cette théologie-là n'aura point de fin, parce que Dieu est inépuisable" (*Foi chrétienne*, 365).

126. Dumas, *Mystique et théologie*, 226, my translation. "une intelligence théologique véritablement théologale, donc pascale."

Chapter Four.   Spiritual Exegesis and/as Salvation

1. Portions of this chapter first appeared as Schlesinger, "Sacrifice as Integrating Principle."

2. Flipper, *Between Apocalypse and Eschaton*, 91.

3. Wood, *Spiritual Exegesis and the Church*, 1.

4. Wood demonstrates this in ibid., 25–51. Her thesis is further extended by Flipper, who contends that this historical theology, especially the relationship between eschatology and history, is the driving force of de Lubac's thought. *Between Apocalypse and Eschaton*.

5. See especially de Lubac, *History and Spirit*, 306–7; *Medieval Exegesis*, 1:227, 241–51; 2:50–58; 3:98–116. See further discussion in Wood, *Spiritual Exegesis and the Church*, 47–49; Schlesinger, "Threefold Body," 189.

6. On this, see de Lubac, *Medieval Exegesis*, 2:54; *History and Spirit*, 306–7. Wood mentions, but does not develop, this connection. *Spiritual Exegesis and the Church*, 47. Flipper recognizes the importance of ecclesiology for de Lubac's theology of history (*Between Apocalypse and Eschaton*, 234–46). However, his discussion does not develop the necessarily ecclesiological bent of de Lubac's theology of history, which results from the fact that the theology of

Notes to Pages 58–61   187

history turns upon the relationship between the two testaments and, hence, the peoples who are related to God through those two economies.

7. See Kevin L. Hughes's suggestion that spiritual exegesis has a "capillary" presence throughout de Lubac's oeuvre. "Spiritual Interpretation of Scripture," 205–23.

8. See Wood, *Spiritual Exegesis and the Church*, 25–51; Hercsik, *Jesus Christus als Mitte der Theologie*, 66–210.

9. de Lubac, "Mysticism and Mystery," 58. "Puisqu'elle se développe sous l'action du mystère reçu dans la foi, mystère qui est celui de l'Incarnation du Verbe de Dieu révélée dans l'Écriture, la mystique chrétienne sera essentiellement une intelligence des Livres Saints. Le mystère en est le sens, la mystique en est l'intelligence" ("Mystique et Mystère," 63).

10. Dumas, *Mystique et théologie*, 286–322.

11. So Kirwan, *Avant-Garde Theological Generation*, 166–68.

12. De Lubac is adamant about this in *Splendor of the Church*, 21, 241–57.

13. Cholvy, *Surnaturel incarné dans la création*, 71, my translation. "La Tradition peut apporter, non des solutions, mais des éclaircissements et permettre de resituer des prises de position qui ne sont que récentes."

14. de Lubac, "Internal Causes," 233–35.

15. de Lubac, *Medieval Exegesis*, 1:24–51, 66–74; 2:176; 3:311–26.

16. Recounted in de Lubac, *At the Service of the Church*, 64–67.

17. Daniélou, *Origène*; Balthasar, *Origenes Geist und Feuer*; *Presence et pensée*. (While focused on Gregory of Nyssa, *Presence et pensée*'s introduction contains important material on Origen.) See further Barnes, "Some Synchronic Moment," 367–411.

18. See de Lubac's own obligatory "rehabilitation" chapters in *History and Spirit*, 15–50. On the twenty years of material gathering, see *At the Service of the Church*, 64–67.

19. de Lubac, *History and Spirit*, 11. "Il ne s'agissait même plus seulement d'exégèse. C'était toute une pensé, toute une vue du monde qui surgissait devant nous. Toute une interprétation du christianisme, dont Origène . . . était d'ailleurs moins l'auteur que le témoin" (*Histoire et esprit*, 9).

20. de Lubac, *Medieval Exegesis*, 1:xiii. "Le présent ouvrage n'est pas une étude allégorique ou spirituelle de l'Écriture: c'est une étude qui se voudrait historique et littérale de ses anciens commentateurs" (*Exégèse médiévale*, 1/1:11).

21. de Lubac, *History and Spirit*, 320, 334–35, 336, 427–507 (esp. 443, 469, 487). See also Wood, *Spiritual Exegesis and the Church*, 22.

22. de Lubac, *History and Spirit*, 427. "De cette vaste doctrine, qui ressurgit à nos yeux comme un palais de rêve à travers la brume d'un lointain passé, que reste-t-il? Selon le biais par où nous cherchons à l'atteindre, nous répondrons: peu de chose, ou, au contraire: tout l'essentiel" (*Histoire et esprit*, 374).

188   Notes to Pages 61–63

23. de Lubac, *History and Spirit*, 489. "L'exégèse spirituelle a depuis longtemps accompli une part essentielle de sa tâche" (*Histoire et esprit*, 429).

24. Hughes, "'Fourfold Sense,'" 457. So also Wood, *Spiritual Exegesis and the Church*, 51; Flipper, *Between Apocalypse and Eschaton*, 98–99. *Contra* Hollon, *Everything Is Sacred*, who throughout operates with the assumption that de Lubac is advocating for a return to patristic and medieval exegetical methodology. Similarly, Robert Louis Wilkin, in his foreword to Vol. 1 of *Medieval Exegesis*, suggests that de Lubac is advocating for a particular form of biblical interpretation (xii). Hans Boersma, on the other hand, recognizes that de Lubac does not call for a return to spiritual exegesis as such. *Nouvelle Théologie and Sacramental Ontology*, 154. See Dumas's assessment: "For de Lubac, one thing is sure: to return to the spiritual understanding of Scripture does not signify to return like the fathers; that would be, on the contrary, a subtle form of betrayal." *Mystique et théologie*, 370, my translation. "Pour Lubac, une chose est sûr: revenir à l'intelligence spirituelle de l'Écriture ne signifie pas y revenir comme les Pères; ce serait au contraire une forme subtile de trahison."

25. de Lubac, *Medieval Exegesis*, 1:xix–xxi; 3:98; *History and Spirit*, 14, 491–93. See discussion in D'Ambrosio, "Henri de Lubac," 367–72.

26. Ayres, "Soul and the Reading of Scripture," 173–90. See also D'Ambrosio, "Henri de Lubac," 384–85.

27. Guibert, *Mystère du Christ*, 412–23; Zwitter, *Histoire en présence de l'Éternel*, 261–80; Cholvy, *Surnaturel incarné dans la création*, 328; Geneste, *Humanisme et lumière du Christ*, 238–39.

28. So Dumas, *Mystique et théologie*, passim.

29. de Lubac, *Medieval Exegesis*, 1:1. "Littera gesta docet, quid credas allegoria, Moralis quid agas, quo tendas anagogia" (*Exégèse médiévale*, 1/1:23). See also Wood, *Spiritual Exegesis and the Church*, 26–46; Flipper, *Between Apocalypse and Eschaton*, 93–96.

30. See discussion in Wood, *Spiritual Exegesis and the Church*, 28; Flipper, *Between Apocalypse and Eschaton*, 94. This terminological plurality provides the evidence from which David Grumett discerns seven different senses of Scripture in de Lubac's writings. *De Lubac: A Guide*, 75–94. While Grumett's treatment gives helpful expression to the various shades of meaning available in the spiritual senses, their multiplication strikes me as needlessly complex, particularly since de Lubac believes that the senses can be distilled to just two: the letter and the spirit. Indeed, see Zwitter's treatment of de Lubac's consistent prioritization of the four senses of the doctrinal form over, though not necessarily to the exclusion of, the three senses of the mystical form. *Histoire en présence de l'Éternel*, 261–80.

31. See, e.g., de Lubac, *Medieval Exegesis*, 1:90–115.

Notes to Pages 63–65   189

32. See ibid., 1:258–59; 2:33–39; *Exégèse médiévale*, 2/2:40, 138–39.

33. See note 24 above. In these passages de Lubac consistently differentiates between the methodology of the four senses of Scripture and the underlying doctrine.

34. Once more, this is the major thesis of Dumas, *Mystique et théologie*, especially 285–361.

35. de Lubac, *Medieval Exegesis*, 1:225; 2:25–37; *History and Spirit*, 190–204. In this twofold form, the second sense is usually referred to as the "spiritual sense," reflecting the Pauline language of letter and spirit (2 Cor. 3:4–6). When all four senses are considered, the spiritual sense tends to be referred to as "allegory" because this allows greater precision vis-à-vis the other two spiritual senses, tropology and anagogy.

36. de Lubac, *Medieval Exegesis*, 2:41, 44, 86. "C'est porquoi, devant certains textes que nous dirions non historiques, surtout lorsque le langage en est figuré, tels que proverbes, paraboles, etc. . . . , on dit volontiers qu'ils n'ont pas de sens littéral" (*Exégèse médiévale*, 1/2:425). So also de Lubac, *History and Spirit*, 111–16. See also Wood, *Spiritual Exegesis and the Church*; Flipper, *Between Apocalypse and Eschaton*, 107–20.

37. de Lubac, *History and Spirit*, 306–16; *Medieval Exegesis*, 1:228–41, 260; 2:98–107; 3:109–11, 140–44; *Exégèse médiévale*, 2/2:109–11. See Flipper's excellent discussion in *Between Apocalypse and Eschaton*, 144–47, especially his language of "the retroactive causality of Christ" (147).

38. de Lubac, *Medieval Exegesis*, 3:98–136.

39. de Lubac, *Christian Resistance to Anti-Semitism*; *At the Service of the Church*, 48–55. See also Gordon, "*Ressourcement* Anti-Semitism?," 614–33.

40. de Lubac, *History and Spirit*, 103–18; *Medieval Exegesis*, 1:226–28, 247; 2:26, 97; 3:143–45.

41. de Lubac, *Medieval Exegesis*, 1:41–69, 201, 226, 247; 3:110–11, 140–46, 211–16, 248. See further Wood, *Spiritual Exegesis and the Church*, 35–37; Flipper, *Between Apocalypse and Eschaton*, 100–115.

42. Flipper, *Between Apocalypse and Eschaton*, 144–49 (147). See also Hercsik, *Jesus Christus als Mitte der Theologie*, 92.

43. de Lubac, *Medieval Exegesis*, 1:105, 162; *History and Spirit*, 457.

44. de Lubac, *Exégèse médiévale*, 2/2:94; *Medieval Exegesis*, 1:237–39; 2:107, 123; 3:97, 106; *History and Spirit*, 461–65; *Catholicism*, 180–81.

45. de Lubac, *Medieval Exegesis*, 1:267. "Le théologien averti . . . tout en assumant les progrès réalisés par la science et en se gardant d'éterniser toutes les formes dans lesquelles s'est librement exprimée jadis la foi dans la divinité de l'Écriture, il reconnaît sans ambages que l'existence d'un double sens, littéral et spirituel, est une donnée inaliénable de la tradition" (*Exégèse médiévale*, 1/1:363).

190   Notes to Pages 65–67

46. de Lubac, *Medieval Exegesis*, 1:258–59; 2:211; *Exégèse médiévale*, 2/2:7–9, 40, 76.

47. de Lubac, *Medieval Exegesis*, 1:xvii–xxi, 266–67; 2:211–14; 3:147, 267; *Exégèse médiévale*, 2/2:76, 80–81, 92–93, 288–89; *History and Spirit*, 491–93. See also Ayres, "Soul and the Reading of Scripture."

48. de Lubac, *Medieval Exegesis*, 1:15–37.

49. de Lubac, *History and Spirit*, 346–48, 446–47; *Medieval Exegesis*, 2:134–43; *Exégèse médiévale*, 2/2:81–86. See also Dumas, *Mystique et théologie*, 289.

50. de Lubac, *Exégèse médiévale*, 2/2:111; *Medieval Exegesis*, 1:225; 2:34. Below I give an account of why this is the case.

51. de Lubac, *Medieval Exegesis*, 2:179–87. See further Zwitter, *Histoire en présence de l'Éternel*, 253–60, 265–75; Dumas, *Mystique et théologie*, 353–61.

52. de Lubac, *Medieval Exegesis*, 2:127. "Le passage de l'allégorie à la tropologie ne comporte point un tel ressaut. Après le sens historique, tous ceux qu'on peut énumérer encore font partie d'un même sens spirituel" (*Exégèse médiévale*, 1/2:549).

53. de Lubac, *Medieval Exegesis*, 2:127–29, 132–34, 179, 183, 186–87, 201–4; *Exégèse médiévale*, 2/2:109–113. See further Flipper, *Between Apocalypse and Eschaton*, 197–99, 231–32.

54. Zwitter, *Histoire en présence de l'Éternel*, 261–80.

55. de Lubac, *Medieval Exegesis*, 1:140–41; 2:1, 19–33; *History and Spirit*, 179–90.

56. de Lubac, *History and Spirit*, 164. "D'une part, donc, nous avions une sorte d'anatomie et de physiologie de l'âme qui, en principe au moins, ne supposait pas la révélation. D'autre part, nous avons une histoire du salut de l'âme en fonction du salut du l'humanité par le Christ, ou un appel au salut de l'âme dans le salut commun de l'Église" (*Histoire et esprit*, 143–44).

57. de Lubac, *Medieval Exegesis*, 1:114, 147. "Selon qu'il précède ou qu'il suit le sens allégorique, c'est-à-dire selon qu'il est rans rapport avec lui ou qu'il est sous sa dépendance. . . . Dans le premier cas, Origène tire du texte sacré diverses «moralités» qui peuvent n'avoir rien de spécifiquement chrétien. . . . Dans le second cas, il expose une ascèse et une mystique d'allure christologique, ecclésiale et sacramentaire . . . toute chrétienne, dans son contenu comme dans sa forme, dans ses aboutissements comme dans sa racine" (*Exégèse médiévale*, 1/1:168, 203). See further de Lubac, *Medieval Exegesis*, 2:33–34; *History and Spirit*, 163–64; Flipper, *Between Apocalypse and Eschaton*, 93–96.

58. de Lubac, *Medieval Exegesis*, 2:132–34.

59. de Lubac, *Exégèse médiévale*, 2/2:109–12; *Medieval Exegesis*, 1:186–87, 201–2; 3:327–419. See also Flipper, *Between Apocalypse and Eschaton*, 160–69; Wood, *Spiritual Exegesis and the Church*, 44–46.

Notes to Pages 67–69   191

60. de Lubac, *Medieval Exegesis*, 1:225–41; *Exégèse médiévale*, 2/2:110.

61. So Flipper, *Between Apocalypse and Eschaton*, 210–20; Wood, *Spiritual Exegesis and the Church*, 59, 63; Schnackers, *Kirche als Sakrament und Mutter*, 164–69.

62. Boersma, *Nouvelle Théologie and Sacramental Ontology*, 151–60.

63. Wood also recognizes a sacramental relationship between letter and spirit, though, as noted above, she goes on to consider the relationship with anagogy. *Spiritual Exegesis and the Church*, 39.

64. Chapter 6 will develop this scholastic terminology further.

65. de Lubac, *Medieval Exegesis*, 1:111. My bracketed substitution. "Il plante la Croix du Christ au centre de toutes choses. . . . L'espace et le temps, la terre et le ciel, les anges et les hommes, l'Ancien Testament et le Nouveau l'univers physique et l'univers moral, la nature et la grâce: tout est embrassé, lié, noué, 'structuré,' unifié par cette Croix, comme tout est dominé par elle" (*Exégèse médiévale*, 1/1:163–64).

66. The centrality of the cross for the supernatural order is affirmed by the mature de Lubac in *Brief Catechesis*, 117–38, especially 167–73. See chapter 1. See also Flipper's account of a structural parallel between the relationship of nature and the supernatural and the relationship between history and allegory. *Between Apocalypse and Eschaton*, 289–92. Both turn upon the novelty of the mystery of redemption in Christ.

67. de Lubac, *Catholicism*, 179. "Si, selon une equivalence qui fut longtemps en usage et don't saint Thomas témoigne encore au début de la *Somme*, on appelle Théologie la science des Écritures, alors on peut dire en verité que toute la Théologie est *Theologia Crucis*, entendant par là *Theologia a Cruce*. C'est la Croix qui dissipe la nuée don't jusqu'alors la Vérité était couverte" (*Catholicisme*, 146).

68. E.g., de Lubac, *History and Spirit*, 198–99, 240–42, 306–10, 316, 363, 460–61; *Medieval Exegesis*, 1:xix, 111, 239–40; 2:53, 92, 101, 134, 179, 183; 3:111, 143–44; *Exégèse médiévale*, 2/2:50–52, 64, 122, 272.

69. de Lubac, *Medieval Exegesis*, 1:239–40. "On peut cependant parler en termes moins généraux. Exégète de l'Écriture, Jésus l'est par excellence dans acte par lequel il accomplit sa mission, à cette heure solennelle pour laquelle il est venu: dans l'acte de son sacrifice, à l'heure de sa mort en croix. . . . En prononçant 'le consummatum est', sur ce gibet que désigne symboliquement la dernière lettre de l'alphabet hébreu, Jésus donne à toute l'Écriture sa consommation. . . . Sa croix est la clé, unique, universelle. Par ce sacrement de la croix, il unit les deux Testaments en un seul corps de doctrine, mêlant les préceptes anciens à la grâce évangélique. . . . Comme la 'récapitulation universelle' s'est effectuée par le Sacrifice de Jésus, ainsi, en même temps, l'ouverture et la condensation définitive de l'ancienne Écriture" (*Exégèse médiévale*, 1/1:324–25, 327). See also *Medieval*

192 Notes to Pages 69–71

Exegesis, 3:111; *Exégèse médiévale*, 2/2:272. Hercsik identifies Christ himself as the *"Schlüssel"* (key) to the two testaments (*Jesus Christus als Mitte der Theologie*, 243), though he goes on to clarify that it is particularly Christ's act in the paschal mystery that holds this position (245–47). Building upon Hercsik, Guibert argues that the paschal mystery is the "synthèse vivante" of de Lubac's works. *Mystère du Christ*, 423–45.

70. de Lubac, *Exégèse médiévale*, 2/2:111–13, 119–20, 122–23 (111).

71. Ibid., 2/2:119, my translation. "Car si l'on peut dater le Nouveau Testament du moment de l'Incarnation, c'est en tant que l'on voit déjà celle-ci préparant l'Acte rédempteur en vue duquel elle s'est accomplie . . . la Nouvelle Alliance a été fondée par lui à la dernière Cène; le voile qui en dissimulait encore la vraie nature n'a été pleinement ôté que par sa mort suivie de sa résurrection et de son ascension, et jusque-là ses disciples aussi bien que lui-même observeraient la Loi juive dans sa lettre." This clarifies the passages where de Lubac speaks as if the incarnation is the content of the allegorical sense (e.g., *Medieval Exegesis*, 1:260; *Exégèse médiévale*, 2/2:511). In the world order that actually exists, the incarnation occurs for the sake of the cross.

72. Significantly, de Lubac has the New Covenant begin at the Last Supper, which, as the institution of the Eucharist, is a sacrificial act. Indeed, according to the Council of Trent, the sacrifice of the Eucharist is identical in content to the sacrifice of the cross (Session 22, "Teaching and Canons on the Most Holy Sacrifice of the Mass" [September 17, 1562], chaps. 1–2 [Tanner, 2:732–36]).

73. de Lubac, *Medieval Exegesis*, 3:143–44. "Voici l'unique Sacrifice, et l'unique Prêtre, et l'unique Victime. Le grand passage est accompli. . . . Voici donc l'holocauste parfait! Voici l'holocauste que jamais Dieu ne dédaignera, celui qui demeure pour toujours devant sa Face" (*Exégèse médiévale*, 2/1:192–93). Similarly, *Exégèse médiévale*, 2/2:45–46.

74. de Lubac, *Medieval Exegesis*, 3:140. See also Hercsik, *Jesus Christus als Mitte der Theologie*, 91–93.

75. de Lubac, *Medieval Exegesis*, 3:140. "En Lui, les 'verba multa' des écrivains bibliques deviennent pour toujours 'Verbum unum.' Sans Lui, au contraire, le lien se dénoue: de nouveau la Parole de Dieu se fragmente en 'paroles humaines'; paroles multiples, non pas seulement nombreuses, mais multiples par essence, et sans unité possible" (*Exégèse médiévale*, 2/1:187–88). See also *Medieval Exegesis*, 1:241–47; *Révélation divine*, 110–15.

76. de Lubac, *Medieval Exegesis*, 3:141–42 (141). "La Parole éternellement prononcée" (*Exégèse médiévale*, 2/1:188).

77. de Lubac, *Medieval Exegesis*, 3:144–46. See O'Sullivan's important discussion of the trinitarian dimensions of de Lubac's theology, especially his theology of the cross. *Christ and Creation*, 391–412. See also Guibert, *Mystère du Christ*, passim, but especially the summary at 449–64.

Notes to Pages 71–72   193

78. *Medieval Exegesis*, 1:260; *Exégèse médievale*, 2/2:511 (indeed, the passage from *Exégèse médiévale* speaks of "*l'incarnation rédemptrice*"). See further Paul McPartlan, *Eucharist Makes the Church*, 62.

79. O'Sullivan, *Christ and Creation*, 43–48, 453.

80. de Lubac, *Medieval Exegesis*, 2:92. "Le Christ et l'Église ne sont qu'un seul grand mystère" (*Exégèse médiévale*, 1/2:502).

81. de Lubac, *Medieval Exegesis*, 2:92. "En cela réside tout le mystère de l'Écriture, tout l'objet d'*allegoria*" (*Exégèse médiévale*, 1/2:502).

82. de Lubac, *Medieval Exegesis*, 2:93; *Exégèse médiévale*, 2/2:50–52, 111–12, 149; *History and Spirit*, 200–201, 243–47. See discussion in Wood, *Spiritual Exegesis and the Church*, 38, 46, 54–68, 144–52; Flipper, *Between Apocalypse and Eschaton*, 227–34; Schlesinger, "Threefold Body," 189–97. Hollon, while noting the importance of the *totus Christus* for de Lubac's theology of spiritual exegesis, suggests that "de Lubac . . . views allegory as the means through which the historical Jesus is transformed into the omnipresent *totus Christus*." *Everything Is Sacred*, 168. Such an understanding is a category error, for it casts the historical Jesus, who is himself the spiritual sense of Scripture, as another literal sense.

83. de Lubac, *Exégèse médiévale*, 2/2:45. Once more we see the cross, sacrifice, and the Trinity bound together.

84. This consideration will be rather central to the discussion in chapter 6 of the relation between the church and the Eucharist.

85. de Lubac, *Exégèse médiévale*, 2/2:45. "La croix du Christ est une machina, que le Christ lui-même a voulu construire afin d'y restaurer et d'y rassembler toutes choses."

86. Ibid., 2/2:47. "Tout la foi de la chrétien va de la Trinité à la Trinité. Enfin, au sommet du toit, brillera la Croix."

87. de Lubac, *Medieval Exegesis*, 2:135. "Le sens tropologique ne suppose donc pas seulement le Mystère du Christ, mais aussi celui de l'Église, qui en est inséparable ainsi qu'on l'a vue. Il suppose, ou plutôt il l'exprime: car si les âmes ne sont chrétiennes que dans l'Église, en revanche 'c'est dans les âmes que l'Église est belle'" (*Exégèse médiévale*, 1/2:559). See also *Histoire et esprit*, 240–42. See further Flipper, *Between Apocalypse and Eschaton*, 173; Hollon, *Everything Is Sacred*, 172–76; Ayres, "Soul and the Reading of Scripture," 185–202.

88. de Lubac, *Medieval Exegesis*, 2:135.

89. de Lubac, *Histoire et esprit*, 211, my translation. "Si variées que soient les circonstances de l'histoire de l'Église ou de la vie de chacun de ses membres, ce Mystère se reproduit toujours, essentiellement le même, car l'Agneau de Dieu ne cesse pas un seul jour d'ôter par son sacrifice le péché de chacun de nous. . . . Cette Pâque ne cesse de se produire en réalité, comme au premier jour. Dieu la renouvelle dans l'âme, et celle-ci doit concourir à son achèvement."

90. de Lubac, *Exégèse médiévale*, 2/2:122, my translation. "Cette face externe du Mystère est passée, comme tout ce qui appartient au temps—le Christ entré dans sa gloire ne souffre plus, ne meurt plus—mais sa face interne demeure. . . . Nous sommes là au cœur de la morale paulinienne."

91. See Guibert's argument that de Lubac's soteriology consists in the interiorization of the mystery of Christ. *Mystère du Christ*, 173–329, esp. 327–29.

92. de Lubac, *Medieval Exegesis*, 2:134. "Toute l'allégorie se concentre dans le mystère de Pâques; mais il nous faut dire encore, avec saint Ambroise: 'Quotannis Jesu Christi Pascha celebratur, hoc est, animarum transitus. . . .' Autrement dit, s'il est vrai que rien n'est supérieur au Mystère du Christ, on ne doit pas oublier que ce Mystère, qui était figuré dans l'Ancien Testament, se réalise encore, s'actualise, s'achève dans l'âme chrétienne" (*Exégèse médiévale*, 1/2:557. Ellipses original).

93. de Lubac, *Medieval Exegesis*, 2:134. "Celle-ci consistant tout entière dans le Mystère du Christ, c'est ce Mystère qui, dans la trogologie, se trouve intériorisé . . . 'in virtute crucis Christi'" (*Exégèse médiévale*, 1/2:558).

94. de Lubac, *Medieval Exegesis*, 2:186–87. "Le premier et le deuxième avènement du Christ sont englobés dans le dernier. . . . Car c'est bien en chacun des membres de son corps mystique que le Christ achève, à la fin des temps, l'œuvre du Père. . . . Ainsi le terme et la voie sont tissés l'un et l'autre, si l'on peut dire, de la même étoffe. . . . La réalité eschatologique atteinte par l'anagogie est la réalité éternelle, en laquelle toute autre a sa son cosommation. . . . Elle constitue 'la Plénitude du Christ'" (*Exégèse médiévale*, 1/2:631–33).

95. de Lubac, *Exégèse médiévale*, 1/2:650, my translation. "Christus seipsum significat . . . translatus est Christus ad Ecclesiam. . . . L'Église sera la plénitude du Christ." See also *Exégèse médiévale*, 2/2:112.

Chapter Five.   Church as the Community of Salvation

1. Balthasar identifies it as such. *Theology of Henri de Lubac*, 105.

2. Simmonds, "Mystical Body," 159–60.

3. de Lubac, *Splendor of the Church*, 17–19; *Motherhood of the Church*, 21–22; *Church: Paradox and Mystery*, 33.

4. *Lumen gentium*, no. 6 (Tanner, 2:852).

5. de Lubac, *Splendor of the Church*, 120–24 (124). "Le concept paulinien de 'Corps du Christ' apparaît le plus apte à intégrer tous les éléments de cette doctrine" (*Méditation sur l'église*, 105). See further Wood, *Spiritual Exegesis and the Church*, 86–89, 93–95.

6. *Lumen gentium*, nos. 6–8 (Tanner, 2:852–55). Grillmeier, "Chapter I: The Mystery of the Church," 1:144–51; Hünermann, "Theologischer Kommentar," 1:363–66.

Notes to Pages 77–79   195

7. For de Lubac's discussion of the various images, see *Splendor of the Church*, 102–24. See further Wood, *Spiritual Exegesis and the Church*, 82–128; Pelchat, *Église mystère de communion*, 77–122.

8. de Lubac, *Catholicism*, 83–111.

9. de Lubac, *Corpus Mysticum*, 88. See further McPartlan, *Eucharist Makes the Church*; Schnackers, *Kirche als Sakrament und Mutter*, 59–64; Doyle, "Henri de Lubac and the Roots of Communion Ecclesiology," 209–27; Wang, "*Sacramentum Unitatis Ecclesiasticae*," 143–58; Moloney, "Henri de Lubac on Church and Eucharist," 331–42.

10. de Lubac, *Catholicism*, 25. "Ainsi l'unité du Corps mystique du Christ, unité surnaturelle, suppose-t-elle un première unité naturelle, l'unité du genre humain" (*Catholicisme*, 3).

11. Even a passing familiarity with *Lumen gentium* will prompt a recognition of de Lubac's influence on the Constitution. Here the overlap is with no. 9 (Tanner, 2:855). I shall not belabor these connections, though, as they are ancillary to my primary concern. For de Lubac's involvement in the Council, especially its ecclesiology, see, e.g., Pelchat, *Église mystère de communion*, 275–350; Riches, "Henri de Lubac and the Second Vatican Council," 121–56; Chantraine and Lemaire, *Henri de Lubac, tome IV*, 282–331.

12. de Lubac, *Catholicism*, 37–39, 367–69 (*Catholicisme*, 14–16, 322–24).

13. de Lubac, *Catholicism*, 39. See the exposition in Guibert, *Mystère du Christ*, 220–80.

14. Guibert, *Mystère du Christ*, 266, my translation. "le don de la révélation totale et définitive qui nous appele à la foi, et le don de l'Église comme société et corps."

15. Ibid., 363–66: "Ainsi, la foi et l'agrégation à son Église, si elles sont bien nécessaires au salut, ne sont pas des conditions surajoutées" (264).

16. Ibid., 267–72.

17. Ibid., 276, my translation. "Étant le Corps du Christ, l'entrée dans ce Corps est participation à la Vie éternelle. Cette Vie éternelle étant l'intime du Père, du Fils et du Saint-Esprit, la participation à ces relations trinitaires, dans la personne du Fils, renouvelle la vie relationnelle de l'homme."

18. Ibid., 277–80. See also Geneste, *Humanisme et lumière du Christ*, 237–53; Cholvy, *Surnaturel incarné dans la création*, 149–67. Of particular note is Édouard Adé's judgment that this grounding of the church in the paschal mystery bears particular relevance for a more familial conception of the church in African theological contexts. "Église-Famille et catholicité," 206.

19. de Lubac, *Church: Paradox and Mystery*, 16–17. See also Pelchat, *Église mystère de communion*, 99–103.

20. *Lumen gentium*, no. 1 (Tanner, 2:849). See also de Lubac, *Church: Paradox and Mystery*, 15–16, 75.

21. de Lubac, *Catholicism*, 76. "Si le Christ est le Sacrement de Dieu, l'Église est pour nous le Sacrement du Christ, elle le représente, selon toute l'ancienne force du terme: elle nous rend le présent en vérité" (*Catholicisme*, 50). Once more, de Lubac was not a lone voice in this regard. See also Rahner, "The Theology of The Symbol," 221–52; Schillebeeckx, *Christ: The Sacrament of the Encounter with God*; Semmelroth, *Kirche als Ursakrament*.

22. Wood, *Spiritual Exegesis and the Church*, 105–28; Schnackers, *Kirche als Sakrament und Mutter*, 74–83; Pelchat, *Église mystère de communion*, 103–6; Simmonds, "Mystical Body."

23. de Lubac, *Splendor of the Church*, 327–34; Wood, *Spiritual Exegesis and the Church*, 96–104; Pelchat, *Église mystère de communion*, 185–88; Schnackers, *Kirche als Sakrament und Mutter*, 181–87.

24. de Lubac, *Paradoxe et mystère de l'église*, 97–98, my translation. "En tant que visible et temporelle, l'Église est destinée à passer. Elle est signe et sacrement: or les signes et les sacrements seront résorbés dans la réalité qu'ils annoncent. Elle est moyen: moyen divin, moyen nécessaire, mais provisoire comme tout moyen." See further *Splendor of the Church*, 64–68; *Catholicism*, 70.

25. de Lubac, *Méditation sur l'église*, 175, my translation. "Il faut qu'elle soit traversée, et non pas à moitié, mais totalement."

26. de Lubac, *Splendor of the Church*, 203.

27. Ibid., 66, 117, 123. See also Wood, *Spiritual Exegesis and the Church*, 41–46, 82.

28. See chapter 4, on the relation between allegory and anagogy, and chapter 7, for de Lubac's anti-Joachimite emphases.

29. de Lubac, *Splendor of the Church*, 68. "Ce sera la manifestation de sa 'vérité.' Ce sera son épiphanie glorieuse et son achèvement" (*Méditation sur l'église*, 56).

30. Ibid., 68–77.

31. Here de Lubac cites *Corpus Mysticum* and *History and Spirit*. I shall return to this notion of truth and its fullness in chapter 7.

32. de Lubac, *Méditation sur l'église*, 175–76, my translation. "Elle se trouve dans un rapport essentiel à notre condition présente, qui ne s'inscrit plus dans le temps des pures figures, mais qui ne comporte pas non plus encore la pleine possession de la 'vérité.' Son second caractère . . . sera donc de ne pouvoir jamais être rejeté comme ayant cessé d'être utile. Ce milieu diaphane, qu'on doit traverser toujours et traverser totalement, on n'a cependant jamais fini de le traverser. C'est toujours à travers lui qu'on atteint ce dont il est le signe. Jamais il ne peut être dépassé, franchi."

33. de Lubac, *Catholicism*, 67–76, 133; *Splendor of the Church*, 64–68, 77–82, 202–3; *Corpus Mysticum*, 66–68, 204; *Church: Paradox and Mystery*, 23–29.

Notes to Pages 82–84   197

34. Cholvy, *Surnaturel incarné dans la création*, 196–97.

35. de Lubac, *Church: Paradox and Mystery*, 2–3; *Motherhood of the Church*, 113–20; *Catholicism*, 62–68; *Splendor of the Church*, 102–11. See further Pelchat, *Église mystère de communion*, 191–96.

36. de Lubac, *Motherhood of the Church*, 75–84.

37. de Lubac, *Church: Paradox and Mystery*, 21.

38. See, e.g., Schnackers, *Kirche als Sakrament und Mutter*, 181–87; Pelchat, *Église mystère de communion*, 185–88; Wood, *Spiritual Exegesis and the Church*, 96–104; Rougé, "'Sicut Maria, ita et ecclesia,'" 176–86.

39. de Lubac, *Méditation sur l'église*, 275, my translation. "La foi catholique à la Sainte Vierge résume symboliquement, dans son cas privilégié, la doctrine de la coopération humaine à la Rédemption, offrant ainsi comme la synthèse ou l'idée-mère du dogme de l'Église. Aussi a-t-on pu dire encore qu'une et l'autre doivent tenir ou crouler ensemble."

40. Ibid., 297, my translation: "Marie fut présentée au Temple, en s'offrant toute à son Dieu elle offrait l'Église avec elle. Quand le Verbe prenant chair en son sein, répandait sur elle ses trésors, il épousait et déjà comblait son Église en la personne de sa Mère. Le *Fiat* de Marie acceptait la pleine réalisation des promesses, pour elle personnellement, mais aussi pour tous collectivement, et c'est au nom de tous que ce *Fiat* était attendu."

41. On this, see Prevot, "Henri de Lubac (1896–1991) and Contemporary Mystical Theology."

42. de Lubac, *Motherhood of the Church*, 66–71.

43. Ibid., 75–84.

44. Ibid., 80–81.

45. Ibid., 85–112.

46. Ibid., 113–20 (113). "Notre participation . . . à la Vie interne de la Divinité" (*Églises particulières dans l'Église universelle*, 189).

47. de Lubac, *Motherhood of the Church*, 120–21; *Splendor of the Church*, 133–44.

48. See, e.g., Gaillardetz, *By What Authority?*; *Teaching with Authority*; Sullivan, *Magisterium*.

49. Henri de Lubac, "Problem of the Development of Dogma," 274–75. "L'état premier de la doctrine . . . le Tout du Dogme" ("Problème du développement du dogme," 2:64–65). See further "Doctrine of Father Lebreton," 338–39.

50. Dumas, *Mystique et théologie*, 83, my translation. "Tout en s'inscrivant dans des problématiques différentes, le 'Dogme' lubacien signifie la même chose que le Mystère."

51. Dumas, *Mystique et théologie*, 84, my translation. "Il faudra également distinguer le Dogme en son état premier—le Christ, Geste d'Amour de Dieu

sur le monde—et les dogmes, ces formulations issues de l'intelligence humaine guidée par l'Esprit de Vérité."

52. de Lubac, "Problem of the Development of Dogma," 274–75. "le Tout du Dogme" ("Problème du développement du dogme," 2:65); *Christian Faith*, 240–59.

53. See chapter 3.

54. de Lubac, *Splendor of the Church*, 241–67 (244). "Jamais il n'aurait l'idée d'en appeler de l'enseignement actuel du Magistère . . . qu'il reçoit tourjours au contraire comme la norme prochaine absolue" (*Méditation sur l'église*, 211).

55. Chantraine and Lemaire, *Henri de Lubac, tome IV,* 336 (quoting a letter from de Lubac dated January 5, 1966). "une certain *intelligentsia* 'pour laquelle tout dogme est pratiquement à rejeter, qui accepte sans critique toutes les suggestions venant des milieux antichrétiens, et ne veut plus rien comprendre de la vie spirituelle. Pour ceux-là, le Concile n'est qu'un premier pas, trop timide encore, dans la voie d'une liquidation générale.'" See further de Lubac, *Motherhood of the Church*, 25–27; Chantraine and Lemaire, *Henri de Lubac, tome IV*, 211–26, 311–38, 413–14, 433–38, 440–44.

56. Chantraine and Lemaire, *Henri de Lubac, tome IV,* 440–44.

57. From a letter to Roger Hamel, October 20 or 26, 1924 (Chantraine, *Henri de Lubac, tome II,* 539–40). "J'ai cette impression bienfaisante qu'il n'y pas tant de choses condamnées qu'on le dit parfois, et qu'en tout cas, ce sont surtout des choses et idées qu ne nous tenterait guère; la pensée se meut bien à travers la théologie, qui lui ouvre de bien vastes horizons, elle peut même sans danger s'abandonner à quelque hardiesse, pourvu que, dans toute sa démarche, elle respecte quelques normes sûres. . . . Avec cela et à condition de ne pas oublier sa condition de pécheur, je crois qu'on peut, sans plus d'embarras, déployer ses ailes."

58. Chantraine, *Henri de Lubac, tome II*, 660–72. On the "groupe Lubac," see 654–60.

59. Dated July 31, 1928 (in ibid., 661–72).

60. Fontoynont (in ibid., 665–67). "Une telle scolastique sera, à plus forte raison, différente de cette sorte d'éclectisme formaliste coupé de tout lien avec la vie, et décidément inassimilable, qui fut en honneur à Jersey, qui reste à des degrés divers la philosophie de beaucoup; et qui tend à dénier le nom scolastique à toute manière de penser qui n'imite pas la sienne."

61. Ibid., 671. "Il est inévitable aussi que beaucoup d'esprits se heurtent à ce qu'il y a d'inassimilable et d'inaccueillant dans ce que beaucoup donnet come étant 'la' scolastique et 'la' doctrine sûre, et se trouvent ainsi repoussés les uns vers les autres."

62. Ibid. "supprimer l'influence du P. de L., c'est supprimer précisément une influence modératrice. . . . Cela va beaucoup plus loin que la question 'progressisme' et 'conservatisme.'"

Notes to Pages 87–90   199

63. de Lubac, *Splendor of the Church*, 264–65. "C'est cette Église hiérar-chique elle-même, et non pas telle que nous pouvons la rêver, mais telle qu'elle existe en fait, aujourd'hui même, que nous appelons notre mère" (*Méditation sur l'église*, 228–29).

64. *Lumen Gentium*, no. 8 (Tanner, 2:854).

65. de Lubac, *Motherhood of the Church*, 178. "Une 'Église' sans structure, invisible et diffuse. . . . la foi chrétienne serait alors évacuée" (*Églises particu-lières*, 49).

66. This is a major theme of Guibert, *Mystère du Christ*, 139–58, 253–63, and is also developed by Cholvy, *Surnaturel incarné dans la création*, 149–71; Geneste, *Humanisme et lumière du Christ*, 245–54.

67. de Lubac, "Mysticism and Mystery," 39, 62. "Si la vie mystique à son sommet consiste dans une union effective à la divinité, elle ne saurait en effet se réaliser que par une grâce surnaturelle, dont le lieu normal est l'Église et dont les conditions normales sont la vie de foi et les sacrements. . . . Il suit de ce qu'on vient de voir que la mystique chrétienne est encore, est nécessairement une mys-tique ecclésiale, puisque l'Incarnation réalise d'abord, dans l'Église, les noces du Verbe et de l'humanité" ("Mystique et Mystère," 46, 67).

68. Guibert, *Mystère du Christ*, 173–329.

69. de Lubac, *Catholicisme*, 14–16, 321–24.

70. Ibid., 82–85.

71. Ibid., 86–88.

72. Geneste's study of de Lubac ends with a vision of "la *concorporatio* eucharistique." *Humanisme et lumière du Christ*, 258–60.

73. Several are collected in Chantraine, *Henri de Lubac, tome II*, 719–42.

74. Ibid., 720. "Il me semble que cette prière, très simple, comprend tout; et que d'ailleurs, la transformation spirituelle en Jésus-Christ est la seule voie qui nous puisse conduire à l'intelligence de son Mystère."

75. de Lubac, *Motherhood of the Church*, 171–72.

76. Ibid., 180–90 (190). "L'Église présidée par un évêque" (*Églises particu-lières*, 55).

77. Ibid., 191–94. Cf. *Lumen Gentium*, no. 26 (Tanner, 2:870–71).

78. Ibid., 231, 257.

79. Ibid., 193–99.

80. Ibid., 199–203 (203).

81. Ibid., 204–6.

82. Ibid., 206–7.

83. Ibid., 234–35, 305–6; *Church: Paradox and Mystery*, 19; "Church in Cri-sis," 318. See also Chantraine and Lemaire, *Henri de Lubac, tome IV*, 68. Beyond de Lubac, see, e.g., Buckley, *Papal Primacy and the Episcopate*; Pottmeyer, *To-wards a Papacy in Communion*; Tillard, *Church of Churches*; *Église locale*.

84. de Lubac, *Motherhood of the Church*, 300.

85. Ibid., 300–304.

86. Ibid., 308–9.

87. Ibid., 305–6.

88. de Lubac, *Églises particulières*, 124, my translation. "Ce certait peut-être lui fair trop d'honneur. . . . Mais l'ancien gallicanisme était purvu d'un appareil doctrinal, il comportait un tradition, il était attaché à des usages vénérables, il s'exprimait dans une culture non seulement ecclésiastique mais humain, peut-être un peu étroite, mais solide, attestée par tant d'œuvres remarquables, tant de noms illustres. Ici, au contraire, on est en face d'une réaction adolescente, d'une idéologie fruste et sans racines, d'un repliement sans grandeur."

89. de Lubac, *Motherhood of the Church*, 305–6.

90. Ibid., 296–97.

91. Ibid., 234–35; de Lubac, *Church: Paradox and Mystery*, 36–37.

92. Chantraine and Lemaire, *Henri de Lubac, tome IV*, 224–27, 440–44, 550–52.

93. de Lubac, *Splendor of the Church*, 241–47.

94. Ibid., 21. "Quand un se refuse les fleurs et les fruits, la branche à laquelle on croit tenir encore n'est plus qu'une branche morte" (*Méditation sur l'église*, 14).

95. de Lubac, "Church in Crisis," 315; *Motherhood of the Church*, 25–27.

96. de Lubac, *Méditation sur l'église*, 194. Noted by Wood, *Spiritual Exegesis and the Church*, 106–7.

97. On para-conciliar immanentism as inverted integralism, see Chantraine and Lemaire, *Henri de Lubac, tome IV*, 212–15; Walsh, "De Lubac's Critique of the Postconciliar Church," 406–8.

Chapter Six. *Corpus mysticum verumque*

1. Portions of this chapter first appeared as Schlesinger, "Integrative Role of Sacrifice."

2. McPartlan, *Eucharist Makes the Church*; Wang, "*Sacramentum Unitatis Ecclesiasticae*," 143–58; Moloney, "Henri de Lubac on Church and Eucharist," 331–42; Wood, *Spiritual Exegesis and the Church*, 53–70; Pelchat, *Église mystère de communion*, 144–59; Doyle, *Communion Ecclesiology*, 56–71; Hemming, "Henri de Lubac: Reading *Corpus Mysticum*," 519–34.

3. de Lubac, *Corpus Mysticum*, 14–36, 75–100.

4. de Lubac, *Splendor of the Church*, 156–57.

Notes to Pages 94–97   201

5. de Lubac, *Corpus Mysticum*, passim, but esp. 3–9, 248–62. See discussion in McPartlan, *Eucharist Makes the Church*, 76–85; Zwitter, *Histoire en présence de l'Éternel*, 281–84.

6. de Lubac, *Corpus Mysticum*, 37–41, 45.

7. Note, though, Hemming's insistence that the ecclesial body not be reduced to the gathered congregation but rather be seen as an eschatological reality of which the gathered community is the effective sign. "Henri de Lubac: Reading *Corpus Mysticum*," 524–28. Also noted by Flipper, *Between Apocalypse and Eschaton*, 238–40.

8. de Lubac, *Corpus Mysticum*, 18–23.

9. Ibid., 32–36, 75–100.

10. Ibid., 23. "Elles aussi, au fond, désignent moins deux objets successifs que, à la fois, deux choses qui n'en font qu'une. Car le corps du Christ qu'est l'Église n'est point *autre* que ce corps et ce sang du mystère" (*Corpus mysticum*, 33, emphasis original).

11. de Lubac, *Corpus Mysticum*, 100–119, 187–247.

12. Ibid., 95–119.

13. de Lubac, *Splendor of the Church*, 97, 126–32; *Motherhood of the Church*, 34; *Church: Paradox and Mystery*, 27, 100.

14. de Lubac, *Corpus Mysticum*, 37. "Toute ce qui touche au mystère de l'autel est copieusement et presque indifféremment qualifié de mystique" (*Corpus mysticum*, 47).

15. de Lubac, *Corpus Mysticum*, 46–47.

16. Ibid., 37–54.

17. de Lubac, *Medieval Exegesis*, 3:19–27.

18. de Lubac, *Corpus Mysticum*, 47. "Le *sacramentum* jouerait donc plutôt le rôle de contenant, d'enveloppe par rapport au *mysterium* qui se cache en lui" (*Corpus mysticum*, 58). Cf. "*Sacramentum* designates . . . the exterior component, the 'envelope.' . . . It is the *sacrum* rather than the *arcanum*. The mystery is the *arcanum* itself. It is the interior component, the reality hidden under the letter and signified by the sign" (*Medieval Exegesis*, 2:21). "Alors *sacramentum* désigne plutôt l'élément extérieur, 'l'enveloppe.' . . . Il et le *sacrum* plutôt qu l'*arcanum*. Le mystère, lui, est cet *arcanum* même. Il est l'élément intérieur, la réalité cachée sous la lettre et signifiée par le signe" (*Exégèse médiévale*, 1/2:399).

19. Hercsik, *Jesus Christus als Mitte der Theologie*, 178–79. See also Flipper, *Between Apocalypse and Eschaton*, 213–17.

20. de Lubac, *Corpus Mysticum*, 49–51. "Un mystère, au sens ancien du mot, est plutôt une action qu'une chose" (*Corpus mysticum*, 60).

21. de Lubac, *Corpus mysticum*, 62–63, my translation: "Il est synthétique et dynamique. Il porte moins sur le signe apparent ou au contraire sur la réalité

202   Notes to Pages 97–99

cachée que sur l'un et l'autre à la fois: sur leur rapport, sur leur union, sur leur implication mutuelle."

22. de Lubac, *Corpus Mysticum*, 37–41.

23. Sacrifice's role in *Corpus Mysticum* is mentioned, but not really developed by Wood, *Spiritual Exegesis and the Church*, 63; McPartlan, *Eucharist Makes the Church*, 62–64, 76–77; Wang, "*Sacramentum Unitatis Ecclesiæ*," 149. It receives more attention in Hauser, "Eucharist and the Historicity of the Faith," 1–33, and in my own previous publications, which form part of the basis of this chapter. Hemming focuses upon the action of the Eucharist for a proper understanding of de Lubac but does not specifically identify the action in sacrificial terms. "Henri de Lubac: Reading *Corpus Mysticum*."

24. de Lubac, *Corpus mysticum*, 70, my translation. "Ici surout il conviendra d'oublier, si commode et si fondée qu'elle soit par ailleurs, la séparation mise par tant de traités modernes entre 'l'Eucharistie comme sacrifice' et 'l'Eucharistie comme sacrement.' Car le sacrement ne se comprend pas sans le sacrifice." See also Hauser, "Eucharist and the Historicity of the Faith," 10.

25. de Lubac, *Corpus Mysticum*, 58–62.

26. de Lubac, *Corpus mysticum*, 74–75, my translation. "Non plus simplement, comme dans le premier cas, 'corpus in mysterio,' mais 'corpus in mysterio passionis.' Ce sera le corps en tant qu'il fait l'objet d'une oblation mystique, elle-même toute relative à cette oblation que le Christ fit de lui-même au terme de sa vie terrestre; le corps en tant qu'engagé dans une action mystique, écho rituel indéfiniment multiplié dans le temps et l'espace de l'Action unique à laquelle elle emprunte son sens."

27. Guibert, *Mystère du Christ*, 228–29; Cholvy, *Surnaturel incarné dans la création*, 192–97. The thematic of the paschal mystery as passage into God will be made explicit in chapter 8 and the coda.

28. de Lubac, *Corpus Mysticum*, 65, 73 (65), emphasis added. "La perspective essentielle de ces textes n'est pas celle d'une présence ou d'un objet, mais celle d'une action et d'un sacrifice" (*Corpus mysticum*, 78). This point is stressed by Hemming, "Henri de Lubac: Reading *Corpus Mysticum*," 524–26. Also noted by Wood, *Spiritual Exegesis and the Church*, 63; McPartlan, *Eucharist Makes the Church*, 63–64; Hauser, "Eucharist and the Historicity of the Faith," 10–11.

29. de Lubac, *Corpus Mysticum*, 65. "d'une action et d'un sacrifice . . . le vocabulaire relatif à cette action et à ce sacrifice est commandé en grande partie par le vocabulaire relatif aux deux Testaments" (*Corpus mysticum*, 78–79).

30. de Lubac, *Corpus Mysticum*, 62–65. See also Zwitter, *Histoire en présence de l'Éternel*, 289–90.

31. de Lubac, *Corpus Mysticum*, 66. "Sacrement de mémoire, elle est aussi sacrement d'espérance" (*Corpus mysticum*, 79–80). See the important discussions in Wood, *Spiritual Exegesis and the Church*, 59–68; Flipper, *Between Apocalypse*

Notes to Pages 99–101   203

and Eschaton, 234–46; Hemming, "Henri de Lubac: Reading *Corpus Mysticum*," 524–28.

32. de Lubac, *Corpus Mysticum*, 66. "Nos deux zones 'cérémonielle' et 'scripturaire' sont confundues" (*Corpus mysticum*, 79).

33. Wood, *Spiritual Exegesis and the Church*, 67.

34. de Lubac, *Corpus Mysticum*, 66–67, emphasis original. "Signe efficace de la charité fraternelle qui fait le lien de ses membres . . . signe efficace de la paix et de l'unité pour laquelle le Christ est mort et vers laquelle, mus par son Esprit, nous tendons. . . . Elle nous signifie donc nous-mêmes—*mysterium nostrum, figura nostra*—en ce que nous avons déjà commencé d'être par le baptême . . . mais surtout en ce que nous devons devinir: en ce sacrement d'unité" (*Corpus mysticum*, 80).

35. This identity of what is memorialized and what is anticipated marks the key difference between my proposal and McPartlan's recognition that "Christ is present from the past, in the ever-presence of his Calvary sacrifice," while "the heavenly Church is present from the future." *Eucharist Makes the Church*, 89. McPartlan suggests that the underlying reality that guides history is the *parousia*'s corporate Christ rather than Calvary's singular sacrifice.

36. Wood, *Spiritual Exegesis and the Church*, 61–62. See also Zwitter, *Histoire en présence de l'Éternel*, 286–322.

37. de Lubac, *Corpus Mysticum*, 65, 201–4. See also Wood, *Spiritual Exegesis and the Church*, 66–67; Hauser, "Eucharist and the Historicity of the Faith," 10.

38. de Lubac, *Corpus Mysticum*, 58–62.

39. Ibid., 63, 193–94; Wood, *Spiritual Exegesis and the Church*, 61–62.

40. de Lubac, *Corpus Mysticum*, 188–206.

41. Ibid., 193–208; de Lubac, *Splendor of the Church*, 68–77, 156–57.

42. de Lubac, *Corpus Mysticum*, 194–95. "*Imago in evangelio*" (*Corpus mysticum*, 218–19 [219]). See also Zwitter, *Histoire en présence de l'Éternel*, 286–94.

43. de Lubac, *Corpus Mysticum*, 197–99.

44. Ibid., 71, 194–96, 198–200. See also, in chapter 4, the articulation of this theme of Christ as both fulfillment and anticipation in the area of spiritual exegesis and, in chapter 5, the articulation of the sacramentality of Christ and the church.

45. de Lubac, *Catholicism*, 76.

46. de Lubac, *Corpus Mysticum*, 64–65.

47. Schnackers, *Kirche als Sakrament und Mutter*, 164–69; Flipper, *Between Apocalypse and Eschaton*, 210–13.

48. de Lubac, *Corpus Mysticum*, 194–95; *Medieval Exegesis*, 2:116, 132–34, 186–87, 201–4. On the identity of content between allegory and anagogy in de Lubac, see Wood, *Spiritual Exegesis and the Church*, 36–46; Flipper, *Between*

204   Notes to Pages 101–102

Apocalypse and Eschaton, 120–26, 163–69. On the *totus Christus* in de Lubac, see Wood, *Spiritual Exegesis and the Church*, 38–46, 54–92; Flipper, *Between Apocalypse and Eschaton*, 227–46; Hemming, "Henri de Lubac: Reading *Corpus Mysticum*"; Zwitter, *Histoire en présence de l'Éternel*, 289.

49. de Lubac, *Corpus Mysticum*, 194–95. "L'Incarnation rédemptrice doit être lui-même considéré comme une vaste liturgie, image terrestre et temporelle de la Liturgie éternelle . . . *Umbra in lege, imago in evangelio, veritas in caelestibus.* Ainsi du sacrifice de l'Église, comparé d'une part aux sacrifices figuratifs et d'autre part à ce qu'on peut appeler le sacrifice céleste" (*Corpus mysticum*, 218–19, emphasis original). See also Zwitter, *Histoire en présence de l'Éternel*, 286–94, 308–9.

50. Wood, *Spiritual Exegesis and the Church*, 61–63. See the development of this insight in Flipper, *Between Apocalypse and Eschaton*, 213–27. It also appears in Zwitter, *Histoire en présence de l'Éternel*, 288, 301–3. Hauser applies this language in a strikingly similar way, though seemingly independent of Wood. "Eucharist and the Historicity of the Faith," 5. This may be explained by the fact that Hauser draws from Donald Keefe, who directed Wood's doctoral dissertation, upon which *Spiritual Exegesis and the Church* is based. McPartlan adverts to *res-sacramentum* language, but without applying it to de Lubac's theology of history in *Eucharist Makes the Church*, 77–79. For de Lubac's own use of the terminology, see, e.g., *Catholicism*, 96–97; *Corpus Mysticum*, 168–77; *Splendor of the Church*, 133.

51. Wood, *Spiritual Exegesis and the Church*, 61–62.

52. Ibid., 62.

53. Hemming, "Henri de Lubac: Reading *Corpus Mysticum*," 528. See also Flipper, *Between Apocalypse and Eschaton*, 238–40; Zwitter, *Histoire en présence de l'Éternel*, 303–11. Cf., e.g., Pickstock, *After Writing*, 158–66.

54. de Lubac, *Corpus Mysticum*, 67. "Le sacrifice extérieur et rituel est aussi le sacrement du 'vrai' sacrifice, de ce sacrifice intérieur et spirituel par lequel se réalise la société sainte de tous ceux qui adhèrent à Dieu" (*Corpus mysticum*, 80).

55. de Lubac, *Corpus Mysticum*, 184, bracketed Latin mine. "On remarquera la force de cette dernière formule, qui nous montre à nouveau le sacrifice de l'Église—de chacun de nous—inséparable désormais, en droit comme en fait, du sacrifice du Christ. Ainsi la considération de l'eau dans son double rapport au mystère eucharistique—mystère de la Passion et mystère de l'Église, mystère du corps déchiré et mystère du corps unifié—ouvrait une voie de plus par où l'on voyait se rejoindre l'idée de la *virtus* et l'idée de la *res*, l'idée de l'union la plus intime au Sauveur et l'idée de l'édification sociale de l'Église, l'idée de l'union de l'Église avec le Christ et l'idée de l'union des membres du Christ entre eux" (*Corpus mysticum*, 207).

Notes to Pages 102–105 205

56. de Lubac, *Corpus Mysticum*, 169–80.

57. Augustine, *Homilies on the Gospel of John* 26.13–15, pp. 460–63. See also de Lubac's summary treatment in *Corpus Mysticum*, 175–77.

58. de Lubac, *Corpus Mysticum*, 40–41, 49, 58, 65–67, 73, 141–42, 164, 200–204.

59. Ibid., 66–68. De Lubac cites *In psalmum* 26; *Sermo* 2.2; *Ep.* 140, 61; *De civitate Dei* 10.6. Elsewhere I have demonstrated that Augustine believed there is an identity between the sacrifice of the cross, the sacrifices of Christians, and the ultimate sacrifice of the *totus Christus*. Schlesinger, "Sacrificial Ecclesiology of *City of God*," 137–55; *Sacrificing the Church*, 33–52.

60. de Lubac, *Catholicism*, 102–11 (109). "Voilà le sacrifice auquel prépare le sacrifice de l'autel" (*Catholicisme*, 81). Hemming comes close to what I am proposing here with his argument that "in fact the *ecclesia* appears from the work done, and *mystically* signifies the body in question. The *ecclesia* does not assemble to do the work, the work only shows the *ecclesia* to have been already assembled, and to belong to something mystically and invisibly wider than itself." "Henri de Lubac: Reading *Corpus Mysticum*," 526. The crucial difference is that Hemming does not explicitly identify "the work" with the eucharistic sacrifice.

61. de Lubac, *Corpus Mysticum*, 88. "A la lettre, donc, l'Eucharistie *fait* l'Église" (*Corpus mysticum*, 104, emphasis original).

62. Chapter 4 documented this in the theology of spiritual exegesis. In *Corpus Mysticum*, see 70–72.

63. de Lubac, *Splendor of the Church*, 68–77, 90–108, 202–12. I will return to this theme in chapter 7.

64. de Lubac, *Catholicism*, 67–76, 133; *Corpus Mysticum*, 66–88, 204; *Splendor of the Church*, 64–68, 77–82, 202–35; *Church: Paradox and Mystery*, 23–29.

65. de Lubac, *Church: Paradox and Mystery*, 23.

66. de Lubac, *Splendor of the Church*, 202–3.

67. de Lubac, *Méditation sur l'église*, 114, my translation. "Tout chrétien participe à l'unique Sacerdoce de Jésus-Christ."

68. de Lubac, *Splendor of the Church*, 137. "Mais ce sacerdoce du peuple chrétien ne concerne pas la vie liturgique de l'Église. Il n'a pas de rapport direct à la confection de l'Eucharistie" (*Méditation sur l'église*, 117).

69. de Lubac, *Splendor of the Church*, 142. "A la messe, le célébrant parle donc au nom de toute la communauté chrétienne" (*Méditation sur l'église*, 121).

70. de Lubac, *Splendor of the Church*, 142. "Mais au moment essentiel, il agit par la vertu du Christ" (*Méditation sur l'église*, 121).

71. See discussion in Berranger, "Le rapport du Christ à l'Église," 169–70.

72. de Lubac, *Splendor of the Church*, 137–38 (138). "L'Église 'hiérarchique' fait l'Eucharistie" (*Méditation sur l'église*, 117).

206 Notes to Pages 105–112

73. de Lubac, *Splendor of the Church*, 142–51. In fact, as de Lubac labored to recover in *Corpus Mysticum*, the very nature of what the Eucharist signifies and effects demands that the whole church be present, for that is precisely what the Eucharist represents.

74. de Lubac, *Splendor of the Church*, 152.

75. de Lubac, *Méditation sur l'église*, 132, my translation. "Il ne serait d'aucun prix, s'il ne suscitait en chaque assistant le sacrifice intérieur . . . notre unité est le fruit du Calvaire. Elle résulte de l'application qui nous est faite à la messe des mérites de la Passion, en vue de la libération finale."

76. Ibid., 114, my translation. "Tout chrétien participe à l'unique Sacerdoce de Jésus-Christ."

77. Ibid., 206, my translation. "Jésus-Christ s'est offert en sacrifice pour que nous ne fassions qu'un dans cette unité des Personnes divines."

78. de Lubac, *Catholicisme*, 298, my translation. "Nous ne sommes pleinement personnels qu'à l'intérieur de la Personne du Fils, par laquelle et en laquelle nous avons part aux échanges de la Vie Trinitaire."

79. de Lubac, *Splendor of the Church*, 77.

80. de Lubac, *Méditation sur l'église*, 64, my translation. "Dans ce 'régime de parfaite intériorité' . . . et il n'y a aura pas d'autre Temple que le Seigneur, lui-même, ni d'autre lumière pour l'éclairer que l'Agneau. L'autel y sera celui des parfums, non plus celui des holocaustes, et l'Église tout entière ne sera plus qu'une seule hostie de louange en Jésus-Christ. Au Jour du Seigneur, quand sera réalisée dans sa perfection la 'catholica societas,' tout se trouvera, comme en Dieu même, à la fois unifié, intériorisé, éternisé parce que 'Dieu sera tout en tous.'"

81. Once more, Hemming approaches this understanding when he speaks of being inserted into "the prayer of Christ," and thereby included in God's "utterance of his Word." "Henri de Lubac: Reading *Corpus Mysticum*," 532. However, he casts this dynamic in terms of prayer rather than explicitly as sacrifice (a more specific member of the genus prayer).

82. These themes are discernible in Guibert, *Mystère du Christ*, 240–60, 449–64; Cholvy, *Surnaturel incarné dans la création*, 388–440; Geneste, *Humanisme et lumière du Christ*, 237–53; Zwitter, *Histoire en présence de l'Éternel*, 308–9, 330–36.

Chapter Seven. Salvation as the Meaning of History

1. Hughes, "Spiritual Interpretation of Scripture," 206. See also the similar, and earlier, observation by Wood, *Spiritual Exegesis and the Church*.

2. For de Lubac's admiration of Joachim, see, e.g., *At the Service of the Church*, 155; *Medieval Exegesis*, 3:327–41. For discussion of de Lubac's views of

and writings on Joachim, see Gardner, "Modern Pentecost," 1–70; Sutton, "Présentation," xxxv–xl; Chantraine and Lemaire, *Henri de Lubac, tome IV*, 649–55; Zwitter, *Histoire en présence de l'Éternel*, 115–207; Geneste, *Humanisme et lumière du Christ*, 198–206. On Joachim more generally, see Reeves, *Joachim of Fiore and the Prophetic Future*; McGinn, *Calabrian Abbot*.

3. Gardner, "Modern Pentecost," 130–258; Figura, "Héritage spirituel de Joachim de Flore," 211–30; Lemaire, "Postérité spirituelle," 14–16.

4. de Lubac, *History and Spirit*, 249–59. Earlier, he mentioned Joachim in passing in *Catholicism*, 118. See also Gardner, "Modern Pentecost," 1–2; Lemaire, "Postérité spirituelle," 15–16.

5. de Lubac, *History and Spirit*, 252. "L'Évangile éternel de celui-ci est l'antithèse et l'antidote anticipé de celui du moine calabrais" (*Histoire et esprit*, 221). See also *Medieval Exegesis*, 3:363.

6. de Lubac, *History and Spirit*, 252. "Bref, il est tout eschatologique" (*Histoire et esprit*, 221). See also Zwitter, *Histoire en présence de l'Éternel*, 127–28.

7. de Lubac, *Medieval Exegesis*, 3:327–419. *Splendor of the Church*, 202–8, also contains a substantive discussion of Joachim, but I reserve discussion of this for later.

8. de Lubac, *Medieval Exegesis*, 3:331–33, 339. See also Zwitter, *Histoire en présence de l'Éternel*, 118–24; Geneste, *Humanisme et lumière du Christ*, 189–201; Figura, "Héritage spirituel de Joachim de Flore," 214–15; Gardner, "Modern Pentecost," 73–86.

9. de Lubac, *Medieval Exegesis*, 3:336, 343. See further Gardner, "Modern Pentecost," 178–80.

10. de Lubac, *Medieval Exegesis*, 3:418–19; *Postérité spirituelle*, 18, 66–67.

11. de Lubac, *Postérité spirituelle*, 13–14. For summaries of de Lubac's historical survey, see, e.g., Figura, "Héritage spirituel de Joachim de Flore," 218–29; Sutton, "Présentation," vi–xxviii; Zwitter, *Histoire en présence de l'Éternel*, 133–207; Gardner, "Modern Pentecost," 86–120.

12. de Lubac, *Medieval Exegesis*, 3:345. "Les interprétations de l'Écriture données par l'abbé de Flore étaient fanaisistes . . . le mal ne serait pas grand, si toutes ces 'fantasmagories' ne découlaient de principes qui ruinent toute l'économie de la révélation chrétienne" (*Exégèse médiévale*, 2/1:464).

13. This is seen especially in the cases of Hegel, Schelling, and Marx (de Lubac, *Postérité spirituelle*, 359–93, 744–72). See also Gardner, "Modern Pentecost," 151–62; Zwitter, *Histoire en présence de l'Éternel*, 189–201.

14. See, e.g., Marjorie Reeves's review of the first volume of *Postérité spirituelle*. "Review of *La manifestation de l'Esprit*," 291–94. She admires it as a work of genuine erudition, yet contends that de Lubac has failed to demonstrate the plausibility of any direct influence of Joachim upon the bulk of his ostensible posterity. This critique is repeated in Reeves and Gould, *Joachim of Fiore and the*

208　Notes to Pages 114–115

Myth of the Eternal Evangel, 10, 24–26. Gardner handily summarizes the basic critiques of de Lubac on this front. "Modern Pentecost," 120–23.

15. Reeves, *Joachim of Fiore and the Prophetic Future*, 6–7.

16. Ibid., 5–7, 13–14, 72–73; McGinn, *Calabrian Abbot*, 112–13, 161–76, 186–87, 192.

17. Reeves, *Joachim of Fiore and the Prophetic Future*, 6–7; McGinn, *Calabrian Abbot*, 162–76, 180–81.

18. McGinn, *Calabrian Abbot*, 124–25.

19. Ibid., 22, 124–25, 137–38, 174–75, 182.

20. See, e.g., the recent plea in Radner, *Profound Ignorance*, 30–31.

21. Gardner, "Modern Pentecost," 124–27.

22. "L'Esprit n'est-il pas dangereusement détaché du Christ, même s'il est toujours enjoyé par lui?" (de Lubac, *Postérité spirituelle*, 66.) Trans: "Isn't the Spirit dangerously detached from Christ, even if it is always enjoyed by him?" "L'Esprit allait être dressé contre l'Église du Christ et par une conséquence fatale contre le Christ lui-même" (ibid., 18). Trans: "The Spirit was to be set against the church of Christ and by a fatal consequence against Christ himself." "Or, par une conséquence fatale, en dissociant de la sorte l'Évangile du Christ, tel qu'il était prêché depuis douze siècles dans l'Église, de cet Évangile éternel, qui sera celui de l'avenir, il dissocie le Christ lui-même de son Esprit" (*Exégèse médiévale*, 2/1:462). Trans: "Now, by a fatal consequence, in disassociating in this way the gospel of Christ, as it had been preached for twelve centuries in the church, from the eternal gospel, which will be that of the future, he disassociated Christ himself from his Spirit."

23. de Lubac, *Medieval Exegesis*, 3:418. "Joachim a compromis . . . la pleine sufisance de Jésus-Christ" (*Exégèse médiévale*, 2/1:558).

24. de Lubac, *Medieval Exegesis*, 3:375. "Toute révélation a été donnée par le Christ et toute œuvre de salut accomplie en Lui" (*Exégèse médiévale*, 2/1:503).

25. de Lubac, *Medieval Exegesis*, 3:375, 381; *Postérité spirituelle*, 43–47.

26. Zwitter, *Histoire en présence de l'Éternel*, 121, my translation. "Lubac explique que l'interprétation joachimite n'a pas seulement poussé plus loin mais radicalement changé l'exégèse traditionelle. Si pour l'exégèse traditionnelle, le défi était l'approfondissement du mystère, l'idée conductrice de Joachim est un secret à trouver ou une énigme (sur le déroulement de l'histoire du monde) à déchiffrer. De cette concordia litterae découle une nouvelle intelligence spirituelle. Le mystère principal, 'révélé' à Joachim à travers sa concorde des deux Testaments, est le mystère du troisième âge."

27. Ibid., 127, my translation. "La nouveauté du Christ n'a donc pas un rapport absolu à l'histoire, elle est seulement transitoire."

Notes to Pages 116–117   209

28. Ibid., my translation. "Si pour Origène l'Évangile éternel reste lié au mystère du Christ, l'Évangile éternel de Joachim se présente plutôt comme le dépassement de ce mystère."

29. Ibid., 128, my translation. "L'eschatologie de l'abbé de Flore est non-christique, puis-qu'elle ne conserve pas la place centrale au mystère pascal."

30. Gardner, "Modern Pentecost," 7–9. See also Figura, "Héritage spirituel de Joachim de Flore," 14–16.

31. See the discussion in chapter 4. See further Gardner, "Modern Pentecost," 178–87.

32. It is touched upon in, e.g., de Lubac, *Medieval Exegesis*, 3:339; *Postérité spirituelle*, 43–47, 373–75, 564–69, 804–11. See discussion in Figura, "Héritage spirituel de Joachim de Flore," 14–16, 29–30; Gardner, "Modern Pentecost," 221–28.

33. Sutton, "Présentation," xxxv, my translation. "Cette même préoccupation était loin d'être étrangère à l'attention que Lubac a portée, en tant qu'historien, aux multiples métamorphoses de la pensée de l'abbé de Flore. Cependant, dans la longue histoire des idées racontée tout au long des dix-huit chapitres de *La Postérité spirituelle*, elle ne fait surface que rarement. En revanche, elle domine la Conclusion de l'ouvrage."

34. de Lubac, *At the Service of the Church*, 156. "Je tiens le joachimisme pour un danger encore actuel et même pressant. Je le reconnais dans le processus de sécularisation qui, trahissant l'Evangile, transforme en utopies sociales la recherche du royaume de Dieu. Je le vois à l'œuvre dans ce qui fut si justement appelé 'l'auto-destruction de l'Église'" (*Mémoire sur l'occasion de mes*, 161).

35. de Lubac, *Postérité spirituelle*, 838, my translation and emphasis.

Impossible de recueillir, dans la foi et l'espérance, la venue de Dieu dans notre histoire, sans retenir, en mémoire indissociable, que l'infini inépuisable nous est donné. . . . Tantôt nous retenons que Dieu s'est donné au temps de sa venue, mais nous pensons que le don, le message et la vie du Christ sont épuisés. Ainsi, il n'y aurait plus d'avenir plus de novation, plus de vie dans une Église figée, sclérosée réduite au passé mort d'une époque, celle qu'il plaît à nos sentiments de retenir. Tantôt, en sens inverse, nous oublions que Dieu s'est donné en personne, absolument, pour croire que tout est à inventer, que l'Église n'a pas d'héritage.

Église du passé, Église du Père sans vie inventive spirituelle; Église figée, morte, des 'intégristes' passéistes. Église du futur, sans recueil du don de Dieu, en défi à l'institution; Église éventée dans un avenir spirituel irréel, Église des 'progressistes.' L'une et l'autre manquent le présent de l'Église; l'une et l'autre sont l'oubli du donné inépuisable de l'infini de Dieu. Et chacun de ces abstractions qui crucifient l'Église risque d'occuper tour à tour chaque chrétien pour ruiner le sens et la réalité vivante de la fidélité. La conversion nécessairement incessant au Dieu de l'Évangile est sans doute la volonté toujours dressée de retrouver sans trêve en l'Église la vérité impartageable du don de Dieu.

36. de Lubac, *At the Service of the Church*, 157. "Pourtant je ne serais loin d'admettre qu'une sorte de semi-joachimisme (peut-être moins infidèle à la visée de Joachim lui-même), don't j'ai parlé à propos de Buchez, fut au contraire la recherche tâtonnante de ce que doit être le développement normal de la Tradition catholique . . . la découverte par l'Église elle-même, au long de son pélerinage, de la perpétuelle fécondité de l'Evangile, d'où, face à chaque situation nouvelle, elle tire . . . nova et vetera" (*Mémoire sur l'occasion de mes écrits*, 161).

37. de Lubac, *Postérité spirituelle*, 520–21 (521), my translation. "'Semi-joachimisme,' disions-nous, qui n'envisage aucun au-delà du christianisme catholique et ne cède à aucune 'interprétation' dissolvante ou déformante du mystère." The main discussion of Buchez is on pp. 477–500. See further Sutton, "Présentation," xxxvi–xxviii; Gardner, "Modern Pentecost," 292–300; Zwitter, *Histoire en présence de l'Éternel*, 179–89.

38. Zwitter, *Histoire en présence de l'Éternel*, 201–7. De Lubac's treatment of Mikiewicz is found in *Postérité spirituelle*, 623–70.

39. Gardner, "Modern Pentecost," 292–300; Zwitter, *L'Histoire en présence de l'Éternel*, 241–46.

40. de Lubac, *At the Service of the Church*, 157. "Pourtant je ne serais loin d'admettre qu'une sorte de semi-joachimisme (peut-être moins infidèle à la visée de Joachim lui-même), don't j'ai parlé à propos de Buchez, fut au contraire la recherche tâtonnante de ce que doit être le développement normal de la Tradition catholique" (*Mémoire sur l'occasion de mes écrits*, 161).

41. de Lubac, *History and Spirit*, 11. "Toute une interprétation du christianisme, dont Origène . . . était d'ailleurs moins l'auteur que le témoin" (*Histoire et esprit*, 9).

42. See Lemaire, "Postérité spirituelle," 24.

43. de Lubac, *At the Service of the Church*, 156. "Au printemps de 1980, j'ai senti que le temps de s'arrêter était venu" (*Mémoire sur l'occasion de mes écrits*, 160). The section of de Lubac, *Postérité spirituelle*, is found on pp. 823–38.

44. de Lubac, *At the Service of the Church*, 156, bracketed French mine (*Mémoire sur l'occasion de mes écrits*, 160).

45. de Lubac, *At the Service of the Church*, 156. "Après coup, je me suis aperçu que le schema de cette conclusion qui manqué était trace en 1952 dans ma *Méditation sur l'Église*, pp. 175–180" (*Mémoire sur l'occasion de mes écrits*, 160). Noted by Lemaire, "Postérité spirituelle," 16–17; Gardner, "Modern Pentecost," 131.

46. Lemaire, "Postérité spirituelle," 17–40.

47. Gardner, "Modern Pentecost," 44–66, 259–61.

48. de Lubac, *Splendor of the Church*, 202. See also Lemaire, "Postérité spirituelle," 17–21; Gardner, "Modern Pentecost," 145–46, 213–21, 228–33, 241–47.

49. de Lubac, *Catholicism*, 76. See the further discussion in chapters 5 and 6.

50. de Lubac, *Splendor of the Church*, 202, bracketed French mine. "Étant le signe d'autre chose, il faut qu'elle soit traversée, et non pas à moitié, mais totalement" (*Méditation sur l'église*, 175).

51. *Méditation sur l'église*, 175–76, my translation. "Cette réalité sacramentaire n'est pas un signe quelconque, provisoire ou changeable à merci. Elle se trouve dans un rapport essentiel à notre condition présente. . . . Son second caractère, indissociable du premier, sera donc de ne pouvoir jamais être rejeté comme ayant cessé d'être utile. Ce milieu diaphane, qu'on doit traverser toujours et traverser totalement, on n'a cependant jamais fini de le traverser. C'est toujours à travers lui qu'on atteint ce dont il est le signe. Jamais il ne peut être dépassé, franchi."

52. de Lubac, *Splendor of the Church*, 202.

53. Ibid., 156–57.

54. For de Lubac's use of the terminology, see, e.g., *Catholicism*, 96–97; *Corpus Mysticum*, 168–75, 246; *Splendor of the Church*, 133. For this salvation-historical application, see, e.g., Wood, *Spiritual Exegesis and the Church*, 61–63; Flipper, *Between Apocalypse and Eschaton*, 213–27; Schlesinger, "Threefold Body," 194–200.

55. de Lubac, *Révélation divine*, 71–77; *Church: Paradox and Mystery*, 14–15. See also the fuller discussion in chapter 4.

56. de Lubac, *Splendor of the Church*, 203; *Catholicism*, 76.

57. de Lubac, *Catholicism*, 202–3; *Corpus Mysticum*, 71. See also the fuller discussion in chapters 4 and 6.

58. Henri de Lubac, *Exégèse médiévale*, 1/2:650, my translation. "Christus seipsum significat." See also *Exégèse médiévale*, 2/2:112.

59. de Lubac, *Corpus Mysticum*, 70–72; *Medieval Exegesis*, 2:92–93; *History and Spirit*, 200–201, 243–47.

60. de Lubac, *Corpus Mysticum*, 24; *Scripture in the Tradition*, 203–4.

61. de Lubac, *Corpus Mysticum*, 188–206. See also the fuller discussion in chapter 6.

62. de Lubac, *Splendor of the Church*, 73–77, 203.

63. de Lubac, *Catholicism*, 67–76, 133; *Splendor of the Church*, 64–68, 77–82, 202–3; *Corpus Mysticum*, 66–68, 204; *Church: Paradox and Mystery*, 23–29.

64. de Lubac, *Splendor of the Church*, 68–77.

65. Ibid., 202. "Étant le signe d'autre chose, il faut qu'elle soit traversée, et non pas à moitié, mais totalement" (*Méditation sur l'église*, 175).

66. de Lubac, *Splendor of the Church*, 68, 74–76.

67. Zwitter, *Histoire en présence de l'Éternel*, 232–33.

68. Lemaire, "Postérité spirituelle," 25, my translation. "la Modernité fait du christianisme un événement historique parmi d'autres, voire une étape à dépasser."

69. Ibid., 25–26.

70. Ibid., 31. See also de Lubac, "Problem of the Development of Dogma," 274–75; *Christian Faith*, 243–57.

71. Gardner, "Modern Pentecost," 142. See also de Lubac, *Christian Faith*, 107.

72. Lemaire, "Postérité spirituelle," 23–29.

73. Ibid., 30–38.

74. Ibid., 32–41.

Chapter Eight.   Salvation as Eschatological Sacrifice

1. These are perhaps most famously explored in Teilhard de Chardin, *Human Phenomenon*; *Divine Milieu*. See also Grumett, *Teilhard de Chardin*; Deane-Drummond, "Sophia, Mary and Eternal Feminine," 215–31; Sutton, "Teilhard de Chardin's Christocentric Trinitarianism," 90–103.

2. de Lubac, *Religion of Teilhard*; *Faith of Teilhard*; *Eternal Feminine*; *Teilhard Explained*; *Teilhard posthume*. In addition, de Lubac edited a volume of correspondence between Teilhard and Maurice Blondel. *Pierre Teilhard de Chardin, Maurice Blondel: Correspondence.*

3. de Lubac, *Vatican Council Notebooks*.

4. Moulins-Beaufort, "Henri de Lubac, avocat de Pierre Teilhard de Chardin," 165–66.

5. de Lubac, *Athéisme et sens de l'homme*, 130–41.

6. Letter from de Lubac to Fessard, CAÉCHL 1963 (H-G 23.01.68), in Chantraine and Lemaire, *Henri de Lubac, tome IV*, 365, my translation. "Du Teilhard et encore du Teilhard, cela me fatigue et m'ennui, d'autant plus que je sens bien tout ce qu'il y a de peu teilhardian en moi."

7. See the evaluations in, e.g., de Lubac, *Religion of Teilhard*, 108, 185–94, 211–15; *Faith of Teilhard*, 40–42, 99–113; *Teilhard Explained*, 37. See also Fédou, "Henri de Lubac lecteur de Teilhard," 110–12.

8. de Lubac, *Teilhard posthume*, 343–44. Perhaps also relevant are the comments on Teilhard's vision of an expanded chastity wherein sex and reproduction have been decoupled to give greater expression to the universality of human love. *Eternal Feminine*, 48–65.

Notes to Pages 127–129   213

9. Teilhard advocates for eugenics in *Human Phenomenon*, 200–202. See the further documentation by Slattery, "Dangerous Tendencies of Cosmic Theology," 69–82, along with the exchange it prompted in Haught, "Trashing Teilhard"; Slattery, "Teilhard & Eugenics." To be fair, Teilhard does resolutely denounce racism in *Human Phenomenon*, 168, 163–64.

10. de Lubac, *Teilhard posthume*, 324.

11. de Lubac, *At the Service of the Church*, 104. These dynamics and developments are more fully traced by Lemaire, "Henri de Lubac, défenseur de Teilhard," 571–86.

12. Fergus Kerr suggests a strong connection between de Lubac's own biography and his tendency to rehabilitate marginalized figures, among whom he includes Origen, Joachim of Fiore, Giovanni Pico della Mirandola, and Teilhard. *Twentieth-Century Catholic Theologians*, 75–77. This may indeed hold for many of these figures, but it most certainly does not accurately describe de Lubac's agenda with Joachim, whose theology of history he resolutely opposed.

13. His appreciation for Teilhard's piety is especially on display in de Lubac, *Faith of Teilhard*, 3–12, 69–88; *Religion of Teilhard*, 221–38.

14. de Lubac, *Teilhard posthume*, 324.

15. de Lubac, *Religion of Teilhard*, esp., 78–91, but also 16–19, 30–33, 65–66. This idea is developed extensively in Pelchat, "Pierre Teilhard de Chardin et Henri de Lubac," 255–73; Wagner, " Henri de Lubac et Pierre Teilhard de Chardin," 212–13.

16. Moulins-Beaufort, "Henri de Lubac, avocat de Pierre Teilhard de Chardin," 180.

17. Grumett, *Teilhard de Chardin*, 8, 37–102. See also Teilhard de Chardin, *Divine Milieu*, 17–68.

18. de Lubac, *Religion of Teilhard*, 11. "Qu'il est facile de laisser tomber, de la pensée d'un auteur, ce qui n'intéresse pas! de n'attribuer à cette part jugée inintéressante qu'une importance minime, ou même de ne pas l'apercevoir! On fausse ainsi de bonne foi la signification de toute une œuvre en en faussant les proportions, même si l'on n'en présente que des analyses exactes. . . . Soit en exemple . . . l'exégèse biblique des Pères de l'Église. Tout entière, elle repose sur la perception aiguë d'un certain rapport, unique en son genre, le rapport des deux 'Alliances' ou des deux 'Testaments,' là est la clé, sans laquelle on ne saurait la comprendre" (*Pensée religieuse*, 11).

19. Ibid., 11–12, 16–19. For other assessments of Teilhard's Christocentrism, see, e.g., Sutton, "Teilhard de Chardin's Christocentric Trinitarianism"; Grumett, "Church, World and Christ," 87–103; Williams, "Traditionalist *Malgré Lui*," 111–12, 17.

20. For another account of Teilhard in terms of the categories of spiritual exegesis, see Ayotte, *Globalization and Multicultural Ministry*.

214   Notes to Pages 130–132

21. Teilhard de Chardin, *Divine Milieu*, 11.

22. He makes a direct appeal to this text in *Religion of Teilhard*, 25. The spirit of this characterization of Teilhard is evident throughout de Lubac's works on him. See especially ibid., 16–19, 28–35, 56–68, 221–38; *Faith of Teilhard*, 3–12, 31–32, 39–43, 45–46, 56–57, 69–77; *Eternal Feminine*, 66–77, 105–6, 165–77; *Teilhard Explained*, 14–17, 34.

23. de Lubac, *Religion of Teilhard*, 22–23; *Eternal Feminine*, 77–84. See also Grumett, *Teilhard de Chardin*, 13–36; "Teilhard at Ore Place," 687–700; King, "A Vision Transformed," 590–605.

24. Teilhard de Chardin, *Human Phenomenon*, 209–15. See further de Lubac, *Religion of Teilhard*, 71, 78–91.

25. de Lubac, *Faith of Teilhard*, 39–40; *Teilhard Explained*, 34–37, 41, 48–49.

26. This is developed at length in the main body of Teilhard de Chardin, *Human Phenomenon*, and presented in summary form in the book's postface (216–23).

27. Ibid., 210–15.

28. de Lubac, *Religion of Teilhard*, 93.

29. Ibid., 69–77, 108–10, 132; *Eternal Feminine*, 77–95; *Teilhard Explained*, 47–50.

30. de Lubac, *Eternal Feminine*, 77–79.

31. Ibid., 80. "Si la réalité nouvelle n'est pas entièrement nouvelle, la réalité ancienne n'en est pas moins entièrement renouvelée" (*Éternel féminin*, 126–27).

32. de Lubac, *Eternal Feminine*, 83–84 (83). "Et de même que les réalités animals—faim, amour, sens de la lute, gout de la proie,—sont encore en nous . . . ainsi, par exemple, la charité surnaturelle se nourrit de nos puissances naturelles d'aimer, tout en les transformant" (*Éternel féminin*, 133–34). See also *Religion of Teilhard*, 127–29.

33. de Lubac, *Religion of Teilhard*, 129. "Que la nature créée demeure elle-même, qu'elle ne soit pas absorbée, annihilée, et que néanmoins elle soit portée à un état tout autre, refondue . . . —et non pas seulement agrandie, prolongée, achevée dans son ordre,—voilà qui suppose l'efficace réalité de ce principe divin auquel la théologie classique a donné le nom de 'surnaturel.' Et la tradition chrétienne s'est plu, on le sait, à reconnaître dans la transformation de l'eau en vin par le miracle de Cana, en même temps qu'un symbole du passage de l'Ancien Testament au Nouveau, un symbole parlant de la divinisation du notre nature par le Christ" (*Pensée religieuse*, 180–81).

34. de Lubac, *Religion of Teilhard*, 322, n. 44. "les paroles de l'ordinaire de la messe, avant l'offrande du calice" (*Pensée religieuse*, 181, n. 4).

35. Teilhard de Chardin, *Human Phenomenon*, 209–15.

36. de Lubac, *Religion of Teilhard*, 74–75.

37. Ibid., 121, my bracketed substitution. "Pas de progress définitif automatique,—mais pas non plus de fin dernière obtenue par la seule action du vouloir humain. Cette fin dernière est divine. Si necessaire et si beau qu'il soit, l'effort de l'Homme, individual ou collectif, ne saurait donc, par lui-même, la procurer, Elle est 'd'un autre ordre.' Le résultat de cet effort n'a jamais par lui-même aucune valeur positivement surnaturelle" (*Pensée religieuse*, 169).

38. de Lubac, *Religion of Teilhard*, 123.

39. Ibid., 157–59; *Teilhard Explained*, 56; *Eternal Feminine*, 41–48, 73. See also Teilhard de Chardin, *Human Phenomenon*, 188–92, 212–13.

40. de Lubac, *Teilhard posthume*, 317. "Aucun n'est naturellement 'charitable.'"

41. de Lubac, *Religion of Teilhard*, 108–20, 137–38; *Teilhard Explained*, 35. Cf. the language of a "humanisme converti" in *Catholicisme*, 323, or of Catholicism as not merely "la seule religion vraie, la seule discipline efficace. . . . Il est la forme que doit revêtir l'humanité pour être enfin elle-même" (*Catholicisime*, 256). Trans: "the only true religion, the only effective discipline. . . . It is the form that humanity must put on to finally be itself."

42. Teilhard de Chardin, *Divine Milieu*, 17–43. See further Grumett, *Teilhard de Chardin*, 37–72.

43. Teilhard de Chardin, *Divine Milieu*, 45–66. See also Grumett, *Teilhard de Chardin*, 73–102.

44. de Lubac, *Religion of Teilhard*, 33–35.

45. Teilhard de Chardin, *Divine Milieu*, 89–131; *Human Phenomenon*, 183–94, 204–15; de Lubac, *Faith of Teilhard*, 29–38; *Religion of Teilhard*, 132–42, 152–60, 195–205; *Teilhard Explained*, 17–21, 54–56, 58–62.

46. de Lubac, *Religion of Teilhard*, 62–63; *Faith of Teilhard*, 30–31, 49–55; *Teilhard Explained*, 17–21, 56–57; *Teilhard posthume*, 288–89, 313–14.

47. de Lubac, *Religion of Teilhard*, 63–64, 68; *Faith of Teilhard*, 45–46, 35–36; *Teilhard Explained*, 16–17, 58–62; *Eternal Feminine*, 167–71; Teilhard de Chardin, *Divine Milieu*, 94–95.

48. de Lubac, *Religion of Teilhard*, 108–9. "La première est la victoire de l'Esprit sur la Matière. . . . Or, se greffant sur cette première victoire, qui en est la condition, une seconde n'est pas moins assurée: la Victoire du Christ ressuscité, don't le Plérôme assurée" (*Pensée religieuse*, 149–50).

49. de Lubac, *Faith of Teilhard*, 126–29; *Religion of Teilhard*, 121, 126.

50. de Lubac, *Religion of Teilhard*, 124–26 (26).

51. de Lubac, *Faith of Teilhard*, 56–57; *Religion of Teilhard*, 64.

52. Teilhard de Chardin, *Messe sur le monde*. See also de Lubac, *Faith of Teilhard*, 57.

53. de Lubac, *Religion of Teilhard*, 65. "Dans l'Eucharistie, mystère central, il contemple et le prolongement de l'Incarnation du Verbe et la promesse de la transfiguration du monde" (*Pensée religieuse*, 88).

54. See de Lubac's qualifications in, e.g., ibid., 65–66; *Faith of Teilhard*, 56–61.

55. Council of Trent, Session 22, "Teaching and Canons on the Most Holy Sacrifice of the Mass" (Tanner, 2:732–36).

56. de Lubac, *Faith of Teilhard*, 48, 68; *Religion of Teilhard*, 58, 132–34, 238; *Eternal Feminine*, 84, 106, 170–72.

57. de Lubac, *Brief Catechesis*, 135. "Sombre drame. . . . Drame sanglant, dont le sommet est au Calvaire" (*Petite catéchèse*, 261).

58. de Lubac, *Brief Catechesis*, 135. "dénouement lumineux" (*Petite catéchèse*, 261).

59. "Second Mémoire du Père Teilhard de Chardin. Au Père Auguste Valensin" (Paris, December 29, 1919), in *Teilhard posthume*, 70–71, my translation: "J'accorde d'abord, sans difficulté, que l'Effort universel du Monde peut-être compris comme *la préparation d'un holocauste*. Par ses acquisitions spirituelles (en lesquelles se résument toutes les autres), le Monde développe essentiellement une capacité, une puissance d'adoration, c'est-à-dire de renoncement. L'utilisation dernière des consciences individuelles et collectives qu'il élabore,—l'act suprême en vue duquel il les nourrit, les affine et les libère, c'est leur retour volontaire à Dieu, et le sacrifice consenti de leur apparente (ou immédiate) autonomie. . . . Tout notre travail, finalement, aboutit à former l'hostie sur qui doit descendre le Feu divin."

60. "Teilhard's Second Paper," in *Pierre Teilhard de Chardin, Maurice Blondel: Correspondence*, 47. "M. Bl. insiste sur deux images, celle du *feu qui dévore* et celle du *feu qui transfigure*. . . . Je me demande si les deux expressions ne sont pas équivalents l'une à l'autre, dans la réalité des choses" (*Teilhard posthume*, 71).

61. "Teilhard's Second Paper," 48, emphasis removed. "Dans l'acte par lequel je décide de me donner à Dieu je passe tout entier. . . . Si . . . du Feu qui doit me refondre, il est également vrai de dire qu'il me consumera et qu'il m'achèvera. Il faut dire de ces Flammes qu'elles dévorent, pour insister sur la grandeur inouïe du renouvellement qu'elles opèrent. Mais il faut ajouter qu'elles conservent, afin de rappeler la persistance, au milieu de la sublimation subie par notre nature, des moindres éléments amassés par notre liberté humaine.— Consumer et transfigurer, pour la Grâce, c'est tout un" (*Teilhard posthume*, 72).

Coda   *Mysterium Crucis*

1. de Lubac, *History and Spirit*, 411. "Or le Logos divin, Image incréée du Père, 'assume' la chair misérable pour la purifier et pour embraser l'univers dans le feu de son holocauste spirituel" (*Histoire et esprit*, 360). See also Zwitter, *Histoire en présence de l'Éternel*, 315.

Notes to Pages 140–142   217

2. Dumas, *Mystique et théologie*, 235–77.

3. de Lubac, *At the Service of the Church*, 112–13. "C'est, je crois bien, depuis assez longtemps l'idée de mon livre sur la Mystique qui m'inspire en tout; c'est de là que je tire mes jugements, c'est lui qui me fournit de quoi classer à mesure mes idées.—Mais ce livre, je ne l'écrirai pas. Il est de tout manière au-dessus de mes forces, physiques, intellectuelles, spirituelles. J'ai la vision nette de ses articulations, je distingue et situe à peu près les problèmes qui devraient y être traités, dans leur nature et dans leur ordre, je vois la direction précise dans laquelle devrait être cherchée la solution de chacun d'eux;—mais cette solution, je suis incapable de la formuler. Tout cela me suffit pour écarter à mesure les vues qui ne sont point émettre, mais tout cela ne prend pas sa forme dernière, la seule qui lui permettrait d'exister. Le foyer m'en échappe toujours. Ce que j'en réalise sur le papier n'est que préliminaire, ou banalités, ou discussions latérales, ou détails d'érudition." *Mémoire sur l'occasion de mes écrits*, 113. My statement "little more" risks appearing dismissive. This is not at all my intent; quite the opposite. What I mean is that de Lubac is far from having imposed some novel framework on his writings, having instead demonstrated an inner logic that de Lubac himself told us was there. See the treatment in Chantraine and Lemaire, *Henri de Lubac, tome IV*, 190–93, which also investigates some archival material in which de Lubac attempts to sketch out his vision for the book on mysticism.

4. de Lubac, "Mystique et Mystère," 37–76.

5. de Lubac, "Mysticism and Mystery," 39. "Il ne peut s'agir assurément pour un chrétien que de l'union au Dieu Tri-personnel de la révélation chrétienne, union réalisée en Jésus-Christ et par sa grâce" ("Mystique et Mystère," 42). On this article, see especially Dumas, *Mystique et théologie*, 153–88; Zwitter, *Histoire en présence de l'Éternel*, 71–85, 323–43; Hollon, "Mysticism and Mystical Theology," 307–25.

6. de Lubac, "Mysticism and Mystery," 40–43. Cf. "Nietzche as Mystic."

7. de Lubac, "Mysticism and Mystery," 43. "Si la vie mystique à son sommet consiste dans une union effective à la divinité, elle ne saurait en effet se réaliser que par une grâce surnaturelle, dont le lieu normal est l'Église et dont les conditions normales sont la vie de foi et les sacrements" ("Mystique et Mystère," 46).

8. de Lubac, "Mysticism and Mystery," 51.

9. Ibid., 52. See also Zwitter, *Histoire en présence de l'Éternel*, 327.

10. de Lubac, "Mysticism and Mystery," 53–54. See further Dumas, *Mystique et théologie*, 154–58; Zwitter, *Histoire en présence de l'Éternel*, 326–29.

11. de Lubac, "Mysticism and Mystery," 57. "intervention gracieuse de Dieu par le don du mystère" ("Mystique et Mystère," 62). See also Zwitter, *Histoire en présence de l'Éternel*, 78–79; Hollon, "Mysticism and Mystical Theology," 316–20. On the theme of image and likeness in de Lubac's thought, see O'Sullivan,

218   Notes to Pages 142–144

Christ and Creation; Moulins-Beaufort, *Anthropologie et mystique*; Nguyen Tien Dung, *Foi au Dieu*, 301–9.

12. See Guibert, *Mystère du Christ*, 195–218; Cholvy, *Surnaturel incarné dans la creation*, 119; O'Sullivan, *Christ and Creation*, 174–201, 277.

13. de Lubac, "Mysticism and Mystery," 57. "Il y a en elle un élément d'espérance eschatologique" ("Mystique et Mystère," 62). See further Dumas, *Mystique et théologie*, 353–61; Zwitter, *Histoire en présence de l'Éternel*, 253–80, 345–67.

14. de Lubac, "Mysticism and Mystery," 58. "La mystique chrétienne sera essentiellement une intelligence des Livres Saints. Le mystère en est le sens, la mystique en est l'intelligence" ("Mystique et Mystère," 63). See also Dumas, *Mystique et théologie*, 285–361; Cholvy, *Surnaturel incarné dans la création*, 316–31; Hollon, "Mysticism and Mystical Theology," 320–24; Zwitter, *Histoire en présence de l'Éternel*, 80–81, 261–80.

15. Dumas, *Mystique et théologie*, 172–77, 222–32, 285–361.

16. Zwitter, *Histoire en présence de l'Éternel*, 261–343.

17. Wood, *Spiritual Exegesis and the Church*, 1.

18. de Lubac, "Mysticism and Mystery," 62. See also Zwitter, *Histoire en présence de l'Éternel*, 281–322, 336–43; Guibert, *Mystère du Christ*, 240–80; and especially the extensive development in Pelchat, *Église mystère de communion*, 77–178.

19. de Lubac, "Mysticism and Mystery," 62. See also Zwitter, *Histoire en présence de l'Éternel*, 81–82.

20. de Lubac, "Mysticism and Mystery," 63. "Ce que nous appelons, dans l'Église catholique, la mystique, n'est que l'actualisation consciente de ce Don de Dieu" ("Mystique et Mystère," 68–69).

21. All of this is documented in chapter 1.

22. See especially Augustine, *City of God* 10.5–6 (pp. 309–10); de Lubac, *Corpus Mysticum*, 66–68; *Catholicism*, 102–11.

23. Thomas Aquinas, *Summa theologiæ* 2-2.85.3–4; 3.48.1–2.

24. de Lubac, *Catholicism*, 37–39. For developments of this theme, see Guibert, *Mystère du Christ*, 139-58; Geneste, *Humanisme et lumière du Christ*, 245–60; Cooper, *Naturally Human, Supernaturally God*, 169–91; O'Sullivan, *Christ and Creation*, 317–18, 378–87.

25. Guibert, *Mystère du Christ*, 329.

26. Pelchat, *Église mystère de communion*, 55–56. Pelchat discerns this viewpoint in de Lubac, *Catholicisme*, 146–49, 322–24; *Histoire et esprit*, 86–91; *Exégèse médiévale*, 1/1:323–28. See also Guibert, *Mystère du Christ*, 457–58. All of this is discussed in chapter 2.

27. See discussion in chapter 5.

28. See, e.g., Guibert, *Mystère du Christ*, 95.

29. See chapter 6.

Notes to Pages 144–147   219

30. See chapter 2.

31. de Lubac, *History and Spirit*, 385–426.

32. Thoroughly documented in chapter 4.

33. E.g., de Lubac, *Medieval Exegesis*, 2:92–93.

34. de Lubac, *History and Spirit*, 421–22. "Écriture, Église, Eucharistie: si'il n'a pas réussi toujours à élucider parfaitement la relation de ces trois termes, Origène a vu du moins qu'ils étaient en rapport. S'installant au centre de la foi, il a fait effort pour les comprendre les uns par les autres. Ce ne serait pas le critiquer, mais le trahir, que de disjoindre ses affirmations à leur sujet. . . . En réalité, la doctrine origénienne veut établir un rapport organique entre ces trois 'corps' du Christ qu'on peut appeler son corps individuel, son corps social et son corps intelligible. Dans cette doctrine, l'Écriture joue un rôle privilégié, parce qu'elle est elle-même Logos. . . . Cependant, remarquons-le, ce n'est pas que dans l'Église, par l'effet de la prédication de l'Église que cette Écriture cesse d'être un simple amas de lettres pour devenir un langage vivant. Quant à cette manducation spirituelle de la Parole, effet de la médiation de l'Écriture, et du sacrement reçu dans l'Église, elle n'est enfin elle-même, dans sa réalité, qu symbolique encore, par rapport à celle qui se fera dans l'autre vie, ou plutôt qui sera l'autre vie" (*Histoire et esprit*, 369–70).

35. Dumas, *Mystique et théologie*, 81, my translation. "[De Lubac] distingue Mystère et mystère(s)—sans grande riguer dans l'usage de la majuscule—pour signifier le Mystère de Dieu ou bien pour désigner un des mystères de la foi. Le Mystère est toujours Mystère-pour-nous. À strictement parler, c'est le Christ, dans l'Esprit-Saint; de manière dérivée est mystère tout ce qui est intimement lié au dessein divin."

36. de Lubac, *History and Spirit*, 424.

37. So Dumas, *Mystique et théologie*, 323–61; Cholvy, *Surnaturel incarné dans la création*, 316–31; Zwitter, *Histoire en présence de l'Éternel*, 253–60, 323–43. See discussion in chapter 3.

38. See chapter 4.

39. de Lubac, *Exégèse médiévale*, 2/2:111, my translation. "Mais, sous cette analogie, quel abîme! Pas plus qu'il n'est la simple lettre d'un texte, ce Fait n'est une simple histoire Il est bien signe, mais signe efficace. Il n'est pas non plus seulement mystère: il est, dans son principe, tout le mystère. La tropologie n'en décrira que le fruit, l'anagogie n'en évoquera que la consommation . . . en réalité ce qu'apporte l'investigation de ces deux derniers sens n'ajoute rien au Mystère du Christ; il ne nous porte pas au-dehors ni au-delà de lui: il en manifeste seulement la fécondité."

40. Ibid., 2/2:113, my translation. "réalité non seulement active et efficace, mais assimilatrice. La vie de l'Église, la vie de l'âme chrétienne, la vie du royaume eschatologique ne sont pas seulement signifiées, ni seulement causées en tant

que signifiées par ce signe efficace qu'est le Mystère du Christ: elles sont constituées tout entières par l'assomption de l'homme à l'intérieur du Mystère du Christ."

41. de Lubac, *Medieval Exegesis*, 2:134. "In virtute crucis Christi" (*Exégèse médiévale*, 1/2:558).

42. de Lubac, *Medieval Exegesis*, 2:141. "Se résume en un mot: la charité" (*Exégèse médiévale*, 1/2:568). See also Zwitter, *Histoire en présence de l'Éternel*, 333.

43. de Lubac, *Medieval Exegesis*, 2:181. "L'une se définit par son objet, et l'autre, par la manière de l'appréhender" (*Exégèse médiévale*, 1/2:624).

44. Zwitter, *Histoire en présence de l'Éternel*, 266. "La première est spéculative, la deuxième contemplative."

45. Dumas, *Mystique et théologie*, 276, my translation. "On pourrait dire que nous sommes finalement en présence d'une double inclusion: de la théologie dans la mystique, et finalement des deux dans le Mystère."

46. de Lubac, *Medieval Exegesis*, 2:187. "L'anagogie réalise donc la perfection et de l'allégorie et de la tropologie, en achevant leur synthèse. Elle n'est ni 'objective,' comme la première, ni 'subjective', comme la seconde. Au-delà de cette division, elle réalise leur unité. Elle intègre le sens total et définitif. Elle vise, dans l'éternité, la fusion du mystère et de la mystique" (*Exégèse médiévale*, 1/2:632–33).

47. Zwitter, *Histoire en présence de l'Éternel*, 279–80.

48. de Lubac, *Exégèse médiévale*, 2/2:122–23 (123), my translation. "Car il n'y a pas de troisième Testament. Le Mystère du Christ, une fois donné, est donné tout entier. Le sens anagogique ne peut être qu'entrevu, mail la réalité qu'il entrevoit est déjà là."

49. de Lubac, *Catholicisme*, 298.

Conclusion

1. I have adopted this phrase from the 2016 Lonergan on the Edge conference held at Marquette University.

2. Recall, though, that this is not due to any *actual* logical inconsistency. The divine mystery presents a surplus of intelligibility, not a lack of it (de Lubac, *Discovery of God*, 117).

BIBLIOGRAPHY

Adé, Édouard. "Église-Famille et catholicité: Une réception africain de 'Méditation sur l'Église.'" In *Henri de Lubac: La rencontre au cœur de l'église*, 201–10. Paris: Cerf, 2006.

Augustine. *The City of God (I–X)*. Edited by Boniface Ramsey. Translated by William Babcock. The Works of Saint Augustine: A Translation for the 21st Century, 1/6. Hyde Park, NY: New City Press, 2012.

———. *The Confessions*. Edited by John E. Rotelle. Translated by Maria Boulding. The Works of Saint Augustine: A Translation for the 21st Century, 1/1. Hyde Park, NY: New City Press, 1997.

———. *Homilies on the Gospel of John (1–40)*. Edited by Allan D. Fitzgerald. Translated by Edmund Hill. The Works of Saint Augustine: A Translation for the 21st Century, 3/12. Hyde Park, NY: New City Press, 2009.

———. *Teaching Christianity*. Edited by John E. Rotelle. Translated by Edmund Hill. The Works of Saint Augustine: A Translation for the 21st Century, 1/11. Hyde Park, NY: New City Press, 1996.

———. *The Trinity*. Edited by John E. Rotelle. Translated by Edmund Hill. 2nd ed. The Works of Saint Augustine: A Translation for the 21st Century, 1/5. Hyde Park, NY: New City Press, 2012.

Ayotte, David John. *Globalization and Multicultural Ministry: A Teilhardian Vision*. New York: Paulist, 2013.

Ayres, Lewis. "The Soul and the Reading of Scripture: A Note on Henri de Lubac." *Scottish Journal of Theology* 61, no. 2 (2008): 173–90.

Balthasar, Hans Urs von. *Mysterium Paschale: The Mystery of Easter*. Translated by Aidan Nichols. San Francisco: Ignatius, 2005.

———. *Presence et pensée: Essai sur la philosophie religieuse de Grégoire de Nysse*. Paris: Beauchesne, 1942.

———. *Theo-Drama: Theological Dramatic Theory, Volume 4: The Action*. Translated by Graham Harrison. San Francisco: Ignatius, 1994.

———. *The Theology of Henri de Lubac: An Overview*. Translated by Joseph Fessio and Michael M. Waldstein. San Francisco: Ignatius, 1991.

———, ed. *Origenes Geist und Feuer: Ein Aufbau aus seinen Schriften*. Salzburg: Otto Müller, 1938.

222   Bibliography

Barnes, Michel René Ponchin. "'Some Synchronic Moment': Gregory of Nyssa, *Théologie Mystique*, and French *Ressourcement.*" *Nova et Vetera* 18, no. 2 (2020): 367–411.

Bernardi, Peter J. *Maurice Blondel, Social Catholicism, and Action Française.* Yamauchi Lectures in Religion, Spring 2009. New Orleans: Loyola University Press, 2009.

Berranger, Olivier de. "Le rapport du Christ à l'Église." In *Henri de Lubac: La rencontre au cœur de l'église*, edited by Jean-Dominique Durand, 165–73. Paris: Cerf, 2006.

Blondel, Maurice. *Action (1893): Essay on a Critique of Life and a Science of Practice.* Translated by Oliva Blanchette. Notre Dame, IN: University of Notre Dame Press, 1984.

Boersma, Hans. *Nouvelle Théologie and Sacramental Ontology: A Return to Mystery.* New York: Oxford University Press, 2009.

Boeve, Lieven. "Revelation, Scripture and Tradition: Lessons from Vatican II's Constitution Dei Verbum for Contemporary Theology: Revelation, Scripture and Tradition." *International Journal of Systematic Theology* 13, no. 4 (2011): 416–33.

Bonino, Serge-Thomas, ed. *Surnaturel: A Controversy at the Heart of Twentieth-Century Thomistic Thought.* Faith and Reason: Studies in Catholic Theology and Philosophy. Ave Maria, FL: Sapientia Press of Ave Maria University, 2009.

Bouillard, Henri. *Conversion et grâce chez S. Thomas d'Aquin.* Paris: Aubier, 1944.

Braine, David. "The Debate between Henri de Lubac and His Critics." *Nova et Vetera* 6, no. 3 (2008): 543–89.

Buckley, Michael J. *Papal Primacy and the Episcopate: Towards a Relational Understanding.* New York: Crossroad, 1998.

Casel, Odo. *The Mystery of Christian Worship*, edited by Burkhard Neunheuser. New York: Crossroad, 1999.

Chantraine, Georges. *Henri de Lubac, tome I: De la naissance à la démobilisation (1896–1919).* Paris: Cerf, 2007.

———. *Henri de Lubac, tome II: Les années de formation (1919–1929).* Paris: Cerf, 2009.

Chantraine, Georges, and Marie-Gabrielle Lemaire. *Henri de Lubac, tome IV: Concile et après-Concile (1960–1991).* Paris: Cerf, 2013.

Chenu, Marie-Dominique. *Aquinas and His Role in Theology.* Translated by Paul Philibert. Collegeville, MN: Liturgical Press, 2002.

Cholvy, Brigitte. *Le surnaturel incarné dans la création: Une lecture de la théologie du surnaturel d'Henri de Lubac.* Paris: Cerf, 2015.

Cooper, Adam G. *Naturally Human, Supernaturally God: Deification in Pre-Conciliar Catholicism.* Minneapolis: Fortress, 2014.

Bibliography   223

Daley, Brian. "Knowing God in History and in the Church: *Dei Verbum* and '*Nouvelle Théologie*.'" In *Ressourcement: A Movement for Renewal in Twentieth-Century Catholic Theology*, edited by Gabriel Flynn and Paul D. Murray, 333–51. Oxford: Oxford University Press, 2012.

———. "The Nouvelle Theologie and the Patristic Revival: Sources, Symbols and the Science of Theology." *International Journal of Systematic Theology* 7, no. 4 (2005): 362–82.

D'Ambrosio, Marcellino. "Henri de Lubac and the Critique of Scientific Exegesis." *Communio: International Catholic Review* 19 (1992): 365–88.

Daniélou, Jean. *Origène*. Paris: Éditions de la table Ronde, 1948.

———. "Le symbolism des rites baptismaux." *Dieu Vivant* 1 (1945): 17–43.

Dansette, Adrien. "Contemporary French Catholicism." In *The Catholic Church in World Affairs*, edited by Waldemar Gurian and M. A. Fitzsimons, translated by James A. Corbet, 230–74. Notre Dame, IN: University of Notre Dame Press, 1954.

Deane-Drummond, Celia. "Sophia, Mary and Eternal Feminine in Pierre Teilhard de Chardin and Sergei Bulgakov." *Ecotheology: Journal of Religion, Nature and the Environment* 10, no. 2 (2005): 215–31.

"Déclaration sur la liberté et la fonction des théologiens dans l'Église." *Concilium* (French edition) 41 (1969): 147–51.

de Lubac, Henri. *Affrontements mystiques*. In *Révélation divine: Affrontements mystiques; Athéisme et sens de l'homme*, edited by Moulins-Beaufort and Georges Chantraine, 243–406. Œuvres Complètes, 4. Paris: Cerf, 2006. First published 1949.

———. *Amida*. In *Aspects du bouddhisme*, edited by Paul Magnin and Dennis Gira, 167–524. Œuvres Complètes, 21. Paris: Cerf, 2012. First published 1955.

———. "Anthropologie tripartite." In *Théologie dans l'histoire*, 1:115–99. Paris: Desclée de Brouwer, 1990.

———. "Apologetics and Theology." In *Theological Fragments*, translated by Rebecca Howell Balinski, 91–104. San Francisco: Ignatius, 1989.

———. "Apologétique et théologie." In *Théologies d'occasion*, 97–111. Paris: Desclée de Brouwer, 1984.

———. *Aspects du Bouddhisme I: Christ et Bouddha*. In *Aspects du Bouddhisme*, edited by Paul Magnin and Dennis Gira, 13–164. Œuvres Complètes, 21. Paris: Seuil, 2012. First published 1951.

———. *Aspects of Buddhism*. Translated by George Lamb. London: Sheed and Ward, 1953.

———. *At the Service of the Church: Henri de Lubac Reflects on the Circumstances That Occasioned His Writings*. Translated by Ann Elizabeth Englund. San Francisco: Ignatius, 1993.

224   Bibliography

———. *Athéisme et sens de l'homme: Une double requête de* Gaudium et spes. Paris: Cerf, 1968.

———. *Augustinianism and Modern Theology.* Translated by Lancelot Sheppard. New York: Herder and Herder, 2000.

———. *Augustinisme et théologie modern.* Edited by Georges Chantraine. Œuvres Complètes, 13. Paris: Cerf, 2008. First published 1965.

———. *Autres paradoxes.* In *Paradoxes,* edited by Georges Chantraine and Michel Sales, 191–293. Œuvres Complètes, 31. Paris: Cerf, 1999. First published 1994.

———. *A Brief Catechesis on Nature and Grace.* Translated by Richard Arnandez. San Francisco: Ignatius, 1984.

———. "Buddhist Messianism?" In *Theological Fragments,* translated by Rebecca Howell Balinski, 371–73. San Francisco: Ignatius, 1989.

———. *Catholicism: Christ and the Common Destiny of Man.* Translated by Lancelot C. Sheppard and Elizabeth Englund. San Francisco: Ignatius, 1998.

———. *Catholicisme: Les aspects sociaux du dogme.* 5th ed. Unam Sanctam, 3. Paris: Cerf, 1952. First published 1938.

———. "Causes internes de l'attenuation et de la disparition du sens du Sacré." In *Théologie dans l'histoire,* 2:13–30. Paris: Desclée de Brouwer, 1990.

———. "Christian Explanation of Our Times." In *Theology in History,* translated by Anne Englund Nash, 440–56. San Francisco: Ignatius, 1996.

———. *The Christian Faith: An Essay on the Structure of the Apostles' Creed.* Translated by Richard Arnandez. San Francisco: Ignatius, 1986.

———. *Christian Resistance to Anti-Semitism: Memories from 1940–1944.* Translated by Elizabeth Englund. San Francisco: Ignatius, 1990.

———. *The Church: Paradox and Mystery.* Translated by James R. Dunne. Shannon, Ireland: Ecclesia Press, 1969.

———. "The Church in Crisis." *Theology Digest* 17, no. 4 (1969): 312–25.

———. "Le combat spirituel." In *Théologie dans l'histoire,* 2:282–95. Paris: Desclée de Brouwer, 1990.

———. "The Conditions of Ontological Affirmation as Set Forth in *L'Action* by Maurice Blondel (1899)." In *Theological Fragments,* translated by Rebecca Howell Balinski, 377–92. San Francisco: Ignatius, 1989.

———. *Corpus Mysticum: The Eucharist and the Church in the Middle Ages.* Edited by Laurence Paul Hemming and Susan Frank Parsons. Translated by Gemma Simmonds, Richard Price, and Christopher Stephens. Notre Dame, IN: University of Notre Dame Press, 2007.

———. *Corpus mysticum: L'eucharistie et l'église au moyen âge: Étude historique.* Edited by Eric Moulins-Beaufort. 2nd ed. (1949). Œuvres Complètes, 15. Paris: Cerf, 2009. First published 1944.

———. *The Discovery of God.* Translated by Alexander Dru, Mark Sebanc, and Cassian Fulsom. Grand Rapids, MI: Eerdmans, 1996.

———. "The Doctrine of Father Lebreton on Revelation and Dogma According to His Anti-Modernist Writings." In *Theology in History*, translated by Anne Englund Nash, 317–65. San Francisco: Ignatius, 1996.

———. *The Drama of Atheist Humanism.* Translated by Edith M. Riley, Anne Englund Nash, and Mark Sebanc. San Francisco: Ignatius, 1995.

———. *Le drame de l'humanisme athée.* Œuvres Complètes, 2. Paris: Cerf, 1998. First published 1945.

———. *Les églises particulières dans l'Église universelle: Suivi de La maternité de l'Église; Et d'une interview recueillie par G. Jarczyk.* Edited by Denis Dupont-Fauville. Œuvres Complètes, 10. Paris: Cerf, 2019. First published 1971.

———. *The Eternal Feminine: A Study on the Poem by Teilhard de Chardin, Followed by Teilhard and the Problems of Today.* Translated by René Hague. London: Collins, 1971.

———. *L'Éternel féminin: Précédé du texte de Teilhard de Chardin.* Paris: Aubier, 1983. First published 1968.

———. *Exégèse médiévale: Les quatre sens de l'ecriture.* 4 vols. Paris: Aubier-Montaigne, 1959–64.

———. "Explication chrétienne de notre temps." In *Théologie dans l'histoire*, 2:232–49. Paris: Beauchesne, 1990.

———. "Faith and Piety in Amidism." In *Theological Fragments*, translated by Rebecca Howell Balinski, 355–69. San Francisco: Ignatius, 1989.

———. *The Faith of Teilhard de Chardin.* Translated by René Hague. London: Burns and Oates, 1965.

———. *La foi chrétienne: Essai sur la structure de symbole des apôtres.* Edited by Éric de Moulins-Beaufort. Œuvres Complètes, 5. Paris: Cerf, 2008. First published 1969.

———. "Foi et devotion dans l'amidisme." In *Théologies d'occasion*, 385–401. Paris: Desclée de Brouwer, 1984.

———. "Le fondement théologique des missions (1941 et 1946)." In *Théologie dans l'histoire*, 2:159–219. Paris: Beauchesne, 1990.

———. *Histoire et esprit: L'intelligence de l'écriture d'après Origène.* Théologie, 16. Paris: Aubier, 1950.

———. *History and Spirit: The Understanding of Scripture According to Origen.* Translated by Anne Englund Nash. San Francisco: Ignatius, 2007.

———. "Homo juridicus." In *Théologie dans l'histoire*, 2:296–99. Paris: Desclée de Brouwer, 1990.

———. "Homo Juridicus." In *Theology in History*, translated by Anne Englund Nash, 502–4. San Francisco: Ignatius, 1996.

———. "Internal Causes of the Weakening and Disappearance of the Sense of the Sacred." In *Theology in History*, translated by Anne Englund Nash, 223–40. San Francisco: Ignatius, 1996.

———. "The Light of Christ." In *Theology in History*, translated by Anne Englund Nash, 201–20. San Francisco: Ignatius, 1996.

———. "La lumière du Christ." In *Théologie dans l'histoire*, 1:203–22. Paris: Desclée de Brouwer, 1990.

———. *Medieval Exegesis: The Four Senses of Scripture*. 3 vols. Grand Rapids, MI: Eerdmans, 1998–2009.

———. *Méditation sur l'église*. Edited by Georges Chantraine, Fabienne Clinquart, and Thierry Thomas. 6th ed. (1985). Œuvres Complètes, 8. Paris: Cerf, 2003. First published 1953.

———. *Mémoire sur l'occasion de mes écrits*. Namur, Belgium: Culture et Vérité, 1989.

———. "Messianisme Bouddhique?" In *Théologies d'occasion*, 403–6. Paris: Desclée de Brouwer, 1984.

———. *More Paradoxes*. Translated by Anne Englund Nash. San Francisco: Ignatius, 2002.

———. *The Motherhood of the Church Followed by Particular Churches in the Universal Church and an Interview Conducted by Gwendoline Jarczyk*. Translated by Sergia Englund. San Francisco: Ignatius, 1982.

———. *Le mystère du Surnaturel*. Œuvres Complètes, 12. Paris: Cerf, 2000. First published 1965.

———. *The Mystery of the Supernatural*. Translated by Rosemary Sheed. New York: Herder and Herder, 2012.

———. "Mysticism and Mystery." In *Theological Fragments*, translated by Rebecca Howell Balinski, 35–69. San Francisco: Ignatius, 1989.

———. "Mystique et Mystère." In *Théologies d'occasion*, 37–76. Paris: Desclée de Brouwer, 1984. First published 1965.

———. "A New Religious 'Front.'" In *Theology in History*, translated by Anne Englund Nash, 457–87. San Francisco: Ignatius, 1996.

———. "Nietzche as Mystic." In *The Drama of Atheist Humanism*, translated by Mark Sebanc. San Francisco: Ignatius, 1995.

———. "La notion du bien et du mal moral dans le Bouddhisme, et spécialement dans l'Amidisme." In *Théologies d'occasion*, 361–84. Paris: Desclée de Brouwer, 1984.

———. "The Notion of Good and Evil in Buddhism and Especially in Amidism." In *Theological Fragments*, translated by Rebecca Howell Balinski, 333–54. San Francisco: Ignatius, 1989.

———. "Un nouveaux 'front' religieuse." In *Théologie dans l'histoire*, 2:250–81. Paris: Desclée de Brouwer, 1990.

Bibliography   227

———. *Nouveaux paradoxes*. In *Paradoxes*, edited by Georges Chantraine and Michel Sales, 67–189. Œuvres Complètes, 31. Paris: Cerf, 1999. First published 1955.

———. *Paradoxe et mystère de l'église suivi de l'église dans la crise actuelle*. Edited by Dennis M. Doyle. Œuvres Complètes, 9. Paris: Cerf, 2010. First published 1967.

———. *Paradoxes*. In *Paradoxes*, edited by Georges Chantraine and Michel Sales, 7–64. Œuvres Complètes, 31. Paris: Cerf, 1999. First published 1945.

———. *Paradoxes of Faith*. Translated by Paule Simon, Sadie Kreilkamp, and Ernest Beaumont. San Francisco: Ignatius, 1987.

———. *La pensée religieuse du père Pierre Teilhard de Chardin*. Edited by Éric de Moulins-Beaufort. Œuvres Complètes, 23. Paris: Cerf, 2002. First published 1962.

———. *Petite catéchèse sur nature et grâce*. In *Esprit et liberté dans la tradition théologique suivi de Petite catéchèse sur nature et grâce*, 197–381. Œuvres Complètes, 14. Paris: Cerf, 2013. First published 1980.

———. *La postérité spirituelle de Joachim de Flore: De Joachim à nos jours*. Edited by Michael Sutton. Œuvres Complètes, 27–28. Paris: Cerf, 2014. First published 1979 (vol. 1) and 1981 (vol. 2).

———. *La prière du père Teilhard de Chardin*. Paris: Librairie Arthème Fayard, 1964.

———. "Le problème du développement du dogme." In *Théologie dans l'histoire*, 2:38–70. Paris: Beauchesne, 1990.

———. "The Problem of the Development of Dogma." In *Theology in History*, translated by Anne Englund Nash, 248–80. San Francisco: Ignatius, 1996.

———. *Proudhon et le Christianisme*. Edited by Jean-Yves Calvez. Œuvres Complètes, 3. Paris: Cerf, 2011. First published 1945.

———. *The Religion of Teilhard de Chardin*. Translated by René Hague. New York: Desclee, 1967.

———. *La révélation divine*. In *Révélation divine: Affrontements mystiques; Athéisme etsens de l'homme*, edited by Eric de Moulins-Beaufort and Georges Chantraine, 35–231. Œuvres Complètes, 4. Paris: Cerf, 2006. First published 1966.

———. *Scripture in the Tradition*. Translated by Luke O'Neill. New York: Crossroad, 2012.

———. "The Search for a New Man." In *The Drama of Atheist Humanism*, translated by Anne Englund Nash. San Francisco: Ignatius, 1995.

———. "'Seigneur, je cherche ton visage': Sur le chapitre XIVe du Proslogion de saint Anselme." *Archives de Philosophie* 39, no. 2 (1976): 201–25.

———. "'Seigneur, je cherche ton visage': Sur le chapitre XIV e du Proslogion de saint Anselme (fin)." *Archives de Philosophie* 39, no. 3 (1976): 407–25.

———. "Spiritual Warfare." In *Theology in History*, translated by Anne Englund Nash, 488–501. San Francisco: Ignatius, 1996.

———. *The Splendor of the Church*. Translated by Michael Mason. 2nd ed. San Francisco: Ignatius, 1999.

———. *Sur les chemins de Dieu*. Edited by Georges Chantraine and François-Emmanuel Duchêne. Œuvres Complètes, 1. Paris: Cerf, 1983. First published 1956.

———. *Surnaturel: Études Historiques*. Edited by Michel Sales. Collection Théologie. Paris: Desclée de Brouwer, 1991. First published 1946.

———. *Teilhard, missionaire et apologiste*. Toulouse: Editions Prière et Vie, 1966.

———. *Teilhard Explained*. Translated by Anthony Buono. New York: Paulist, 1968.

———. *Teilhard posthume: Réflexions et souvenirs, précédé de Blondel—Teilhard de Chardin: Correspondance 1919* (two books). Edited by Jean-Pierre Wagner. Œuvres Complètes, 26. Paris: Cerf, 2008. First published 1977 (first book) and 1965 (second book).

———. "The Theological Foundation of the Missions (1941 and 1946)." In *Theology in History*, translated by Anne Englund Nash, 367–427. San Francisco: Ignatius, 1996.

———. "Tripartite Anthropology." In *Theology in History*, translated by Anne Englund Nash, 1:117–200. San Francisco: Ignatius, 1991.

———. *The Un-Marxian Socialist: A Study of Proudhon*. Translated by R. E. Scantlebury. New York: Sheed and Ward, 1948.

———. *Vatican Council Notebooks*. Edited by Loïc Figoureux. Translated by Andrew Sefanelli and Anne Englund Nash. 2 vols. San Francisco: Ignatius, 2015–16.

———, ed. *Pierre Teilhard de Chardin, Maurice Blondel: Correspondence*. Translated by William Whitman. New York: Herder and Herder, 1967.

Demers, Bruno. "Les 'nouvelles' notions de Révélation et de Foi de Dei Verbum et La Catéchèse." *Lumen Vitae* 68, no. 1 (2013): 19–35.

DeMeuse, Eric. "'The World Is Content with Words': Jansenism between Thomism and Calvinism." In *Beyond Dort and* De Auxiliis: *The Dynamics of Protestant and Catholic Soteriology in the Sixteenth and Seventeenth Centuries*, edited by Jordan Ballor, Matthew Gaetano, and David Sytsma, 245–76. London: Brill, 2019.

Doyle, Dennis M. *Communion Ecclesiology: Visions and Versions*. Maryknoll, NY: Orbis, 2000.

———. "Henri de Lubac and the Roots of Communion Ecclesiology." *Theological Studies* 60, no. 2 (1999): 209–27.

Dumas, Bertrand. *Mystique et théologie d'après Henri de Lubac*. Paris: Cerf, 2012.

Bibliography   229

Fédou, Michel. "Henri de Lubac lecteur de Teilhard vision scientifique et expérience chrétienne." *Gregorianum* 97, no. 1 (2016): 101–21.

Feingold, Lawrence. *The Natural Desire to See God According to St. Thomas Aquinas and His Interpreters.* 2nd ed. Ave Maria, FL: Sapientia Press of Ave Maria University, 2010.

Figura, Michaël. "L'héritage spirituel de Joachim de Flore dans l'interprétation de Henri de Lubac." *Communio: Revue catholique internationale* 24, nos. 5–6 (1999): 211–30.

Flipper, Joseph S. *Between Apocalypse and Eschaton: History and Eternity in Henri de Lubac.* Minneapolis: Fortress, 2015.

Gaillardetz, Richard R. *By What Authority? Foundations for Understanding Authority in the Church.* 2nd ed. Collegeville: Liturgical Press, 2018.

———. *Teaching with Authority: A Theology of the Magisterium in the Church.* Collegeville, MN: Michael Glazier, 1997.

Gaillardetz, Richard R., and Catherine E. Clifford. *Keys to the Council: Unlocking the Teaching of Vatican II.* Collegeville, MN: Liturgical Press, 2012.

Gardner, Patrick X. "An Inhuman Humanism." In *T&T Clark Companion to Henri de Lubac,* edited by Jordan Hillebert, 225–46. London: Bloomsbury T&T Clark, 2017.

———. "Modern Pentecost: Henri de Lubac on Atheism and the Spiritual Posterity of Joachim of Fiore." Ph.D. diss., University of Notre Dame, Notre Dame, IN, 2015.

Garrigou-Lagrange, Reginald. "La nouvelle théologie où va-telle?" *Angelicum* 23 (1946): 126–45.

Geneste, Philippe. *Humanisme et lumière du Christ chez Henri de Lubac.* Paris: Cerf, 2016.

Gilson, Etienne. *The Christian Philosophy of St. Thomas Aquinas: With a Catalog of St. Thomas's Works.* Translated by L. K. Shook. New York: Random House, 1956.

———. *The Philosopher and Theology.* New York: Random House, 1962.

———. *The Philosophy of St. Bonaventure.* Translated by Illtyd Trethowan and F. J. Sheed. New York: Sheed and Ward, 1938.

———. *Thomist Realism and the Critique of Knowledge.* Translated by Mark A. Wauck. San Francisco: Ignatius, 1986.

Gordon, Joseph K. "*Ressourcement* Anti-Semitism? Addressing an Obstacle to Henri de Lubac's Proposed Renewal of Premodern Christian Spiritual Exegesis." *Theological Studies* 78, no. 3 (2017): 614–33.

Grillmeier, Aloys. "Chapter I: The Mystery of the Church." In *Commentary on the Documents of Vatican II,* edited by Herbert Vorgrimler, translated by Kevin Smyth, 1:138–52. New York: Herder and Herder, 1967.

Grogin, R. C. *The Bergsonian Controversy in France, 1900–1914*. Calgary: University of Calgary Press, 1988.

Grumett, David. "Church, World and Christ in Teilhard de Chardin." *Ecclesiology* 1, no. 1 (2004): 87–103.

———. *De Lubac: A Guide for the Perplexed*. London: T&T Clark, 2007.

———. "De Lubac, Grace, and the Pure Nature Debate." *Modern Theology* 31, no. 1 (2015): 123–46.

———. *Henri de Lubac and the Shaping of Modern Theology: A Reader*. San Francisco: Ignatius, 2020.

———. "Teilhard at Ore Place, Hastings, 1908–1912." *New Blackfriars* 90, no. 1030 (2009): 687–700.

———. *Teilhard de Chardin: Theology, Humanity and Cosmos*. Leuven, Belgium: Peeters, 2005.

Guibert, Étienne. *Le mystère du Christ d'après Henri de Lubac*. Paris: Cerf, 2006.

Haught, John F. "Trashing Teilhard: How Not to Read a Great Religious Thinker." *Commonweal*, 2019.

Hauser, Daniel. "The Eucharist and the Historicity of the Faith." *Saint Anselm Journal* 8, no. 2 (2013): 1–33.

Healy, Nicholas J. "The Christian Mystery of Nature and Grace." In *T&T Clark Companion to Henri de Lubac*, edited by Jordan Hillebert, 181–203. London: Bloomsbury T&T Clark, 2017.

———. "Henri de Lubac on Nature and Grace: A Note on Some Recent Contributions to the Debate." *Communio: International Catholic Review* 35 (2008): 535–64.

Heaps, Jonathan Robert. "The Ambiguity of Being: Medieval and Modern Cooperation on the Problem of the Supernatural." Ph.D. diss., Marquette University, Milwaukee, WI: 2019.

Hemming, Laurence Paul. "Henri de Lubac: Reading *Corpus Mysticum*." *New Blackfriars* 90 (2009): 519–34.

Hercsik, Donath. *Jesus Christus als Mitte der Theologie von Henri de Lubac*. Frankfurt am Main: Josef Knecht, 2001.

Hillebert, Jordan. *Henri de Lubac and the Drama of Human Existence*. Notre Dame, IN: University of Notre Dame Press, 2021.

———. "Introducing Henri de Lubac." In *T&T Clark Companion to Henri de Lubac*, edited by Jordan Hillebert, 3–27. London: Bloomsbury T&T Clark, 2017.

Hollon, Bryan C. *Everything Is Sacred: Spiritual Exegesis in the Political Theology of Henri de Lubac*. Eugene, OR: Cascade, 2009.

———. "Mysticism and Mystical Theology." In *T&T Clark Companion to Henri de Lubac*, edited by Jordan Hillebert, 307–25. London: Bloomsbury T&T Clark, 2017.

Hughes, Kevin L. "The 'Fourfold Sense': De Lubac, Blondel and Contemporary Theology." *Heythrop Journal* 42 (2001): 451–62.

———. "The Spiritual Interpretation of Scripture." In *T&T Clark Companion to Henri de Lubac*, edited by Jordan Hillebert, 205–23. London: Bloomsbury T&T Clark, 2017.

Hünermann, Peter. "The Final Weeks of the Council." In *History of Vatican II*, edited by Joseph A. Komonchak and Giuseppe Alberigo, translated by Matthew J. O'Connell, 5:363–483. Maryknoll, NY: Orbis, 2006.

———. "Theologischer Kommentar zur dogmatischen Konstitution über die Kirche *Lumen Gentium*." In *Herders theologischer Kommentar zum zweiten vatikanischen Konzil*, edited by Peter Hünermann and Bernd Jochen Hilberath, 2nd ed., 1:263–563. Freiburg, Germany: Herder, 2004.

Hütter, Reinhard. "Aquinas on the Natural Desire for the Vision of God: A Relecture of Summa Contra Gentiles III, c. 25, Après Henri de Lubac." *Thomist: A Speculative Quarterly Review* 73, no. 4 (2009): 523–91.

———. "*Desiderium naturale visionis Dei—Est autem duplex hominis beatitudo sive felicitas*: Some Observations about Lawrence Feingold's and John Milbank's Recent Interventions in the Debate over the Natural Desire to See God." *Nova et Vetera* 5, no. 1 (2007): 81–183.

Kerr, Fergus. "A Different World: Neoscholasticism and Its Discontents." *International Journal of Systematic Theology* 8, no. 2 (2006): 128–48.

———. *Twentieth-Century Catholic Theologians: From Neoscholasticism to Nuptial Mysticism*. Malden, MA: Blackwell, 2007.

King, Ursula. "A Vision Transformed: Teilhard de Chardin's Evolutionary Awakening at Hastings." *Heythrop Journal* 54, no. 4 (2013): 590–605.

Kirwan, Jon. *An Avant-Garde Theological Generation: The Nouvelle Théologie and the French Crisis of Modernity*. Oxford: Oxford University Press, 2018.

Komonchak, Joseph A. "Theology and Culture at Mid-Century: The Example of Henri de Lubac." *Theological Studies* 51 (1990): 579–602.

Labourdette, Marie-Michel. "La théologie et ses sources." *Revue Thomiste* 46 (1946): 353–71.

Larsen, Sean. "The Politics of Desire: Two Readings of Henri de Lubac on Nature and Grace." *Modern Theology* 29, no. 3 (2013): 279–310.

Lemaire, Marie-Gabrielle. "Henri de Lubac, défenseur de Teilhard: Un cas de conscience." *Nouvelle Revue Théologique* 139 (2017): 571–86.

———. "La postérité spirituelle de Joachim de Flore, esquisse d'une conclusion." *Bulletin de l'Association Internationale Cardinal Henri de Lubac* 16 (2014): 14–41.

Lenehan, Kevin. "Unfolding in Friendship: Revelation and the Analogy of Friendship in *Dei Verbum*." *Pacifica: Australasian Theological Studies* 29, no. 2 (2016): 175–91.

232   Bibliography

Leo XIII. *Aeterni Patris*. August 4, 1879. http://w2.vatican.va/content/leo-xiii/en/encyclicals/documents/hf_l-xiii_enc_04081879_aeterni-patris.html.

Livingston, James C. *Modern Christian Thought*. 2nd ed. Vol. 1. Minneapolis: Fortress, 2006.

Lonergan, Bernard J. F. *Grace and Freedom: Operative Grace in the Thought of St. Thomas Aquinas*. Edited by Frederick E. Crowe and Robert M. Doran. Collected Works of Bernard Lonergan, 1. Toronto: University of Toronto Press, 1988.

———. *Insight: A Study of Human Understanding*. Edited by Frederick E. Crowe and Robert M. Doran. Collected Works of Bernard Lonergan, 3. Toronto: University of Toronto Press, 1992.

———. *Verbum: Word and Idea in Aquinas*. Edited by Frederick E. Crowe and Robert M. Doran. Collected Works of Bernard Lonergan, 2. Toronto: University of Toronto Press, 1997.

Long, D. Stephen. "Knowing God." In *T&T Clark Companion to Henri de Lubac*, edited by Jordan Hillebert, 269–87. London: Bloomsbury T&T Clark, 2017.

Long, Steven A. *Natura Pura: On the Recovery of Nature in the Doctrine of Grace*. Moral Philosophy and Moral Theology. New York: Fordham University Press, 2010.

Loughlin, Gerard. "*Nouvelle Théologie*: A Return to Modernism?" In *Ressourcement: A Movement for Renewal in Twentieth-Century Catholic Theology*, edited by Gabriel Flynn and Paul D. Murray, 36–50. Oxford: Oxford University Press, 2012.

Maréchal, Joseph. *Le Point de départ de la métaphysique: Leçons sur le développement historique et théorique du problème de la connaissance*. 5 vols. Paris: Desclée de Brouwer, 1944.

McCool, Gerald A. *Catholic Theology in the Nineteenth Century: The Quest for a Unitary Method*. New York: Seabury, 1977.

———. *From Unity to Pluralism: The Internal Evolution of Thomism*. New York: Fordham University Press, 1989.

McDermott, John M. "De Lubac and Rousselot." *Gregorianum* 78, no. 4 (1997): 735–59.

———. *Love and Understanding: The Relation of Will and Intellect in Pierre Rousselot's Christological Vision*. Rome: Università Gregoriana Editrice, 1983.

McGinn, Bernard. *The Calabrian Abbot, Joachim of Fiore in the History of Western Thought*. New York: Macmillan, 1985.

McPartlan, Paul. *The Eucharist Makes the Church: Henri de Lubac and John Zizioulas in Dialogue*. London: T&T Clark, 1996.

Meconi, David Vincent. "The Incarnation and the Role of Participation in St. Augustine's Confessions." *Augustinian Studies* 29, no. 2 (1998): 61–75.

Bibliography   233

Meszaros, Andrew. "Revelation in George Tyrrell, Neo-Scholasticism, and Dei Verbum." *Angelicum* 90, no. 3 (2014): 535–68.

Mettepenningen, Jürgen. *Nouvelle Théologie—New Theology: Inheritor of Modernism, Precursor of Vatican II*. London: T&T Clark, 2010.

Milbank, John. *The Suspended Middle: Henri de Lubac and the Debate Concerning the Supernatural*. 2nd ed. Grand Rapids, MI: Eerdmans, 2014.

———. *Theology and Social Theory: Beyond Secular Reason*. 2nd ed. Oxford: Blackwell, 2006.

Moloney, Raymond. "De Lubac and Lonergan on the Supernatural." *Theological Studies* 69, no. 3 (2008): 509–27.

———. "Henri de Lubac on Church and Eucharist." *Irish Theological Quarterly* 70 (2005): 331–42.

Moulins-Beaufort, Éric de. *Anthropologie et mystique selon Henri de Lubac : "L'esprit de l'homme," ou la présence de Dieu en l'homme*. Études lubaciennes, 3. Paris: Cerf, 2003.

———. "Henri de Lubac, avocat de Pierre Teilhard de Chardin." In *Pierre Teilhard de Chardin face à ses contradicteurs*, edited by Philippe Capelle-Dumont, François Euvé, and Jean Duchesme, 165–80. Paris: Parole et Silence, 2006.

Mulcahy, Bernard. *Aquinas's Notion of Pure Nature and the Christian Integralism of Henri de Lubac: Not Everything Is Grace*. New York: Peter Lang, 2011.

Murphy, Francesca Aran. "The Influence of Maurice Blondel." In *T&T Clark Companion to Henri de Lubac*, edited by Jordan Hillebert, 57–71. London: Bloomsbury T&T Clark, 2017.

Nguyen Tien Dung, François-Xavier. *La foi au Dieu des chrétiens, gage d'un authentique humanisme: Henri de Lubac face à l'humanisme athée*. Paris: Desclée de Brouwer, 2010.

Nichols, Aidan. "Henri de Lubac: Panorama and Proposal." *New Blackfriars* 93, no. 1043 (2012): 3–33.

Nolte, Ernst. *Three Faces of Fascism: Action Française Italian Fascism, National Socialism*. New York: Holt, Rinehart and Winston, 1966.

O'Sullivan, Noel. *Christ and Creation: Christology as the Key to Interpreting the Theology of Creation in the Works of Henri de Lubac*. Oxford: Peter Lang, 2008.

———. "An Emerging Christology." In *T&T Clark Companion to Henri de Lubac*, edited by Jordan Hillebert, 327–48. London: Bloomsbury T&T Clark, 2017.

Pelchat, Marc. *L'Église mystère de communion: L'Ecclésiologie dans l'œuvre de Henri de Lubac*. Paris: Éditions Paulines and Médiaspaul, 1988.

234 Bibliography

———. "Pierre Teilhard de Chardin et Henri de Lubac: Pour une nouvelle synthèse théologique à l'âge scientifique." *Laval théologique et philosophique* 45, no. 2 (1989): 255–73.

Pickstock, Catherine. *After Writing: On the Liturgical Consummation of Philosophy*. Oxford: Blackwell, 1998.

Pius X. *Pascendi Dominici Gregis*. September 8, 1907. http://w2.vatican.va/content/pius-x/en/encyclicals/documents/hf_p-x_enc_19070908_pascendi-dominici-gregis.html.

———. *Sacrorum antistitum*. September 1, 1910. http://w2.vatican.va/content/pius-x/la/motu_proprio/documents/hf_p-x_motu-proprio_19100901_sacrorum-antistitum.html.

Pius XII. *Humani Generis*. August 12, 1950. http://w2.vatican.va/content/pius-xii/en/encyclicals/documents/hf_p-xii_enc_12081950_humani-generis.html.

Portier, William L. "What Kind of a World of Grace? Henri Cardinal de Lubac and the Council's Christological Center." *Communio: International Catholic Review*, no. 39 (2012): 136–51.

Pottmeyer, Hermann J. *Towards a Papacy in Communion: Perspectives from Vatican Councils I and II*. New York: Herder and Herder, 1998.

Prevot, Andrew. "Henri de Lubac (1896–1991) and Contemporary Mystical Theology." In *A Companion to Jesuit Mysticism*, edited by Robert A. Maryks, 279–303. London: Brill, 2017.

Prévotat, Jacques. "Note sur Auguste Comte, Charles Maurras, et le christianisme." In *Le drame de l'humanisme athée*, xxi–xxviii. Œuvres Complètes, 2. Paris: Cerf, 1998.

Radner, Ephraim. "Early Modern Jansenism." In *The Oxford Handbook of Early Modern Theology, 1600–1800*, edited by Ulrich Lehner, Richard A. Muller, and A. G. Roeber, 436–50. Oxford: Oxford University Press, 2016.

———. *A Profound Ignorance: Modern Pneumatology and Its Anti-Modern Redemption*. Waco, TX: Baylor University Press, 2019.

Rahner, Karl. "The Concept of Mystery in Catholic Theology." In *Theological Investigations*, Electronic Centenary Edition, 4:36–73. Limerick, Ireland: Centre for Theology, Culture and Values, 2005.

———. "The Theology of The Symbol." In *Theological Investigations*, Electronic Centenary Edition, 4:221–52. Limerick, Ireland: Centre for Theology, Culture and Values, 2005.

Ratzinger, Joseph. "Dogmatic Constitution on Divine Revelation." In *Commentary on the Documents of Vatican II*, edited by Herbert Vorgrimler, translated by William Glen-Doepel, 3:155–272. New York: Herder and Herder, 1969.

Reeves, Marjorie. *Joachim of Fiore and the Prophetic Future*. New York: Harper & Row, 1977.

———. "Review of *La manifestation de l'Esprit selon Joachim de Fiore* by Henry Mottu: *La Postérité spirituelle de Joachim de Flore, Tome 1: De Joachim à Schelling*." *Journal of Theological Studies* 32, no. 1 (1981): 287–94.

Reeves, Marjorie, and Warwick Gould. *Joachim of Fiore and the Myth of the Eternal Evangel in the Nineteenth Century*. Oxford: Clarendon, 1986.

Riches, Aaron. "Henri de Lubac and the Second Vatican Council." In *T&T Clark Companion to Henri de Lubac*, edited by Jordan Hillebert, 121–56. London: Bloomsbury T&T Clark, 2017.

Rober, Daniel A. *Recognizing the Gift: Toward a Renewed Theology of Nature and Grace*. Minneapolis: Fortress, 2016.

Rougé, Matthieu. "'Sicut Maria, ita et ecclesia': La culte de Marie, signe d'une Église pleinement eucharistique." In *Henri de Lubac: La rencontre au cœur de l'église*, edited by Jean-Dominique Durand, 176–86. Paris: Cerf, 2006.

Rousselot, Pierre. *L'intellectualisme de saint Thomas*, 3rd ed. Paris: Beauchesne, 1936.

———. *Intelligence: Sense of Being, Faculty of God*. Translated by Andrew Tallon. Milwaukee, WI: Marquette University Press, 1999.

Routhier, Gilles. "Finishing the Work Begun: The Trying Experience of the Fourth Period." In *History of Vatican II*, edited by Joseph A. Komonchak and Giuseppe Alberigo, translated by Matthew J. O'Connell, 5:49–177. Maryknoll, NY: Orbis, 2006.

Rowland, Tracey. "Neo-Scholasticism of the Strict Observance." In *T&T Clark Companion to Henri de Lubac*, edited by Jordan Hillebert, 29–55. London: Bloomsbury T&T Clark, 2017.

Sauer, Hanjo. "The Doctrinal and the Pastoral: The Text on Divine Revelation." In *History of Vatican II*, edited by Joseph Komonchak and Giuseppe Alberigo, 4:195–231. Maryknoll, NY: Orbis, 2003.

Schillebeeckx, Edward. *Approches théologiques*. Translated by P. Bourgy. Vol. 3. Brussels: CEP, 1967.

———. *Christ: The Sacrament of the Encounter with God*. New York: Sheed and Ward, 1963.

———. "L'église et Le monde." *Do-C: Documantatie Centrum Concile* (French ed.) 3, no. 142 (1964).

———. "L'église et l'humanité." *Concilium* 1, no. 1 (1965): 57–78.

———. "Kerk en wereld." *Tijdschrift voor Theologie* 4 (1964): 386–99.

Schlesinger, Eugene R. "The Eucharistic Poverty of the Church in the Theologies of Jon Sobrino and Hans Urs von Balthasar." *Theological Studies* 77, no. 3 (2016): 627–51.

———. "The Integrative Role of Sacrifice in the Theology of Henri de Lubac." *International Journal of Systematic Theology* 20, no. 3 (2018): 402–22.

———. *Missa Est! A Missional Liturgical Ecclesiology.* Minneapolis: Fortress, 2017.

———. "The Sacrificial Ecclesiology of *City of God* 10." *Augustinian Studies* 47, no. 2 (2016): 137–55.

———. *Sacrificing the Church: Mass, Mission, and Ecumenism.* Lanham, MD: Lexington Books/Fortress Academic, 2019.

———. "The Threefold Body in Eschatological Perspective: With and Beyond Henri de Lubac on the Church." *Ecclesiology* 10, no. 2 (2014): 186–204.

Schloesser, Stephen. *Jazz Age Catholicism: Mystic Modernism in Postwar Paris, 1919–1933.* Toronto: University of Toronto Press, 2005.

Schnackers, Hubert. *Kirche als Sakrament und Mutter: Zur Ekklesiologie von Henri de Lubac.* Regensburger Studien zur Theologie, 22. Frankfurt am Main: Peter Lang, 1979.

Semmelroth, Otto. *Die Kirche als Ursakrament.* Frankfurt am Main: J. Knecht, 1955.

Simmonds, Gemma. "The Mystical Body: Ecclesiology and Sacramental Theology." In *T&T Clark Companion to Henri de Lubac*, edited by Jordan Hillebert, 159–79. London: Bloomsbury T&T Clark, 2017.

Slattery, John P. "Dangerous Tendencies of Cosmic Theology: The Untold Legacy of Teilhard de Chardin." *Philosophy and Theology* 29, no. 1 (2017): 69–82.

———. "Teilhard & Eugenics: A Response to John Haught." *Commonweal*, 2019.

Sternhell, Zeev. *Neither Right nor Left: Fascist Ideology in France.* Translated by David Maisel. Berkeley: University of California Press, 1986.

Sullivan, Francis A. *Magisterium: Teaching Authority in the Catholic Church.* Eugene, OR: Wipf and Stock, 2002.

Sutton, Agneta. "Teilhard de Chardin's Christocentric Trinitarianism." *New Blackfriars* 92, no. 1037 (2011): 90–103.

Sutton, Michael. "Henri de Lubac: Reflections on Atheist Humanism, Joachism, and Totalitarianism." *Gregorianum* 97, no. 1 (2016): 79–100.

———. "Présentation." In *La postérité spirituelle de Joachim de Flore: de Joachim à nos jours*, by Henri de Lubac, i–lvi. Œuvres Complètes, 27–28. Paris: Cerf, 2014.

Swafford, Andrew Dean. *Nature and Grace, A New Approach to Thomistic Ressourcement.* Cambridge: James Clarke and Co., 2014.

Tanner, Norman, ed. *Decrees of the Ecumenical Councils.* 2 vols. Washington, DC: Georgetown University Press, 1990.

Teilhard de Chardin, Pierre. *The Divine Milieu: An Essay on the Interior Life*. Translated by Bernard Wall. London: Harper & Brothers, 1960.

———. *The Human Phenomenon*. Translated by Sarah Appleton-Weber. Brighton, UK: Sussex Academic Press, 1999.

———. *La messe sur le monde*. Paris: Seuil, 1965. First published 1923.

"La Théologie et ses sources: Reponse." *Recherches de science religieuse* 33, no. 4 (1946): 385–401.

Tillard, Jean-Marie R. *Church of Churches: The Ecclesiology of Communion*. Translated by R. C. de Peaux. Collegeville, MN: Liturgical Press, 1992.

———. *L'Église locale: Ecclésiologie de communion et catholicité*. Paris: Cerf, 1995.

Wagner, Jean-Pierre. "Henri de Lubac et Pierre Teilhard de Chardin: Le sens d'une hospitalité." *Revue des sciences religieuses* 77, no. 2 (2002): 199–214.

———. *La théologie fondamentale selon Henri de Lubac*. Paris: Cerf, 1997.

Walsh, Christopher J. "De Lubac's Critique of the Postconciliar Church." *Communio* 19 (1992): 404–32.

Wang, Lisa. "*Sacramentum Unitatis Ecclesiasticae*: The Eucharistic Ecclesiology of Henri de Lubac." *Anglican Theological Review* 85, no. 1 (2003): 143–58.

Williams, A. N. "The Traditionalist *Malgré Lui*: Teilhard de Chardin and *Ressourcement*." In *Ressourcement: A Movement for Renewal in Twentieth-Century Catholic Theology*, edited by Gabriel Flynn and Paul D. Murray, 111–24. Oxford: Oxford University Press, 2012.

Wood, Jacob W. "Henri de Lubac, Humani Generis, and the Natural Desire for a Supernatural End." *Nova et Vetera* 15, no. 4 (2017): 1209–41.

———. *To Stir a Restless Heart: Thomas Aquinas and Henri de Lubac on Nature, Grace, and the Desire for God*. Washington, DC: Catholic University of America Press, 2019.

Wood, Susan K. "The Nature-Grace Problematic within Henri de Lubac's Christological Paradox." *Communio: International Catholic Review* 19 (1992): 389–403.

———. *Spiritual Exegesis and the Church in the Theology of Henri de Lubac*. Eugene, OR: Wipf and Stock, 2010.

Zwitter, Alek. *L'Histoire en présence de l'Éternel: L'eschatologie d'Henri de Lubac*. Paris: Cerf, 2019.

INDEX

Action Française, 23, 171n12
Adam (biblical), 7
Aeterni Patris (Leo XIII), 40–44, 179n32
allegory, 65–68, 123, 147, 148, 152
  sacrifice and, 72–74
  supernatural and, 135
Amidism, 31–33
anagogy, 65–68, 123, 147, 148–49, 152
anti-humanism, 21–25
anti-Joachimite, xxvi
anti-modernist oath, 47–48
anti-Pelagianism, 7
anti-semitism, 63–64
anti-Theists, 24–25
"Apologétique et théologie" (de Lubac), xvi, xvii, 51, 54
Approches théologiques (Schillebeeckx), 17
Aspects of Buddhism (de Lubac), 30–33
atheism, xix, xxiii–xxiv, 15, 167n87
  atheist humanism and, 21–25, 170n3
At the Service of the Church (de Lubac), 23, 116, 217n3
Augustine, xxiv, xxv, 4, 56–57, 102, 163n31, 166n64
  Augustinian position and, 143
  on sacrifice, 205n59
  Surnaturel and Augustinianism, 6–9

authentic humanism
  atheist humanism and, 21–25, 170n3
  Buddhism and, 29–33
  Christian humanism and, 25–29
  as salvation, 20–34
  true humanism and, 33–34
authoritarian political movements, xiii, 171n12
authority, 83–87
Ayres, Lewis, 62

Baianism, 12, 163n31
Baius, Michael, 6–8
Balthasar, Hans Urs von, xv, xix
baptism, 82
Benedict XVI, 90–91
Bergson, Henri, 22, 41–42
bishops, 89–90
Blondel, Maurice, 26, 128, 163n23, 163n31, 182n66, 184n98
  Teilhard de Chardin and, 138–39
body
  church as, 94–95
  in *Corpus Mysticum*, 94–107
  ecclesial, 77, 100–101, 103–7, 122–23
  historical, 120–21
  Holy Trinity and, 79
  human, 81
  identity of, 97–98, 103, 123
  of Jesus Christ, xxvii, 72, 77–79, 94–107, 120–23, 143, 152

238

mysticism and, 94–107, 121–23, 144
resurrection and, 81, 98–99
sacramental, 121–22
sacrifice and, 94–103, 120–23
"true," 94–95
See also Eucharist
Boersma, Hans, xxiii, 67–68, 179n27, 188n24
Bouillard, Henri, 42
Braine, David, 161n10
Brief Catechesis on Nature and Grace, A (de Lubac), 14–17
Buchez, Philippe, 117–18
Buddhism
de Lubac and, 4, 29–33
humanism and, xxiv, 29–33
soteriology and, 30–33

Calvary, 98, 102–3, 203n35
Catholic Church. *See* church
Catholicisme (de Lubac), xviii–xix, 25–29, 68–69
salvation in, 78–79
Catholic theology, xiii
Thomistic milieu and, 39–44, 179n27
See also specific topics
CELAM. *See* Latin American Episcopal Conferences
change, xiii–xv. *See also* Christian novelty
Chantraine, Georges, xv, 85, 180n45
charity, xxv, 13, 56, 147
as bond of unity, 107–8
Christian, 30–31
gift of, 28–29
humanism and, 28–29
sacramentality and, 107–8
Chenu, Marie-Dominique, 42
Cholvy, Brigitte, 8, 11–12, 60, 161n10

Christian charity, 30–31
Christian Faith, The (de Lubac), xvii, xxiv
Christian humanism, 25–29, 144, 149. *See also* humanism; humanity
Christian novelty (Christian newness), xxv, 34, 151–53
continuity, discontinuity, and, 131–33
Old and New Testament and, 58–59, 64–68
renewal and, xiv–xv
sacrifice in, 73–74
salvation and, 131–33
soteriology and, xiv–xv
Christocentrism, 129–30
Christogenesis, 152
church
Action Française and, 23, 171n12
authority of, 83–87
baptism and, 82
bishops and, 89–90
as body, 94–95
change and, xiii–xiv
clergy and, 83–84
Comte and Catholic Church, 22–23
Dei Filius and, xvi–xviii, 48, 55–56, 154–55
as dependent upon Jesus Christ, 79–82
ecclesia discens, 82
ecclesia docens, 82
ecclesial antecedence and, 82–88
episcopal college and, 89–90
Eucharist and, 88–91, 94, 99–103
faith and, 56
hierarchy of, 82–83, 86–87
humanity and, 144
identity of, 104–5, 117

Church (*cont.*)
  integralism and, 27–28
  Jesus Christ and, 72–73, 77–82,
    94–95
  liturgy and, 61–62, 72, 101
  local or particular, 89–90
  Lumen gentium and, 77, 79, 87, 105,
    195n11
  magisterium and, 84–87
  Mass and, 103, 105, 136–37
  ministerial priesthood and, 105–6
  mother, maternity, and, 82–84, 87
  mysticism in, 87–88
  Origen on, 145–46
  as particular and universal, 88–91
  Radical Orthodoxy and, xxii
  sacramentality of, 79–82, 118–20
  sacrifice and, xxv, 96–97, 100–107
  salvation and, xxv, 17, 77–93
  self-destruction of, 116–17
  universality of, 88–91
  Vatican II and, 77, 90–91
clergy, 83–84
Comte, Auguste, 22–23, 171n12
conciliar anachronism, xv–xix
Concilium (journal), 16–17, 85–86,
  91
consciousness, 32–33
Constitution on Revelation. *See Dei
  Verbum*
Constitution on the Catholic Faith.
  See Dei Filius
contemplation, 53–55
continuity, 131–33
Corpus Mysticum (de Lubac), 54–55,
    78, 92
  body in, 94–107
  on church's sacrificial center, 96–97
  church's sacrificial destiny in, 103–7
  Eucharist in, 94, 97–98, 206n73
  sacrifice in, 94–108

  sacrificial anticipation in, 98–103
  sacrificial memorial in, 97–98
  Scripture and, 97–98
cosmic Christ, 133–34
creation, xviii, 6, 10–13, 45–46
cross, 29, 33–34
  cruciformity and, 129–30
  mysterium crucis and, 140–49
  sacrifice and, 69–72, 98–103
  Scripture's meaning and, 68–74
  spiritual exegesis and, 68–74
  tree of life and, 32
  truth and, 69
crucicentrism, 33–34
cruciformity, 129–30

Daniélou, Jean, 158n21
Darwin, Charles, 130
Dei Filius (Constitution on the
    Catholic Faith), xvi–xviii, 39–44,
    48, 55–56, 154–55, 159n24
Dei Verbum (Constitution on Reve-
    lation), xviii
de Lubac, Henri
  "Apologétique et théologie" lecture
    by, xvi, xvii, 51, 54
  Aspects of Buddhism, 30–33
  At the Service of the Church, 23, 116,
    217n3
  on authority, 85–86
  *A Brief Catechesis on Nature and
    Grace*, 14–17
  Buddhism and, 4, 29–33
  Catholicisme, xviii–xix, 25–29,
    68–69, 78–79
  The Christian Faith, xvii, xxiv
  Corpus Mysticum, 54–55, 78, 92,
    94–108, 206n73
  The Discovery of God, xxiv, 39
  Dumas and, 140–41
  on gender, 83

History and Spirit, 60–61, 112–18, 140
  on Joachim of Fiore, 112–18
Medieval Exegesis, 92, 100, 113
Meditation sur l'église, 4, 92, 119
The Mystery of the Supernatural, 12–13, 14
  "Mystique et Mystère," xx, xxvi–xxvii, 38, 141, 217n3
nexus mysteriorum and, xvi–xvii, 146, 151–56
Petite catéchèse, 8
La postérité spirituelle, 118–20
The Religion of Teilhard de Chardin by, 129
  speculative theology and, 153–54
  spiritual posterity of, 112–18
The Splendor of the Church, xvii, xxi, 104
Surnaturel, xxiii, 3–9
  systematization of, 154
  on Teilhard de Chardin, xxvi, 125–39
  "Tripartite Anthropology," 9–10
  Vatican I and, xv–xviii, 90–91, 152–53
  Vatican II and, xiii–xiv, xv, 85, 90–91, 125–26, 152–53, 158n13
  See also specific topics
Descartes, René, 39
Descoqs, Pedro, 172n24
desire
  for God, 13–14, 37
  for happiness, 37
discontinuity, 131–33
Discovery of God, The (de Lubac), xxiv, 39
"distich," 62–63
Divine Milieu (Teilhard de Chardin), 127, 129–31, 133
divinization, 15, 18–19, 132–33

dogma
  Dumas on, xvii
  faith and, 56–57
  humanism and, 25–29
  mysteries, mystery, and, xvii–xix, 84–85, 151–52
Dumas, Bertrand, 188n24
  de Lubac and, 140–41
  on dogma, xvii
  on mysticism, xx, 50, 140–41, 148
  on spiritual intelligence, 54–55

Easter, 143
ecclesia discens (learning church), 82
ecclesia docens (teaching church), 82
ecclesial antecedence, 82–88
ecclesial body
  history and, 122–23
  Jesus Christ and, 77, 100–101, 103–7, 122–23
  sacrifice and, 122–23
ecclesiology, 77–78, 81–82, 88, 104–5. *See also* church
economy, of New Testament, 104–5
Enlightenment, 65
episcopal college, 89–90
eschatology, 148
  eschatological sacrifice and, 125–39
"eternal gospel," 112–16
Eucharist
  church and, 88–91, 94, 99–103
  in *Corpus Mysticum*, 94, 97–98, 206n73
  cosmic, 136–39
  history and, 121
  Holy Trinity and, 70–71, 106–8
  New Testament and, 100
  Old Testament and, 100, 121
  sacrifice and, xxv, 97–107, 136–39, 144, 192n72

Eucharist (*cont.*)
   salvation and, 88–93, 99–103,
      106–8, 136–39
   in Scripture, 99–100, 102–3
   Teilhard de Chardin and, 136–39
eugenicism, 126–27, 213n9
evolution, 130–31

faith
   church and, 56
   Dei Filius and, xvi–xviii, 39–44, 48,
      55–56, 154–55, 159n29
   dogma and, 56–57
   knowledge and, 51–57
   reason and, 39–40, 51–52
   revelation, reason, and, 39–40,
      55–57
   spiritual intelligence and, 53–55
   truth and, 51–52
fascism, 171n12
fermentum, 89–90, 95
fideism, 39
First Vatican Council. *See* Vatican I
Flipper, Joseph, 64, 159n29,
      160nn33–34, 186n6
Fontoynont, Victor, 85–87
freedom, 13, 21
French liberalism, 23

Gallicanism, 90
Gardner, Patrick, 114, 118, 119, 124
gender, 83
gift
   of charity, 28–29
   Jesus Christ's gift and humanism,
      33–34, 74
   of love, 11
   of redemption, 29, 33–34
   sacrifice as, 73–74
   of salvation, 79, 155
Gilson, Étienne, 42, 179n30

God
   desire for, 13–14, 37
   grace and, 6–8
   Holy Trinity and, 6, 57
   image of, 10, 38–39, 45
   as inexhaustible, 57
   journey to, 56–57
   knowledge of, 37–39, 45–48, 55–57
   love and, 11–12, 28–29
   mystery of, xvi, 142, 146, 149
   as salvation, 37–39, 55–57
   See also Word of God
grace
   acceptance of, 45–46
   deifying, 18–19
   God and, 6–8
   gratuity of, 9–14
   Holy Trinity and, 3, 9–14, 18–19
   humanity and, 7, 18–19
   intellectualism and, 45–46
   in Old and New Testament, 8
   redemption and, 14–18
   salvation and, 6–9, 13, 17–18
   soteriology, nature, and, 3–19
   spirit and, 9–14
   supernatural and, 6–9, 18–19, 24
gratuity, 9–14
Grumett, David, 188n30
Guibert, Étienne, xx, 79, 88, 143,
      160n1

happiness, 37
Hauser, Daniel, 202n23, 204n50
Hemming, Laurence Paul, 101–2,
      201n7, 202n23, 205n60, 206n81
history
   ecclesial body and, 122–23
   Eucharist and, 121
   historical body and, 120–21
   Jesus Christ of, 133–36
   meaning of, 111–24

Index   243

mystery and, 147–48
mysticism and, xix–xx, 147–48
ontology and, xxii–xxiii
outcome of, 140
pivot of, 123–24
sacramental body and, 121–22
sacramentality of, 118–20
sacrifice and, 155
salvation, xxiii, xxvi, 111–24, 134–36, 152
soteriology between ontology and, xxii–xxiii
spiritual posterity and, 112–18
Teilhard de Chardin on, 133–36, 140
History and Spirit (de Lubac), 60–61, 112–18, 140
Holy Trinity
  body of Christ and, 79
  divinization and, 18–19
  Eucharist and, 70–71, 106–8
  grace and, 3, 9–14, 18–19
  humanity and, xxvi–xxvii, 18–19, 70–72, 79, 154–55
  love and, 147, 155
  mystery of, 48
  mysticism and, xx, 143, 148–49
  paths of God and, 57
  revelation of, 48–49, 56–57
  sacrifice and, 106–8
  salvation through, xxvi, 49, 155
  saving acts and, xxiv
  Scripture and, 113
  spiritual exegesis and, 70–72
  supernatural and, 18–19, 48
  Word of God and, 6
Huby, Joseph, 30
human body, 81
Humani generis (Pope Pius XII), 4–5
humanism
  anti-humanism, 21–25

atheist, 21–25, 170n3
authentic, 20–34
Buddhism and, xxiv, 29–33
in *Catholicisme*, 25–29
charity and, 28–29
Christian, 25–29, 144, 149
dogma and, 25–29
Jesus Christ's gift and, 33–34, 74
mysticism and, 21–22
salvation and, 20–34, 144
social collectivism and, 26–29
supernatural and, xxiii–xxiv, 23, 27–29
true, 33–34
humanity
  church and, 144
  fulfillment of, 11–12
  grace and, 7, 18–19
  Holy Trinity and, xxvi–xxvii, 18–19, 70–72, 79, 154–55
  beyond intellectualism, 44–47
  mystery of, 38–39, 149, 150–51
  mysticism and, 38–39
  nature and, 13, 16, 47–48, 54
  revelation and, xviii, 47–49
  salvation of, xviii, xx–xxi, xxvi–xxvii, 6–9, 87–88
  sin and, 16
  spirit and, 9–14, 47
Human Phenomenon, The (Teilhard de Chardin), 127, 129–30, 132–33
Hume, David, 39
humility, 15, 56–57
Hütter, Reinhard, 161n10

identity
  of church, 104–5, 117
  of Jesus Christ's body, 97–98, 103, 123

image
  of God, 10, 38–39, 45
  mysticism, "likeness," and, 10,
    38–39, 142
integralism, 27–28
intellectualism
  beyond, 44–47
  authority and, 85–87
  Catholic theology and, 39–44
  contemplation and, 53–55
  creation and, 45–46
  grace and, 45–46
  Joachim of Fiora and, 112–18
  knowledge and, 39–47, 51–52
  mystery and, 39–47, 53–55
  reason and, 39–42, 47–48
  Rousselot and, 42, 44–45, 54
  scholasticism and, 41–44, 85–87,
    153–54, 162n20
  spirit and, 44–47
  spiritual intelligence and, 53–55, 59
  Teilhard de Chardin and, 128
  Thomistic milieu and, 39–44,
    179n27

Jansen, Cornelius, 6–8, 163n25
Jesuits, xix, 4–5
Jesus Christ
  body of, xxvii, 72, 77–79, 94–107,
    120–23, 143, 152
  change through, xiv–xv
  Christ's passion and, 72–73
  church and, 72–73, 77–82, 94–95
  cosmic Christ and, 133–34
  death of, 29, 98, 124
  ecclesial body and, 77, 100–101,
    103–7, 122–23
  historical body and, 120–21
  of history, 133–36
  humanism and gift of, 33–34, 74
  identity of Christ's body, 97–98,
    103, 123

Last Supper and, 69–70, 192n72
mystery of, xxvi, 72–74, 146–49,
  158n21
mysticism and, 143–44
Omega and, 125, 129, 131–36
passing into, 62–68
passion of, 72–73, 105
pivot of history and, 123–24
sacramental body and, 121–22
sacramentality and, 95, 97–98,
  118–20
saving acts of, xxiv
Scripture and, 62–68
totus Christus and, 77, 100–101,
  103–7, 122–23
truth of, 50–51
Virgin Mary and, 80, 82–83
See also cross; resurrection; sacrifice; salvation
Joachim of Fiora, 67, 104, 112–18,
  124
John Paul II, 90–91
Judaism, 63–64

Kant, Immanuel, 39, 41–42
Keefe, Donald, 204n50
kenosis, 15
Kerr, Fergus, 213n12
knowledge
  faith and, 51–57
  of God, 37–39, 45–48, 55–57
  beyond intellectualism, 44–47
  intellectualism and, 39–47,
    51–52
  mystery and, 37–57
  paradox of, 52–53
  spiritual intelligence, contempla-
    tion, and, 53–55
Komonchak, Joseph, 171n12

Labourdette, Marie-Michel, 46
Last Supper, 69–70, 192n72

Latin American Episcopal Conferences (CELAM), 89
learning church (*ecclesia discens*), 82
Lemaire, Marie-Gabrielle, 85, 119, 124
Leo XIII, 40–44, 179n32
liberalism, 23
liberation theology, 16
"likeness," 10, 38–39, 142
liturgy, 61–62, 72, 101
local church, 89–90. *See also* church
Lonergan, Bernard, xix, 179n27
love, 152, 212n8
  God and, 11–12, 28–29
  Holy Trinity and, 147, 155
  sacrifice and, 147, 155
Lumen gentium, 77, 79, 87, 105, 195n11

magisterium, 84–87
manualism, 41
Maréchal, Joseph, 42, 180n45
marginalization, 127–28, 213n12
Martelet, Gustave, 158n13
Marxism, 23–24, 25, 172nn24–25
Mass, 103, 105, 136–37
maternity, 82–84, 87
matter, 102–3
Maurras, Charles, 23, 172n24
McCool, Gerald, 178n14, 179n30
McGinn, Bernard, 114
McPartlan, Paul, 203n35
Medieval Exegesis (de Lubac), 92, 100, 113
Meditation sur l'église (de Lubac), 4, 92, 119
memorialization, 97–98, 100, 102–3
Mickiewicz, Adam, 118
Milbank, John, xxii–xxiii, 8, 162n16
ministerial priesthood, 105–6
modernism, 178n16

mother, 82–84, 87. *See also* Virgin Mary
Moulins-Beaufort, Éric de, 126, 128
Mulcahy, Bernard, 161n10
mystère du Christ d'après Henri de Lubac, Le (Guibert), xx
mystery
  contemplation and, 53–55
  of God, xvi, 142, 146, 149
  history and, 147–48
  of Holy Trinity, 48
  of humanity, 38–39, 149, 150–51
  intellectualism and, 39–47, 53–55
  of Jesus Christ, xxvi, 72–74, 146–49, 158n21
  knowledge and, 37–57
  mysteries, mystery, and dogma, xvii–xix, 84–85, 151–52
  mysterium crucis and, 140–49
  mysticism and, xix–xxii, 140–48, 159n29
  myth and, 22
  nexus mysteriorum and, xvi–xvii, 146, 151–56
  paradox and, 37, 50–53
  Paschal, 24, 168n89
  of redemption, xxiv, 141–46
  of resurrection, 143–44, 158n21
  revealed and apprehended, 47–57
  sacrifice and, 147–48, 149
  of Scripture, 145–47, 149
  spiritual exegesis and, 59
  spiritual intelligence and, 53–55
  in Vatican I, xvii–xviii
  in Vatican II, xviii
Mystery of the Supernatural, The (de Lubac), 12–13, 14
mysticism
  anagogy and, 148–49
  body and, 94–107, 121–23, 144
  in church, 87–88
  Dumas on, xx, 50, 140–41, 148

mysticism (*cont.*)
history and, xix–xx, 147–48
Holy Trinity and, xx, 143, 148–49
humanism and, 21–22
humanity and, 38–39
image, "likeness," and, 10, 38–39, 142
Jesus Christ and, 143–44
meaning of, 88
mystery and, xix–xxii, 140–48, 159n29
in "Mystique et Mystère," xx, xxvi–xxvii, 141, 217n3
of Nietzsche, 21–22
salvation and, xx–xxi, 88, 143–44
in Scripture, 59, 87–88, 142–43
theology and, 50, 140, 148, 150
"Mystique et Mystère" (de Lubac), xx, xxvi–xxvii, 38, 141, 217n3
Mystique et théologie d'après Henri de Lubac (Dumas), xx
myth, 22

natural selection, 126–27, 130
nature
gratuity of grace and, 9–14
humanity and, 13, 16, 47–48, 54
salvation and, 6–9, 13, 17–18
sin and, 12
social collectivism and, 26–27
soteriology, grace, and, 3–19
spiritual intelligence and, 54
supernatural and, 3–4, 16, 23, 27, 48, 132–33
neo-scholasticism, 41
New Testament, 146
Christian novelty and, 58–59, 64–68
economy of, 104–5
Eucharist and, 100
grace in, 8

Joachim of Fiora and, 113–14
Scripture and, 62–72
transition to, xxv
See also Scripture
nexus mysteriorum
de Lubac's use of, xvi–xvii, 146, 151–56
"organic unity," conciliar anachronism, and, xv–xix
Nichols, Aidan, 159n29
Nietzsche, Friedrich, 21–22, 171n12

Old Testament, 146
Christian novelty and, 58–59, 64–68
Eucharist and, 100, 121
grace in, 8
sacrifice and, 98, 100
Scripture and, 62–72
transition from, xxv
See also Scripture
Omega, 125, 129, 131–36
ontology, xxii–xxiii
"organic unity," xv–xix
Origen, 64, 147–48
on church, 145–46
History and Spirit and, 112–16, 118, 140
on Scripture, 60–61, 145–46

paganism, 13–14, 171n12
papacy, 90–91. *See also specific popes*
paradox
of knowledge, 52–53
mystery and, 37, 50–53
of spirit, 10
paschal mystery, 24, 168n89
passion, of Jesus Christ, 72–73, 105
paths of God (*Sur les chemins de Dieu*), 57
Pelagianism, 7, 12, 27

Pelchat, Marc, 143
Petite catéchèse (de Lubac), 8
Pius X, 178n16
Pius XI, 23
Platonism, xxii, 14, 160n32, 160n34
politics, 23–24, 86–87
   authoritarian political movements
     and, xiii, 171n12
Pope Pius XII, 4
positivism, 22–23
postérité spirituelle, La (de Lubac),
   118–20
power, 21–22, 102–3
priesthood, 105–6
Promethean aspirations, 21–22
Proudhon, Pierre-Joseph, 24–25,
   28–29, 172n30

racism, 63–64
Radical Orthodoxy, xxii, 101, 160n32
Rahner, Karl, 17, 158n21
rationalism, 39, 51, 53–54
reason, 41–42, 47–48
   Enlightenment and, 65
   faith and, 39–40, 51–52
   revelation, faith, and, 39–40, 55–57
redemption
   gift of, 29, 33–34
   grace and, 14–18
   mystery of, xxiv, 141–46
   renewal and, xiv–xv
   sacrifice and, xxiii–xxiv
   salvation and, xxi, 49, 82–83
Reeves, Marjorie, 114
Religion of Teilhard de Chardin, The
   (de Lubac), 129. *See also*
   Teilhard de Chardin, Pierre
renewal, xiv–xv
ressourcement, xxii, 43, 87, 92, 152
   Dei Verbum and, xviii
   meaning of, 153

Scripture and, 59–62
   spiritual exegesis as, 59–62
resurrection
   body and, 81, 99
   mystery of, 143–44, 158n21
revelation
   Dei Verbum and, xviii
   faith, reason, and, 39–40, 55–57
   of Holy Trinity, 48–49, 56–57
   humanity and, xviii, 47–49
   of mystery, 47–57
   soteriology and, 48–49
Rousselot, Pierre, 30, 128, 179n27,
   180n45, 184n98
   intellectualism and, 42, 44–45, 54

sacramental body, 121–22
sacramentality
   charity and, 107–8
   of church, 79–82, 118–20
   of history, 118–20
   Jesus Christ and, 95, 97–98, 118–20
   sacramental hermeneutic and,
     67–68
sacrifice
   allegory and, 72–74
   Augustine on, 205n59
   body and, 94–103, 120–23
   in Christian novelty, 73–74
   Christocentrism and, 129–30
   church and, xxv, 96–97, 100–107
   in *Corpus Mysticum*, 94–108
   cosmic, 136–39
   cross and, 69–72, 98–103
   ecclesial body and, 122–23
   eschatological, 125–39
   Eucharist and, xxv, 97–107, 136–39,
     144, 192n72
   as gift, 73–74
   historical body and, 120–21
   history and, 155

sacrifice (*cont.*)
  Holy Trinity and, 106–8
  love and, 147, 155
  ministerial priesthood and, 105–6
  mystery and, 147–48, 149
  Old Testament and, 98, 100
  redemption and, xxiii–xxiv
  sacramental body and, 121–22
  sacrificial anticipation, 98–103
  sacrificial language and, xxiii–xxiv
  sacrificial memorial and, 97–98
  salvation as, 125–39
  supernatural and, xxiii
salvation
  authentic humanism as, 20–34
  in *Catholicisme*, 78–79
  Christian novelty and, 131–33
  church and, xxv, 17, 77–93
  cosmic Christ and, 133–34
  Eucharist and, 88–93, 99–103,
    106–8, 136–39
  evolution's culmination and con-
    vergence in Christ, 130–31
  as gift, 79, 155
  God as, 37–39, 55–57
  history, xxiii, xxvi, 111–24, 134–36,
    152
  through Holy Trinity, xxvi, 49, 155
  humanism and, 20–34, 144
  of humanity, xviii, xx–xxi, xxvi–
    xxvii, 6–9, 87–88
  as meaning of history, 111–24
  mysticism and, xx–xxi, 88, 143–44
  nature, grace, and, 6–9, 13, 17–18
  redemption and, xxi, 49, 82–83
  as sacrifice, 125–39
  Scripture and, 68–72
  as social, 78–79
  social collectivism and, 78–79
  spiritual exegesis and, 58–74
  supernatural and, xxiv, 7–9, 17–18

  truth and, 50–51
  Vatican II and, 17
  See also redemption
saving acts, xxiv
Schillebeeckx, Edward, 16–18
scholasticism, 41–44, 85–87, 153–54,
    162n20
Scripture
  Corpus Mysticum and, 97–98
  cross as meaning of, 68–74
  Eucharist in, 99–100, 102–3
  four senses of Scripture and their
    doctrinal form, 62–68
  Holy Trinity and, 113
  Jesus Christ and, 62–68
  mystery of, 145–47, 149
  mysticism in, 59, 87–88, 142–43
  New Testament and, 62–72
  Old Testament and, 62–72
  Origen on, 60–61, 145–46
  ressourcement and, 59–62
  rhyme about, 62–63
  salvation and, 68–72
  spiritual exegesis and, 60–74
  spiritual intelligence of, 59
  spiritual interpretation of, 145–47
  supernatural and, 64–65
  as Word of God, 60–62, 145
Second Vatican Council. *See* Vatican
    II
self-destruction, 116–17
semi-Joachimism, 114–18
sin, 7, 21, 48
  humanity and, 16
  nature and, 12
social collectivism
  humanism and, 26–29
  salvation and, 78–79
soteriology
  Buddhism and, 30–33
  Christian novelty and, xiv–xv

nature, grace, and, 3–19
between ontology and history,
  xxii–xxiii
revelation and, 48–49
speculative, xxii–xxiii
speculative soteriology, xxii–xxiii
speculative theology, 153–56
spirit. *See also* Holy Trinity
grace and, 9–14
humanity and, 9–14, 47
intellectualism and, 44–47
paradox of, 10
transformation of, 151–52
of Vatican I, 154–55, 220n1
spiritual exegesis, xxv, 112, 142
cross and, 68–74
Holy Trinity and, 70–72
mystery and, 59
as *ressourcement*, 59–62
salvation and, 58–74
Scripture and, 60–74
of Teilhard de Chardin, 125–29,
  133–34
spiritual intelligence, 53–55, 59
spiritual posterity, 112–18
Splendor of the Church, The (de
  Lubac), xvii, xxi, 104
supernatural
allegory and, 135
Augustine and, 6–9
cosmic Christ and, 133–34
divinization and, 15, 18–19, 132–33
God, love, and, 11–12
grace and, 6–9, 18–19, 24
Holy Trinity and, 18–19, 48
humanism and, xxiii–xxiv, 23, 27–29
nature and, 3–4, 16, 23, 27, 48,
  132–33
sacrifice and, xxiii
salvation and, xxiv, 7–9, 17–18
Scripture and, 64–65

Sur les chemins de Dieu (paths of
  God), 57
Surnaturel (de Lubac), xxiii
Augustinianism and, 6–9
controversy of, 3–6
criticism of, 5–6
Suspended Middle, The (Milbank), 8
symbolism, 53–54

teaching church (*ecclesia docens*), 82
Teilhard de Chardin, Pierre, xiii–xiv,
  140
Blondel and, 138–39
Christian novelty and, 131–33
Christocentrism and, 129–30
cosmic Christ and, 133–34
death of, 127
Divine Milieu by, 127, 129–31, 133
Eucharist and, 136–39
eugenicism and, 126–27, 213n9
evolution and, 130–31
on history, 140
The Human Phenomenon by, 127,
  129–30, 132–33
intellectualism and, 128
Jesus of history and, 133–36
de Lubac on, xxvi, 125–39
Omega and, 125, 129, 131–36
spiritual exegesis of, 125–29, 133–34
theology. *See also specific topics*
Catholic, xiii, 39–44, 179n27
liberation, 16
mysticism and, 50, 140, 148, 150
speculative, 153–56
in Vatican I, 154–55
in Vatican II, 155
Thomas Aquinas (Saint), xxiv, 4,
  40–43, 68–69, 143
Thomistic milieu, 39–44, 179n27
totus Christus, 77, 100–101, 103–7
ecclesial body and, 122–23

tree of life, 32
de Trinitate ex hominibus, 82–88
"Tripartite Anthropology" (de Lubac), 9–10
tropology, 65–68, 147, 148, 152
"true body," 94–95
true humanism, 33–34
truth
  cross and, 69
  faith and, 51–52
  of Jesus Christ, 50–51
  salvation and, 50–51
  spiritual intelligence and, 53–55

unity, xvii
utopianism, 23–25

Valensin, Auguste, 138
Vatican I (First Vatican Council)
  Dei Filius and, 39–44
  de Lubac and, xv–xviii, 90–91, 152–53
  mystery in, xvii–xviii
  spirit of, 154–55, 220n1
  theology in, 154–55
Vatican II (Second Vatican Council)
  Aeterni Patris and, 43–44

church and, 77, 90–91
Concilium and, 16–17, 85–86, 91
de Lubac and, xiii–xiv, xv, 85, 90–91, 125–26, 152–53, 158n13
Lumen gentium and, 77
mystery in, xviii
on non-Christian religions, 30
salvation and, 17
speculative theology and, 155
theology in, 155
Vichy regime, 21–22
Virgin Mary, 80, 82–83, 135

Wagner, Jean-Pierre, 128, 159n24
Will to Power, 21–22
Wood, Jacob, 161n10, 162n16
Wood, Susan, xxii–xxiii, 92, 99–101, 142, 160n33, 204n50
Word of God, 26
  clergy and, 83–84
  Holy Trinity and, 6
  Scripture as, 60–62, 145
  Word after our Fall, xviii
World War II, 22, 63–64

Zwitter, Alek, 115, 118, 148, 188n30

EUGENE R. SCHLESINGER is a lecturer in the Department of Religious Studies at Santa Clara University. He is the author of *Sacrificing the Church: Mass, Mission, and Ecumenism.*

Milton Keynes UK
Ingram Content Group UK Ltd.
UKHW021048100324
439084UK00003B/70